Praise for
The Course in Miracles Experiment

"Oh, *this is fun!* And so easy! *The Course in Miracles Experiment* is the dream vehicle for harnessing Pam Grout's brilliance, realism, and sense of humor. It's also the dream vehicle that will help turn your thoughts into the things and events of your life."

— **Mike Dooley,** *New York Times* best-selling author of *Infinite Possibilities*

"With candid wit and light-hearted humor, Pam Grout takes the mystifying and esoteric text of '*A Course in Miracles*' and makes it easily understood through her unique style and amusing examples. This is a must-read for followers of The Course. Pam makes it easy to integrate the spiritual principles of this teaching into your everyday life. I just love this book! Thank you for writing it, Pam!"

— **Anita Moorjani,** *New York Times* best-selling author of *Dying to Be Me* and *What If This Is Heaven?*

"Entertaining and enlightening! Pam Grout shows us how to experience miracles in our beautifully mysterious and messy lives."

— **Robert Holden,** best-selling author of *Holy Shift!: 365 Meditations on A Course in Miracles*

THE COURSE IN MIRACLES

Experiment

ALSO BY PAM GROUT

BOOKS

Art & Soul, Reloaded: A Yearlong Apprenticeship for Summoning the Muses and Reclaiming your Bold, Audacious, Creative Side (also available as an audiobook)*

Thank & Grow Rich: A 30-day Experiment in Shameless Gratitude and Unabashed Joy (also available as an audiobook)*

E-Cubed: Nine More Energy Experiments That Prove Manifesting Magic and Miracles Is Your Full-Time Gig (also available as an audiobook)*

E-Squared: Nine Do-It-Yourself Energy Experiments That Prove Your Thoughts Create Your Reality (also available as an audiobook)*

Jumpstart Your Metabolism: How to Lose Weight by Changing the Way You Breathe

Living Big: Embrace Your Passion and Leap into an Extraordinary Life

Kansas Curiosities: Quirky Characters, Roadside Oddities & Other Offbeat Stuff

Colorado Curiosities: Quirky Characters, Roadside Oddities & Other Offbeat Stuff

Girlfriend Getaways: You Go Girl! And I'll Go, Too

You Know You're in Kansas When . . . :
101 Quintessential Places, People, Events, Customs,
Lingo, and Eats of the Sunflower State

Recycle This Book: And 72 1/2 Even Better
Ways to Save "Yo Momma" Earth

God Doesn't Have Bad Hair Days: Ten Spiritual Experiments
That Will Bring More Abundance, Joy, and Love to Your Life

The 100 Best Vacations to Enrich Your Life

The 100 Best Worldwide Vacations to Enrich Your Life

The 100 Best Volunteer Vacations to Enrich Your Life

CARD DECK

The Oracle of E: A 52-Card Deck and Guidebook
to Manifest Your Dreams (with Colette Baron-Reid)*

*Available from Hay House
Please visit:

Hay House USA: www.hayhouse.com®
Hay House Australia: www.hayhouse.com.au
Hay House UK: www.hayhouse.co.uk
Hay House India: www.hayhouse.co.in

***

THE COURSE IN MIRACLES

Experiment

A STARTER KIT FOR REWIRING YOUR MIND (AND THEREFORE THE WORLD)

PAM GROUT

HAY HOUSE, INC.
Carlsbad, California • New York City
London • Sydney • New Delhi

Published in the United States by: Hay House, Inc.: www.hayhouse.com® • *Published in Australia by:* Hay House Australia Pty. Ltd.: www.hayhouse.com.au • *Published in the United Kingdom by:* Hay House UK, Ltd.: www.hayhouse.co.uk • *Published in India by:* Hay House Publishers India: www.hayhouse.co.in

Cover design: Mary Ann Smith
Interior design: Julie Davison

Cataloging-in-Publication Data is on file at the Library of Congress

Tradepaper ISBN: 978-1-4019-5750-6
E-book ISBN: 978-1-4019-5751-3
Audiobook ISBN: 978-1-4019-5752-0

14 13 12 11 10 9 8 7 6 5
1st edition, January 2020
Printed in the United States of America

This product uses responsibly sourced papers and/or recycled materials. For more information, see www.hayhouse.com.

For Taz
I could never live without you.
So I don't.

Go forth, my book, and help destroy
the world as we know it.
— RUSSELL BANKS

CONTENTS

Preface xv

Lessons 1–50 1

BOOM! Review I: Lessons 51–60 53

Lessons 61–80 66

BOOM! Review II: Lessons 81–90 87

Lessons 91–110 99

BOOM! Review III: Lessons 111–120 120

Lessons 121–140 131

BOOM! Review IV: Lessons 141–150 151

Lessons 151–170 162

BOOM! Review V: Lessons 171–180 183

Lessons 181–200 195

BOOM! Review VI: Lessons 201–210 216

Lessons 211–220 227

Welcome to Nirvana! Or Part II: Lessons 221–365 237

From the bottom of my heart 384

About the Author 385

PREFACE

May I waste my heart on fear no longer.

— JOHN O'DONOHUE

Google Translate is a champ at decoding Korean pop songs and unraveling Brazilian FB memes.

But what if the words you're trying to decipher are in English, your native tongue?

A Course in Miracles, a self-study program designed to bring about spiritual transformation, made its debut nearly 45 years ago. Millions of copies have been sold. But for many of us, the massive thought overhaul promised by the Course still reads like Urdu. What does it mean that I'm supposed to live in infinite peace?

When I began blogging about my own recalcitrant trek into *A Course in Miracles*, a journey I repeat every year, I was stunned by the number of eavesdroppers. Even though I was obviously "counseling" myself, people seemed to dig overhearing it. Readers began posting comments like:

"Ohh! So that's what forgiveness means?"

"Ohh! So that's how you access this secret invisible resource?"

"Ohh! So that God guy's not a sadistic jerk, after all?"

Almost immediately, readers urged me to compile my posts into a book. They liked that I made the Course "accessible," "light-hearted," "user-friendly." They liked that I made spiritual awakening fun.

So essentially, I have been summoned. I have been guided (it's a "thing" we Course students expect) to create the book you're holding in your hands.

The Course in Miracles Experiment is my somewhat cheeky translation of the Workbook from *A Course in Miracles*. Like the original, it covers 365 lessons, one for each day of the year.

Feel free to use it in tandem with the original or as a substitute.

Instead of posing high and mighty theories, the workbook, both the original and this knock-off, offers simple thought experiments to use on the daily. It invites readers to take spiritual practices out for a spin so they can witness life-altering results with their own two eyes.

None of the lessons are difficult. They require no major time commitment. They have but one purpose: to gently unravel all thoughts that impede our natural sense of joy and peace.

"God has no name." — *A Course in Miracles*

You'll notice the terminology in my version is slightly different. Okay, it's completely different. Case in point: the word "God"—more baggage than a Samsonite store, completely misconceived, the coolest force on the planet. That's why I rarely call it God.

Talk about triggering PTSD. That simple three-letter word is the last place most of us would turn to find meaning and joy and freedom. As someone once told me, "I have nothing against God. It's his fan club to which I take exception."

This book uses a variety of synonyms to describe the timeless, the eternal, the vast mystery of life itself. The Dude. The Mothership. The Universe. Field of Infinite Potentiality. Divine Buzz, Radiant X. Super God. Pick one, use 'em all, or better yet, come up with your own.

Because here's the thing. This unseen energetic force is the biggest badass on the planet. Why wouldn't everyone want to feel this buzz? To use its infinite power? To enjoy its guidance and blessings?

Who am I to pontificate about *A Course in Miracles*?

"Never once did God scan the room for the best example of holy living and send that person out to tell others about him. He always sent stumblers and sinners. I find that comforting."

— NADIA BOLZ-WEBER

The above question, by the way, came from my own head. I don't profess to be an expert of much of anything. I'm a seeker and, over the years, have explored everything from rebirthing, ho'oponopono, and tapping, to Abraham-Hicks and Byron Katie's "The Work." I keep coming back to the Course because, well, it just seems like my path. It's not everybody's tomato nor does it profess to be. All roads, as they say, lead to Rome. I like it because I'm a sucker for miracles and being happy.

A Course in Miracles was "scribed" between 1967 and 1972 by two professors at Columbia University who were frustrated with department infighting and aggressive office politics. Bill Thetford, head of medical psychology, proclaimed in exasperation one day, "There has GOT to be a better way."

An invisible voice, which began pouring forth through Helen Schucman, his research assistant, claimed to offer that "better way." As you can imagine, Helen was a bit freaked out that a disembodied voice was posing in her life as "Dear Abby." Nevertheless, she reluctantly agreed to listen, Bill agreed to take dictation, and, after seven interminable years, they compiled 200 photocopies of the voice's rather long-winded message.

Four years later, in 1976, the channeled 669-page text, 365 daily lessons, and Manual for Teachers was turned into a hardback by the Foundation for Inner Peace. In 1979, Johnny Carson endorsed Gerald Jampolsky's *Love Is Letting Go of Fear*, the first of many books spawned from the Course principles. Its popularity grew from there.

The Course ascribes to no particular religion or dogma. No sacrifice is required. With the help of the same invisible voice that spoke to Helen, anyone who asks can train their mind to see the world in an entirely new light.

Even a f**up like me. Before I became a serious student of *A Course in Miracles*, I was the last person anyone would have nominated to play a part in The Dude's little project here on earth.

At the time, my boyfriend, the last in a long series of boyfriends, had kicked me out of the house we shared in rural Connecticut.

To top it off, I was seven months pregnant, was (obviously) unmarried, and had nary a clue where to go. Even worse, it was mid-July and the air conditioner in the little blue Toyota in which I'd stuffed most of my earthly possessions was on the fritz.

Temperatures averaged 100 degrees as I set out across the country, big as a house, pointed in the general direction of Breckenridge, Colorado.

Clearly, something needed to change.

The Course, which I ultimately began to follow in earnest, had the audacity to suggest I was responsible for my train wreck of a life. It implied that if I would simply let go of all my mad fixations—my "he done me wrong" blockages, and all the other clutter I'd picked up about the way the world works— I could actually be happy. It suggested that the only reason I wasn't experiencing big-ass love and swimming in perpetual abundance was because my consciousness was on red alert.

My thoughts viewed the world as my sworn enemy. In short, it challenged the very foundation of my life.

I didn't let go without a fight.

My conversations with the Voice went something like this:

"But what about all my problems? I must analyze and fix them."

"Let go!" the Voice seemed to suggest.

"But what about good and evil, right and wrong?"

"Resign now as your own teacher," the Voice clearly advised.

"But . . . but . . ."

Slowly, inch by inch, I gave up the reins to my beliefs and old mental constructs. It began to occur to me that if I had the power to create such an ongoing disaster, I might also have the power to create a life I could enjoy.

The Course pulls no punches, going so far as to guarantee that "perfect peace and perfect joy are my inheritance." All I have to do is give up my belief in deprivation and lack.

"But that's so hard," I whined.

"It's not hard." The Voice was insistent. "It's your natural state. It's just very different than the way most people think."

I also learned from the Course that the tall blonde chick in the mirror isn't really me. The depressed pregnant woman driving the blue Toyota cross-country was nothing but a false identity I'd been taught to assume by a world that worships separation and limitations.

By focusing in on that little "self," I completely missed my connection to this other thing, this bigger thing that many call God.

I had completely imprisoned myself by zeroing in on this rickety body that was never—no matter how many face creams I used, no matter how many downward-facing dogs I did, no matter how many Wayne Dyer books I read—going to be good enough.

And that's what the Course is about: Taking the wrecking ball to mental constructs that have imprisoned us for far too long. Taking the focus off the limited self we see in the mirror and putting it on the glorious field of potentiality (the FP) that allows us to connect to all that is.

It's about letting go and surrendering to the all-loving, all-powerful energy force that's bigger, bolder, brighter, and, yes, stranger than anything we've yet seen. This Sacred Buzz is life itself.

Life, which—no matter how many walls we erect, no matter how seriously we screw up—is always there waiting with arms open wide.

New Sh*t Has Come to Light

*You are a miracle, capable of creating in
the likeness of your Creator. Everything else
is your own nightmare, and does not exist.*

— A Course in Miracles

A Course in Miracles proposes a revolutionary overhaul of everything we now believe.

Like quantum physics that overthrew Newton's reality of colliding pool balls, the Course presents an outright challenge to the fundamental nature of reality.

Everything we think we know, everything we believe to be fact is backwards, wrong side up.

Boiled down, that's the first 50 lessons of *A Course in Miracles*. What we think is true, even what we call factual knowledge, is the exact opposite of how the world really is.

Our culture feeds us a bullsh*t line about the world being scary. It teaches us to protect ourselves, claims possibilities are finite.

The Course is designed to prove none of that is true. It's designed to undo and retrain our minds. Which rewires and changes everything in our lives.

So shall we begin:

Lesson 1: Nothing I see means anything.

For one measly minute, simply look around the room, out the window, whatever happens to be in your line of sight and say: this lamp doesn't mean anything, this TV doesn't mean anything, this computer doesn't mean anything.

That's it. As the Course says, you don't have to believe it. You don't even have to like it. Just follow the damned instructions.

CIRCUS FREAK SHOW

We are all captives of a story.

— DANIEL QUINN

For more than 100 years, physicists have known that Newton's classical view of physical reality doesn't work at its core. The subatomic realm so defies all reason and logic that most scientists, scared to endanger their academic credentials, have more or less ignored the fact that life is nothing like we pretend it is.

In fact, the world is so freaky—particles popping up out of nowhere, time slowing down and speeding up, particles reacting and communicating with each other even when separated by thousands of miles— that the main thing scientists have done with this information is develop technology for blowing each other up, sending text messages and nuking leftover black-eyed peas.

We now have inscrutable proof that the two main fundaments of physical reality—space and time—are as shaky as a *Jenga* tower.

And that's what *A Course in Miracles* is all about. It advocates the idea that consciousness creates the material world. It says we humans decide in advance how we're going to experience life, that we choose beforehand what we want to see.

The problem is, we all look at the world with a giant chip on our shoulder.

So to change the course of my life, I must actively see and expect a different reality. Way too often, I devote my time and attention (my consciousness, if you will) to things I don't want. But it's nothing more than a bad habit. And like any bad habit, it can be changed with deliberate daily effort.

That's why I go through the Course lessons every year. That's why "training my mind" is priority numero uno.

In Lesson 2 (I have given everything I see all the meaning that it has for me), I simply take a quick minute, look around, and acknowledge that I have given meaning to whatever happens to cross my view.

For example, I'm currently giving meaning to a big globe, a peace tree I purchased from an artist in Haiti, an encaustic painting I made when writing a story for *Cooking Light* about art camps in Carmel. That's it! Look around. Take note of the things to which you've given meaning.

SNEAKING PAST THE BOUNCER OF MY LIMITED THINKING

Enlightenment is the unlearning of the thought system that dominates the planet.

— MARIANNE WILLIAMSON

Picture a big, muscle-bound bouncer, a Dwayne (the Rock) Johnson type. His arms are crossed and he's got that "no way, no how" look on his face.

Anyone with a lick of sense can figure out it'd be best to come back later, to try again when Mr. Tough isn't so diligently blocking the entry.

Our current beliefs about the world are just like that bouncer. They block all the joy, peace, and other Divine goodies the Universe so desperately wants to bestow.

A Course in Miracles is about clearing our minds, about undoing beliefs we think are absolute fact.

Enter Lesson 3: I do not understand anything I see (in this room, out the window, etc.). Again, we simply take a moment or two to look around and say, "I do not understand this pillow. I do not understand this cat. I do not understand this hand."

Remember, you don't have to believe these lessons. You just have to do them.

Because our old beliefs are dominated by fear, separation, and limitations, and because our brains look for proof of our beliefs, we collapse the wave (a physics term that describes plucking a single superposition from all possible superpositions) that supports our beliefs. Once it's collapsed, the other superpositions are no longer visible.

As we surrender old certainties (the world is flat, the table is solid, what we can't see with our physical eyes does not exist), a new, kinder, more loving reality comes gushing in.

So sure, I may think I understand this pillow, this cat, this hand. But it's possible I don't.

And I'm willing to surrender my feeble interpretations so the infinite and incomparable, my natural state, can glide effortlessly by that now-superfluous bouncer.

FIRE THE NEGATIVE COMMITTEE THAT MEETS INSIDE YOUR HEAD

Most of what goes on in your mind doesn't deserve
your attention. It's a tiring and terrifying time machine.

— JIM CARREY

If there was a loud speaker projecting the voice in my head, I would have been committed years ago. This insistent voice rarely, if ever, stops yammering.

It seems to think it's Simon Cowell, that it's getting paid to judge, analyze, dissect, and label everything.

What a huge relief to discover that all my mental verbalizing means nothing.

Lesson 4 of *A Course in Miracles* says this: My thoughts do not mean anything.

For a minute or two whenever I think about it, I stop and notice my thoughts (the roommate in my head, as Michael Singer calls it) and simply repeat:

"This thought that I'm running late doesn't mean anything."

"This thought that I need to pick up the house doesn't mean anything."

"This thought that it's really cold outside doesn't mean anything."

Believe me, it's extremely liberating to realize that the running commentary that dominates my consciousness is not who I really am.

DON'T GET EVEN. GET ODD.

In an exuberant state of joy, you are at peace with everything about you . . . there is no thing unconquerable, no thing unreachable.

— RAMTHA

My friend's mother, who is visiting from her homeland of China, can't speak English. She likes to walk around the neighborhood and because she's friendly and always waves, neighbors often attempt to strike up a conversation. Her mom smiles and, even though she can't understand a word, says, "I love you. I love you. Good-bye."

The Dude is like my friend's mother. It sees me as perfect, beautiful, an amazing creation and can't understand the unhinged dialog that runs like a ticker tape through my mind. It just keeps saying, "I love you. I love you."

Lesson 5 from *A Course in Miracles* says: I am never upset for the reason I think.

It might seem like I'm upset because of something happening out there (politics, my mean stepfather, a snow bomb wreaking havoc with the electric grid), but it's always, 100 percent of the time, something that's happening within me.

Life itself is never painful. It's simply a mirror of my beliefs. And just like I don't look in the mirror, notice my mascara is smudged, and then try to "fix it" on the mirror itself, I can't really "fix" my problems out there. I "fix" my problems by recognizing them as a case of mistaken identity and then changing the inner belief, the inner cause.

Three or four times today, I'm asked to search my mind for any source of upset (worry, fear, depression) and to simply acknowledge that no matter its façade, its cause is not what I think.

Instead of getting even (with that problem that appears to be out there), I get odd by going inside and knowing that, despite all appearances, the Dude, like my friend's mother, is simply saying, "I love you. I love you. I love you."

WONDER WOMAN'S
TRUE SUPERPOWER

If you need to stop an asteroid, call Superman.
If you need to solve a mystery, call Batman. But if
you need to end a war, call Wonder Woman.

— GAIL SIMONE

Anyone who has ever attended one of my workshops knows I LOVE Wonder Woman. I have T-shirts, action figures, even underwear.

And while I applaud Gal Gadot's cinematic portrayal of our first female superhero, I wasn't down with all the violence.

A true changemaker would never perpetuate the "old way." A true changemaker would see that slaying bad guys just keeps the crazy going.

I will never be truly free until I move beyond the mistaken belief that bad guys exist.

Which is precisely the message in Lesson 6: I am upset because I see something that is not there.

So sure, I can work to overcome all the "evils," the "bad guys," the "problems."

Or I can retrain my mind to see a different reality.

Don't get me wrong. I still LOVE Wonder Woman. I will continue to stand in Wonder Woman pose.

And I will remind myself (three times today, according to my Workbook lesson) that just like movies aren't real, all those upsets I think I see are nothing but holograms that will radically change, not by fighting them, not by poking spears into their guts, but when I train my mind to see them differently.

MAXIMIZE 60 SECONDS
OF EVERY MOMENT

Now thyself.

— MEL BROOKS

Oh, good! You're still here!

Yesterday's lesson has a tendency to irk newbies. They tend to get plugged in by the Course's seeming suggestion that things like Sandy Hook and the Holocaust are illusions or holograms. "It doesn't seem quite right," a reader pointed out, "to ignore the fact that people died."

Since this relates to Lesson 7 (I see only the past), I'd like to share my take on it.

When I focus on the past, I ignore the astounding love and grace of right now. When I truly experience *this* moment (which is unique in all the world and has never happened before) tears roll down my cheeks. It's that beautiful. I often don't notice because I see only the past.

So it's not about ignoring tragedy. It's about NOT ignoring what's possible right in this moment.

It reminds me of the story about a pair of celibate monks. While crossing a river, they noticed a beautiful young woman struggling over the rocks. One of them quietly put her on his back and carried her across. The other monk silently stewed about the indiscretion as they continued their journey: *That's against our vows. We're not supposed to touch female flesh.* Finally, able to bear it no longer, he questioned his comrade, who replied, "I set her down four hours ago. It seems you're the only one still carrying her."

By now you know the drill: Look around and repeat. I see only the past in, say, this candle, that face, that notebook. Three times for a moment each should suffice.

In this moment, anything is possible, and everything is here.

I myself don't want to miss it.

THE WRECKING BALL

There comes a point when you know, without doubt, without hesitation, that you cannot go back to your old life. You cannot be who you once were and also have a new life with new riches.

— JULIE MCINTYRE

The past sometimes comes in handy. Like when ordering a pair of sneakers on Zappo's. Eliminates a lot of back and forth shipping if I know I wear a size 9. Or when I come to an intersection. Knowing what that red octagonal sign means prevents unnecessary collisions.

But other than a few useful details, the past is mostly a prison. It prevents me from seeing and experiencing life as it is now.

When I continue to regurgitate my past, the glorious field of infinite potentiality (the FP) can't get in. Nothing can ever change.

Lesson 8: My mind is preoccupied with past thoughts.

I know it might seem rather pointless to look at my thoughts four or five times today and call them out as the posers they are.

But it doesn't matter what I think of the exercises. It just matters that I do them. What's pointless are all the invalid decisions and assumptions I've made about what's best for me.

Today, I surrender my defenses, my fool bullheadedness and my convictions that I must figure everything out. I fall back into the loving arms of the Universe, whose sole purpose is to dish up my good.

A TRAGEDY AND COMEDY
ALL ROLLED INTO ONE

*Keep it light, so light that the pull of old, sad stories cannot
keep you from playing, dancing—cannot hold you down.*

— TONI LABAGH

My mind is like the jukebox in a sticky, smoke-filled bar. It has been playing the same old records for years. Yesterday it kept dropping quarters in the Country & Western slot. Maybe you've heard a few favorites: "Poor Me, Not Again," "I Really Must Be a Loser."

What a considerable relief to learn those familiar oldies are nothing but erroneous ideas. That they simply are not true.

For years, I actually believed my thoughts. I presumed something was wrong with me, that I wasn't doing life right.

Yesterday, the old melodies started playing in my mind. Because I know every word by heart, I joined right in. The old verses are as familiar to me as old Supremes songs—only mine are usually out of tune.

Before the Course, I could keep those lyrics going for days. I am so grateful I now watch my thoughts from a distance. I now know not to take them seriously, not to adopt them as my identity.

Even better is knowing there's another consciousness, a jubilant, gleeful, brilliant consciousness that invites me to boogie on a much better dance floor.

Lesson 9 (I see nothing as it is now) doesn't pressure me to believe I'm seeing the past, the false, the old familiar jukebox standards.

It just asks for a teensy bit of willingness. Maybe a spoonful. And to apply (I don't see this banana, this table, this laptop as it is now) three or four times today. The bigger thing will take it from there.

TRANSCENDING THE CHATTY ASSHAT IN MY HEAD

We cannot create anew with the same ole, same ole, same ole.

— SHERRIE TAYLOR-JONES

Once, when interviewing a visiting Indian guru, Larry King pointed to his turbaned head and asked, "How does it get so quiet in there?" The Swami answered, "It IS quiet in there. That's the natural state."

Everything else (the incessant mental verbalizing) is a crutch we non-Swami types use to buffer the world. The never-ending chatter narrates the world, slicing and dicing it to fit our personal story. Its purpose is to keep us distracted and disoriented.

Most of us are too close to the "roommate in our head" to be objective, to fully realize its overriding power over us.

As Lesson 10 of *A Course in Miracles* says: My thoughts do not mean anything.

After years of siding with the thoughts in our head, it can be confrontational to hear our "precious thoughts" mean nothing. To learn they're useless mental commotion devised to filter reality.

It doesn't even matter if the thoughts tell us nice things. Doesn't matter if they spout spiritual wisdom or tell us we should proceed immediately to the nearest bed and pull the covers up over our head. Either way, that voice is not us.

Just for kicks, stop for a second and make the voice in your head say, "John Jacob Jingleheimer Schmidt." Now, make it say it in a sultry voice.

See? It's at your command. And it's busy, night and day.

We mistakenly believe this ongoing sideline color commentary keeps us safe. But, as we learn in the Course, the nonstop vocalizing keeps us trapped. It keeps us from knowing who we really are.

So today, take it from Larry King's swami and start to observe the "roommate in your head."

Realize that chatty voice is not you. And know true freedom comes the moment you allow yourself to transcend it.

THE FUNHOUSE MIRROR

*Just remember life is all an illusion . . . it's your creation
and you can dismantle it and re-create at will.*

— NANETTE MATHEWS

We live in a quantum age where people can instantaneously Snapchat each other across the globe, shatter a kidney stone with nothing but a laser beam, and use little handheld devices to buy tickets to *Hamilton*.

Yet in our thinking, in our application of these new truths, we've barely budged. We're more than a century into this new quantum reality and very few of us consistently use these startling new processes in our personal lives.

Lesson 11 (My meaningless thoughts are showing me a meaningless world) sounds kinda bleak at first. But all it means is I'm still using industrial age thinking. I'm still investing my thoughts—my power, if you will—in victimhood, in this idea that life happens to me. This warped view of reality wouldn't be an issue if thoughts were mere puffs of smoke, blown away by the next breeze. But, as quantum reality has proven, my thoughts and beliefs (my consciousness) can and do create worlds.

All the people in my life, the circumstances, the "good" and "bad" are the out-picturing of my thoughts.

This lesson begins to introduce the main thesis from my book *E-Squared.*[*] My thoughts create my reality. My thoughts determine the world I see.

In three practice periods, simply look around and repeat the lesson, trusting that, while it might seem absurd, it has the power to break to pieces the indoctrination and programming that currently holds you hostage. Remind yourself that, silly as they seem, these lessons enable you to tune in to an ongoing Divine Broadcast of love that wants to be known and expressed through you. It's the bedrock of who you are.

---

[*] *E-Squared,* like this book, was adapted from the Course. In it, I pointed out the Dude's ongoing PR problem. That those who claimed to be his minions were not doing him (I prefer the less masculine pronoun "it") justice.

FIRST, REWIRE
THE INNER LIFE

Don't put the past in the cupboard of your flesh.

— CLAUDIA RANKINE

Bill Thetford, the Columbia professor whose plea for "a better way" launched the Course, suggested this: If a particular lesson or word or concept doesn't resonate, just rip that sucker out.

Today's lesson is the first RSO. Instead, I choose one of its side notes: "I get whatever I focus upon."

When I give up meaningless thoughts and ideas (and that's any thought of fear or distress or uneasiness), I begin to notice a more pleasing reality. So here's a story about erasing meaningless thoughts and assumptions.

Anand Giridharadas is a young Indian-American journalist whose book, *True American*, won all sorts of Best Book of the Year awards. It's about a Texas vigilante who walked into a Dallas mini-mart ten days after 9/11 and shot Raisuddin Bhuiyan, an enterprising Muslim immigrant from Bangladesh.

Bhuiyan survives, ends up getting to know his swastika-tattooed perpetrator, befriends his daughter, even tries to free him from death row. Let's just say the book is incredibly inspiring and shows that beneath the labels (our meaningless thoughts) is a much deeper story.

But this lesson features Giridharadas himself. He's 30-something, politically liberal, very PC. The other day a middle-aged white guy came to install a stove in his Brooklyn apartment. The white guy asks, "So . . . where are you from?"

That all-too-familiar question always raises red flags. *Here we go again. Another redneck racist making assumptions about my brown skin.*

But he chose to give up that meaningless thought.

Rather than deliver his stock, wiseass answer (Cleveland, because well, he was born and raised by Indian immigrants in Cleveland), he decided to give him the answer he knew he wanted. "I was born in Cleveland, but my family comes from India."

The stove repairman smiled and said, "That's what I thought. My brother married a woman from India. She has become the light in our family. We were a pretty dysfunctional family and then she turned everything around."

So, yes, it's easy to assume I know the way people are, the way this day is going to play out, but once I give up my meaningless thoughts, a beautiful new indescribable happiness is free to come streaming in.

13

PAPER, PLASTIC, OR THE TEEMING DAZZLE OF LIFE ITS OWN SELF

Withdraw your faith in distortions and invest in only what is true.

— A COURSE IN MIRACLES

A couple of years ago, I was invited (for free) on a cruise to Bermuda with three sexy chefs from the Bravo show, *Top Chef.*

There were private cooking classes, Quick Fire challenges, and meet and greets with bad boy celebrity chefs Ash Fulk, Angelo Sosa, and Spike Mendelsohn.

While this travel writing assignment certainly illustrates how miracles started rapping on my door when I began giving up meaningless ideas, my point is the cardboard cutouts. When I first arrived on the ship, I took a selfie with a cardboard cutout of the three guests of honor.

The purpose of ACIM's first 50 lessons is to notice that everything my eyes show me is a cardboard cutout. It's a picture of the past frozen in time, serving as a stand-in for the real thing.

Once I decide life is a certain way, the cardboard cutout is all I can see. My crafty brain literally reconstructs an empty shell, a caricature of the teeming life that exists in every now moment.

I can't really see the people, the events, my own backyard, not as they are now. Three or four times today, I stop and notice that I am looking at a cardboard cutout of my story. And I remind myself that as long as I do, the invisible grace and never-ending abundance remain invisible.

I'm happy to report that later during said cruise, I was able to take a selfie with the real deal, the flesh-and-blood chefs themselves. And let me just say (because whatever happens on a Top Chef Cruise stays on a Top Chef Cruise) the cardboard cutout paled in comparison.

MAKE IT FUN. MAKE IT YOURS.

*When it comes to revolution, we need big
doses of passion and audacity.*

— CHE GUEVARA

A Course in Miracles is like anything. You make it what you want it to be. My guiding philosophy: If it's not fun, it's not sustainable.

So I can be bothered by the language. Yes, Lesson 14 uses the controversial G word.

Or I can appreciate it for the rebellious and revolutionary program it is. I can notice the part about ditching my own personal house of horrors, the line about moving toward perfect safety and perfect peace.

Tony Hsieh, CEO of Zappo's, is the poster boy for making perceived un-fun things fun. In fact, he walked away from the first company he built (he was 27 and it was worth $265 million) because it didn't bring joy.

Zappo's (which does) is built on weirdness, creativity, being adventurous, and doing whatever it takes to give love. In corporate speak, love equals customer service, but, take it from me, it's love, pure and simple.

Like the Course, Tony eschews perfection ("jump in fast, make mistakes, it's all okay") and old paradigms. On a dare, he named his venture capital firm Venture Frogs (who does that?), and every day, he does something outside the business norm—like dye his hair red or wear a mohawk.

He lives in an Airstream, spends most of his non-working time outdoors (says he has the world's largest front porch), and knows without a doubt that if it's not fun, it's not worth doing.

So if a guy who doesn't even like shoes (he owns three pairs) can turn a billion-dollar online shoe company into a rockin' good time (a tour of their Las Vegas headquarters is better than a self-help seminar), I'm thinking we can transform this wordy blue book into weird, boisterous, meaningful fun.

So today, I'm gonna whoop and holler and recognize that anything that disturbs me, anything that isn't out-and-out gorgeous or doesn't ooze with big-ass fun is an illusion I concocted. And poof! I have the power to make it disappear. Sometimes, I even ask politely.

The Ultimate Billboard

I began to have this gnawing suspicion that this
voice in my head—while presenting itself as my trusted ally—
might actually be the enemy.

— JOSH RADNOR

At the end of interviews, I'm often asked, "If you could leave our listeners with one final piece of wisdom, what would it be?" In other words, what would I emblazon if I had a personal billboard?

I often hem and haw. Me? Wisdom? Or I run through the gazillion lessons I've picked up along my path to peace. Chief among them is pull myself back up when I land, near daily, flat on my face.

But finally, I've come up with a nugget of truth that, for me, vanquishes all others.

Nothing could be more vital than to be suspicious of the voice in my head.

This inner critic/taskmaster is loud. It's nonstop. And it does not, I repeat, it does not have my best interests at heart.

This demonic voice that insists on running the show is terrified. Because it knows. It knows it's an impostor. It knows its time is limited. And it knows that if and when I take my attention off its whiny, complaining voice, I will discover this other occupant in my head.

This other voice is a lot gentler. More patient. And it points toward the intangible, immeasurable, fundamentally spiritual things that defy every obnoxious missive the loudmouth has been shouting in my ear from the time I noticed I was encased in a body.

Beginning to recognize that the critical/naggy voice is not "me" is the starting gate for any spiritual path. Lesson 15 (My thoughts are images that I have made) is the recognition there is something bigger and unseen going on. Three times today, I stop and notice that this puzzle, this cereal bowl, this spoon are all images I have made.

I can't guarantee the obnoxious voice will eventually shut up. It probably won't. But as I recognize it's just making stuff up, I can call it out, I can say, "Oh really!" when it gets on its insufferable megaphone.

LIKE A ROOM
WITHOUT A ROOF

*My whole life has been an effort to find freedom—
freedom from myself, freedom from my own fears.*

— HELEN MIRREN

As a journalist, I was taught that the lede (the opening paragraph) of any story is my big chance to catch a reader's attention. Tell them who, what, where, when, and how—right up front.

A Course in Miracles doesn't do that. It tills the soil, prepares me slowly for the insanely radical notion that I'm not so much "observing reality" as I am creating it.

I get why people scoff. It's the exact opposite of every single lesson on planet earth. To suggest the world is not independent of my thoughts is alarming. And how could it possibly be true that the majority of my thoughts are meaningless? That sounds preposterous.

So I'll try to explain:

Any thought that falls into one of the following categories is basically meaningless:

I'm separate and all alone.
I'm limited to this body.
If I can't see it with my eyes, it doesn't exist.

Every thought that falls into one of these categories is meaningless. Or rather, it's simply NOT TRUE. It only appears that way because I secretly (or not so secretly) put my attention there.

The first few lessons of the Course serve as a giant eraser to gently remove all meaningless thoughts. To create space for things that actually ARE true. Things like ease and grace, being connected to an intensely alive energy field, knowing my purpose is to illuminate dark places.

Lesson 16 (I have no neutral thoughts) dispels the belief that my thoughts have no effect. It goes so far as to say that there is NO EXCEPTION to this fact. My every thought either furthers the illusion (the meaningless) or it furthers the truth that, rather than face reality, I actually create reality.

CHANGE YOUR STORY, CHANGE YOUR LIFE

The universe as we know it is a joint product
of the observer and the observed.

— PIERRE TEILHARD DE CHARDIN

Several years ago, *People* magazine sent me to interview the runner-up on the reality show *The Bachelor*.

The assignment was to find out if reality shows truly depict reality. Although we reporters are taught to be objective and simply report facts, I'm savvy enough to know that reality, like beauty, is in the mind of the beholder.

The bachelorette I interviewed was very clear that reality shows are anything but true. Early on, she was cast by producers as a certain character, a particular personality type (namely, the partier) and then everything that fit that story line was shown on TV and everything that didn't was left on the cutting room floor.

Even though we may not be television producers, we all edit our life experiences to fit the stories we make up. If our story line is that our boss is a jerk, for example, everything that furthers that plot goes straight to the active part of our brain.

If our story is that our significant other is lazy, everything that jibes with that scenario is registered and magnified.

The gazillion good things our boss and our partners do get left on the cutting room floor.

We literally can't see them. Likewise, if we believe life is hard or that money is difficult to come by, we find evidence to further that story line in our lives.

Lesson 17 (I see no neutral things) is an important step in identifying cause and effect as it operates in the world. It's a spiritual law as reliable as gravity. I magnetize into my life whatever my non-neutral thoughts focus upon.

Here's the routine:

I do not see a neutral _____ because my thoughts about _____ are not neutral.

Three times today, I'm asked to look about and recognize that I'm seeing nothing that is neutral.

WE'RE ALL IN THIS TOGETHER

It is all about love and how we all are connected.

— MARK WAHLBERG

In 2018, Ellen Pompeo (you probably know her as Meredith Grey on *Grey's Anatomy*) became the highest-paid actress on a television drama. She walked away from contract negotiations with a cool $575,000 per episode. Not bad for a kid from blue-collar Boston whose mom died of an overdose when she was just five.

It also represents Lesson 18: I am not alone in experiencing the effects of my seeing. In an interview with *The Hollywood Reporter*, Pompeo said she became empowered by watching Shonda Rhimes, the creator of *Grey's Anatomy*. As Shonda grew into her own power, as she shook off the shackles of the old paradigm (of not being worthy, of not being paid as well as her male counterparts), Ellen was able to do it, too.

And that's just the starting line for not being alone in the effects of my perceptions.

In fact, the majority of my interactions with others occur in the nonphysical realm. All those thoughts I think I'm privately keeping to myself? They're not really private. I might as well bellow them over an intercom. Subtly, everyone is getting the message anyway.

Whether aware of it or not, I am connected to a giant database and am constantly exchanging energy, not only with those in my inner circle, but with every being on the planet.

Today, in three or four quick practice periods, I'm asked to look around, pick a couple of random subjects, and say:

"I am not alone in experiencing the effects of how I see _____."

For example, I am not alone in experiencing the effects of how I see that African mask, those sunglasses, that water bottle.

How I see these things affects how others see them, maybe not a terribly useful concept when it comes to water bottles, but think how pertinent and healing to change how I see, say, a serial killer or a ruthless dictator. Or for that matter, the creepy FB commenter who called me a full-fledged idiot and New Age fraud.

THE TRAFFIC COP
INSIDE YOUR BRAIN

I love swimming in the great question of what is real, true, what's
happening here in this thing called life.

— GRACE BELL

So there's one more reality sand trap from which we need to escape. For years, we've known our brains produce thoughts. But it's only partially true.

Research in neuroplasticity shows our brains are constantly being rewired with new pathways forming and others falling dormant. At birth, our neurons have some 7,500 connections. Slowly, over time, these connections get pruned away and discarded. So technically it's our thoughts (or our beliefs) that create our brains.

And because our brains, like cranky old uncles, do not like to be wrong, they literally make stuff up. They construct reality to fit our beliefs, creating patterns and filling in blanks to reflect our dominant ideas, wishes, and emotions.

They even dump chemicals (our brains contain the equivalent analogs of all the naughty Schedule 2 substances—opioids, cannabinoids, hallucinogens, etc.) to match our beliefs. Some studies even suggest that all drugs are placebos, meaning they work because we think they will. A Course in Miracles says, "Well, duh!"

Our brains are such talented forgers, weaving a detailed and compelling tapestry of perception, that it never occurs to us to question the reality they manufacture.

Lesson 19 asks us to question everything. Three times today, we're asked to stop and remember cause and effect are never separate. And since we now know our brains play tricks, altering our neurochemistry and translating our personal HTML into vibrations and pictures that we mistake for reality, we plead for help.

We sincerely ask that all lines of leftover, outmoded, no-longer-working code be eliminated until we see nothing but our new miracle plan.

WHEN 1+1=3

Shall we let terror simplify the world to good and evil?
Or shall we lean toward one another, recognize our need,
and cherish all magnetic nudges toward inclusion?

— KIM STAFFORD

Lesson 20 (I am determined to see) asks me to step up my game. It asks me to commit to seeing truth and to remind myself of my commitment a couple of times an hour. It doesn't ask me to do 50 push-ups or love my enemies even once.

It asks me to briefly remember that if I make any exceptions or leave any situation or person out of the equation, I'm gonna experience the same old world.

Rather than be against anyone or anything, it asks me to see unity, peace, love, joy for all. It asks me to see the truth in the oppressed AND the oppressor, in the bullied AND the bully.

Opposition only perpetuates the old paradigm of winners and losers, of somebody being left out of the equation.

Remember the story from Lesson 12 about the Bangladeshi store clerk who decided to forgive the swastika-tattooed vigilante who shot him? What he discovered, when he became "determined to see" is that his shooter had come from broken parents, broken schools, a broken prison system. He grew up knowing that if his mom had been able to scrape together just 50 more bucks, she'd have aborted him. Is it any wonder he might have a slight bit of anger and resentment?

Today, I see and create a radically new vision, one where everyone wins, everyone gets a seat at the table.

21

THE SKY IS NOT FALLING

God is a comedian playing to an audience too afraid to laugh.

— VOLTAIRE

For years, my friend's sister-in-law threatened to boycott Kenny Rogers for using crass language in his song "Lucille."

"Why," she demanded to know, "would anybody write a song about 400 children crapping in the field?"

Ummm . . . because he didn't.

Like life that I sometimes misconstrue as "frustrating" or "pointless" or "hard," she misconstrued Kenny's lyrics, which actually go: "With four hungry children and a crop in the field."

In Lesson 21, I become determined to give up all thoughts "of crapping children." Any thought that makes me unhappy (even just a little bit) is misconstrued. And I am determined to see each one differently.

Even little ones that I tend to overlook. Five times today (for just a minute), I'm asked to search my mind for any person or situation that seems less than perfect. Doesn't matter how small.

And then I simply tell myself:

I am determined to see _____ (name of bozo) differently.

I am determined to see _____ (whatever sky-is-falling-run-for-cover thought that occurs) differently.

Any thought (even a tiny one) is fair game.

No longer using my thoughts to attack myself

*If beating ourselves up worked, we'd
all be thin, rich and happy by now.*

— CHERYL RICHARDSON

My friend Anita Moorjani wrote an amazing book called *Dying to Be Me*. It's about her four-year bout with cancer and the NDE (near death experience) that completely revolutionized her ideas about life and death.

Not long after returning from the other side and quickly healing from the stage four lymphoma that had ravaged her body, she got out of bed (she'd been unable to walk for months before), shuffled into the bathroom, and nearly fell over in shock when she saw her withered frame staring at her in the mirror. She looked herself straight in the eye and made this solemn vow: "I will NEVER do this to you again."

Until she got cancer, Anita says she was afraid of everything. Like so many of us, she was a people pleaser. She worked hard to be liked, to be a "good person," to be spiritual, to be a good employee. She tried to eat right. She says she worried constantly about microwaves, plastic containers, red meat, getting, you guessed it, cancer.

In other words, she was the poster child for Lesson 22: What I see is a form of vengeance.

At first read, this sounds pretty harsh, but when I hear stories like Anita's (or even pay attention to the running commentary in my own head), I realize how vengeful I often am . . . especially in my judgments of myself. I would never dream of speaking to anyone the way I often speak to myself.

This lesson also celebrates the joyous news that my countless fears and critical thoughts are NOT REAL. I learn there's an escape. Five times today, I look around and acknowledge that all I fear does not exist.

Anita had to die and go to what we call heaven to realize this precious truth. I get to do it today by simply asking for help to see life differently.

IT'S YOU, BOO!

There's a difference between knowing the path and walking the path.

— MORPHEUS, *THE MATRIX*

Lesson 23 may be the best news yet. It offers the secret key to the ocean of love that all these spiritual practices keep promising. It offers escape from the closed psychological structures that cause our pain, our problems.

It says: I can escape from the world I see by giving up attack thoughts.

This lesson succinctly explains that cause and effect is the organizing principle of the universe.

It says point blank, "There is no point in lamenting the world. There is no point in trying to change it."

The world is merely an effect of my thoughts. That's worth repeating. My thoughts and beliefs about the world are its cause. In quantum physics, it's called the observer effect.

So while there's no point in fighting to change the world, there is HUGE BENEFIT in changing my thoughts. That's why this workbook's daily practice is so important. Why Morpheus said there's a difference between knowing the path and walking the path.

Like it or not, I am the image maker of the world. This is shout-it-from-the-rooftop groovy because all I have to do is change my thoughts and beliefs. Once I do, the world changes automatically. Beautiful experiences rise up. Joy, beauty, love, and peace show up.

It's also worth mentioning that—despite what self-help books and therapy sessions preach—changing my thoughts and beliefs is a simple matter of asking for help.

That Voice that wouldn't stop pestering Helen Schucman is also eager to commune with me. With you.

24

HIRE THE STUNT DOUBLE

*Put down the script. You don't have to be an actor
in that drama anymore.*

— JERRY COLONNA

The brain is basically a bureaucrat. It looks at the past, applies it to the present and uses it as a map to predict the future. It literally makes up stories.

Lesson 24 (I do not perceive my own best interests) points out that in no situation is my perception accurate. How can I accurately decide on the best course of action when my brain distorts reality?

Today in five two-minute practice periods, I'm asked to honestly search my mind, to examine various situations and enumerate all the things I want to happen.

*In the situation involving _____, I would like _____
to happen, and _____ to happen.*

It quickly becomes apparent that I'm placing demands that have nothing to do with the situation and that many of these intentions are contradictory. Having no unified outcome is a setup for disappointment.

Which is why today's a good time to reemphasize the bennies of practicing the Course. I don't go through these lessons to be "more spiritual" or win brownie points with the Dude.

I do it solely because I CAN USE THE HELP.

When Matt Damon reprised his role as Jason Bourne in the fifth installment of the popular movie series, he was nine years older than the last time he'd played the titular character. Although he was still able to perform the fight scenes, he conceded to let a stunt double jump out of helicopters and madly speed through the streets of Berlin.

All of us have a stunt double—an inner voice that this Course calls the Holy Spirit. And unlike our brains, it always knows the best course of action.

This voice is not just available for Helen Schucman or Eckhart Tolle or, for that matter, Matt Damon, who must have been listening to his voice when he dropped out of Harvard to pursue acting.

The Voice is available to each and every one of us. And it always knows how to transcend ordinary experience and identify with the bigger part of ourselves.

Moral of this lesson? Fire your brain. Hire your stunt double.

25

THE HOME DEPOT OF
SPIRITUAL PRACTICES

*Do not bend reality to your tiny experience or limit
its purpose to your little personal thoughts.*

— A COURSE IN MIRACLES

The universe is kinda like Home Depot, offering an unlimited selection of tools to further my good.

Lesson 25 (I do not know what anything is for) assures me that every single person, every single thing that happens is in my best interest.

But instead of repeating that wordy mantra, I prefer to channel Hans Schultz. He's the fictional sergeant to Colonel Wilhelm Klink in the old TV series *Hogan's Heroes*.

Even though Schultz knew about the shenanigans of the Allied POWs who were running special operations from Stalag 13, he was famous for proclaiming to his inept colonel, "I know nothing" in a clipped, German accent.

I repeat that line (complete with the accent) quite often. In fact, it has become an important line item in my spiritual practice.

I have learned that any time I think I've figured something out, any time I believe I've found the route to this intention or that dream, I promptly proceed to get in my own way.

My understanding is sorely limited. But when "I know nothing," like Hans Schultz, I leave the gates wide open for blessings to rush in.

Six times today, I will remember Hans Schultz and thank him for proving that inspiration and important spiritual practices can come from anywhere.

TWO WORDS OR TEN?

If you could observe the physiological changes that take place in your body when you're in negative states, you would stop immediately.

— ECKHART TOLLE

In a funny skit on *MadTV*, Bob Newhart plays a shrink offering "Stop it!" therapy. A client named Katherine comes to him with panic attacks. She's frantic about being buried alive in a box.

Newhart's Dr. Switzer asks, "Has anyone ever tried to bury you in a box?"

Katherine: "No, but thinking about it makes my life horrible. I can't go through a tunnel or be in an elevator or in a house, anything boxy."

Dr. Switzer: "I'm going to say two words. I want you to listen very, very carefully."

Katherine: "Should I write them down?"

Dr. Switzer: "We find most people can remember them."

Of course, his two words (Stop it!) weren't what Katherine really wanted to hear. She wanted to go on and on about being bulimic, about having self-destructive relationships with men, about her germ phobia, being afraid to drive.

Like Dr. Switzer's two words, Lesson 26 (My attack thoughts are attacking my invulnerability) isn't what most of us want to hear. It basically says any thought that's not of love is an attack upon ourselves, an attack upon our invulnerability.

If it's true nothing can hurt me (as this lesson promises), maybe I could actually benefit from Dr. Switzer's comical five-minute, five-dollar therapy.

Instead, I'm asked to stop for two minutes, six different times today, and recognize that any thought of worry, anger, depression, or foreboding is an actual knife I thrust into my psyche.

In each of the two-minute sessions, I review a painful situation:

I am concerned about _____.

And then I'm asked to go over all possible outcomes.

I am afraid _____ will happen.

After naming each outcome I fret about, I simply tell myself, "That thought is an attack upon myself."

Attack thoughts (which make up the bulk of my incessant thinking) create a false image of who I really am. Slowly, but surely, as I start identifying my attack thoughts, I can give them to what I like to call the Holy S.*

It won't tell me to "Stop it!" but it will gently remind me that none of those thoughts are true. None of them can change who I really am: Invulnerable and forever free.

---

* You may have heard it called Holy Spirit. Helen called it the Voice.

WRITING A
DIFFERENT CAPTION

There is a quiet light that shines in every heart. . . .
It is what illuminates our minds to see beauty,
our desire to seek possibility and our hearts to love life.

— JOHN O'DONOHUE

Each week, The New Yorker, on the last page, offers a blank cartoon. Readers are invited to compose and submit clever captions. When I wrote this, for example, the back page featured a giant gingerbread man lying in a hospital bed with six doctors in chef hats peering down upon him.

Editors choose three caption finalists and then readers vote.

It never ceases to amaze me how widely varying the captions are. One simple cartoon, three astoundingly different captions.

This popular contest demonstrates just how completely different individual perceptions are. We may think everyone sees the world just like we do. But au contraire, my friends.

ACIM Lesson 27 says: Above all else I want to see.

I want to let go of my false perceptions, my own personally captioned cartoon. I want only to see the insanely beautiful truth in everything. In everyone.

That sycamore tree in my yard is literally pulsing with life. The sky overhead offers a stunning new canvas each day. Each of my fellow humanoids are, as Hafiz says, "God speaking." Today, I remind myself over and over again (four times an hour if possible) that "vision has no cost to anyone" and that every time I truly look at life without blinders, I send innumerable blessings out into the world.

WHEN THE UNIVERSE
STARTS SAYING, "HEY GIRL!"

*There is no end to the adventures that we can have
if only we seek them with our eyes open.*

— JAWAHARLAL NEHRU

When we truly commit to wanting to see things differently, blessings start showing up. Or rather we become open enough to notice. We begin to recognize we're not really separate from that table, that seashell, that "nasty politician."

Gail, a newbie to one of my possibility posses,* bebopped in the other day brimming with excitement. She couldn't wait to give her report.

She began her Saturday, as the Course recommends, asking for "a perfect day." She didn't specify what that entailed. She simply put in the order.

Right away, her phone rang. A friend had two tickets for a Master Gardener's tour. Would she like to join? Then she was treated to lunch, had an enlightening visit with yet another friend and then ended the evening at a Beatles reunion concert swaying and singing "All You Need Is Love" with an entire room of happy humanoids.

We, of course, applauded. That's what possibility posses do. But secretly I was wondering, Is it too early to tell her that every day can be like that? Would it harsh her mellow to reveal that *A Course in Miracles* promises "perfect days" every single day?

Lesson 28 (Above all else I want to see things differently) is crystal clear. Once we no longer bind our lives to our preconceived ideas, no longer define today in past terms, no longer limit our experience to our personal little thoughts, our days offer infinite value, full of happiness and hope.

---

* A possibility posse is a group that gets together to talk possibility, quantum physics, and the miraculous world we choose to see. Let me repeat—*we choose* to look for and register magic. That is our intention, our sole purpose. We're a support group, I guess you could say, for warding off the more prevalent story of lack and limitation.

QUESTION AUTHORITY

It's not denial. I'm just selective about the reality I accept.

— CALVIN AND HOBBES

The first thing I learned in journalism school is "question your source." Is the source reliable? Knowledgeable? Are the "facts" being presented scientifically provable?

This standard journalistic practice is especially useful when deciding which of the voices in the chorus of your head to listen to.

In Lesson 29, I learn love is in everything I see.

But if it's absolute fact that love is in everything, why do I see pain and dysfunction? Why am I afraid?

When thoughts like this arise, it's time to question your source. Who is this voice that screams, "Get me out of here. Make this stop?"

In my case, it's always my own made-up story, a petty, whiny voice that pouts, crosses its arms, and says, "Off with her head." The Course calls it my ego. I've nicknamed it the chatty asshat.

Six times today, for two minutes, I will consciously choose to see nothing but love. In everything. If the chatty asshat starts yammering, as its wont to do, I will question the source and realize that if what it's telling me frightens me or causes me to doubt my worth, it's just—as Faulkner calls it—my little postage stamp of reality.

THE DIVINE BUZZ
AND ME: A LOVE STORY

A feeling of peace and well-being spread through her veins.

— ANN PATCHETT

While I was brunching with my friend Judy, she asked if I was up for an experiment. She has been using psychologist Arthur Aron's 36 questions. It's a device, according to an essay in *The New York Times'* Modern Love column, for accelerating intimacy.

I think I surprised us both with my answer to question 4: What would constitute a "perfect" day for you?

Typical answers include things like being at the beach, sipping drinks with umbrellas, getting a massage.

I said (and I was as surprised as Judy) that my perfect day had nothing to do with activities or events. It has to do with my head space, with feeling the Divine Buzz that, at times, almost overwhelms me. I'm not even sure how to describe it. A sense of joy, a sense of life's fierce beauty. It's almost as if I could spontaneously combust with sheer rapture.

When those days (well, more like minutes of some days) happen, it matters not what I'm doing.

Believe me, I've had many of the "perfect" days promoted by the marketing machine—exotic vacations, five-star hotels, mountaintop lodges. But nothing compares to being on the frequency of the Divine Buzz.

The perks we think we want are cool. I'm often astonished by the things I'm invited to do as a travel writer. But those things don't guarantee happiness or "perfect" days. I managed to be miserable on a jungle safari in Brazil. My head wanted to be back home. My thoughts were judgy, insecure, lost.

The only requirement for a perfect day is having a happy mind. ACIM Lesson 30 says it like this: Love is in everything I see because Love is in my mind. When I join with what I see rather than hold it apart, I lock in the Divine Buzz. I will be grateful for this connection every chance I get and will therefore have a "perfect" day.

THERE'S A PARTY GOING ON RIGHT HERE

A miracle is the answer to any problem.

— MARIANNE WILLIAMSON

A Course in Miracles has lots of pages, lots of words, but it boils down to this: once we relinquish our old thought system, love becomes our M.O., and miracles and blessings are all we see.

As we let go of the creaky, has-been thought system that's currently playing out on our planet, we move . . .

From fear to love.

From problem state to possibility state.

From limitations to absolutely anything can happen.

And it starts with getting Lesson 31: I am not the victim of the world I see.

For five minutes, two or three times today, I'm asked to remember that the world out there is a result of the world in here. I hope you see me pointing at my head.

Once I let go of my belief (my thought system) that whatever problem seems to be plaguing me is ABSOLUTE TRUTH, a bigger picture (also known as a miracle) starts to emerge.

WE ARE ALL THOMAS EDISON

There is no end. There is no beginning.
There is only the infinite passion of life.

— FEDERICO FELLINI

In the quantum world, there's no such thing as absolutes. No one reality is truer than any other.

The quantum field is an infinite mashup of possibilities. It contains countless waves, dancing around in countless states, countless positions, countless possibilities. Each has its own energy and frequency.

It isn't until the waves are measured—or chosen—that they coalesce into one material reality, thus destroying the original configuration where "all is possible." Once we decide that, say, "life's a struggle" or that "people always disappoint me," we collapse that wave and lose touch with all the rest.

Lesson 32 explains it like this: I have invented the world I see.

So today I ask myself, do I want to continue inventing a world out of my complaints?

Or do I want to invent a world from oneness and joy and peace?

The material world as it's currently configured is based on fear. It's based on the belief that everything is out to get us: our politicians, our food, our bodies (which we examine regularly for breakdowns in yearly checkups), other countries, even our lovers, whom we've been warned to examine for signs that "he's just not that into us." Every news report, every commission, every political speech, every self-help book is based on our unending fascination with "what's wrong." We take pills, we buy energy drinks, we twist ourselves into yoga poses, we chant, we meditate, we pray to some nebulous deity in a fruitless search to correct all the wrong in our lives. Or the wrong we've been warned is coming.

The Course tells us that by treating, analyzing, and working so diligently to annihilate problems, we give them the power to govern us. By exercising such extreme efforts to "avoid" our inevitable demise, we actually facilitate the very demise we're hoping to avert.

So today, I acknowledge that I "made this world up" (in two 3- to 5-minute practice periods) and I commit to using my brilliant inventor mind—not to complain or whinge or look for problems—but to envision a luminous, happy, beautiful world for everyone.

THE HANGOVER, PART III

*Like all bullies, fear wants you to believe
it's tougher than it really is.*

— CRAIG FERGUSON

I'm happy to report I didn't see *The Hangover Part III*. Didn't even see the second in the trilogy.

What this one-star summer bomb demonstrates is my tendency to repeat myself again and again, day after day.

I get stuck in a loop, worshipping the same thoughts into form, seeing the same things I saw yesterday.

Lesson 33 assures me: There is another way of looking at the world. A simple shift of perception (practiced five minutes in the morning and five before bed) unlocks a treasure chest of new possibilities.

Ed McMahon (or his successor) could knock on my door with the magazine sweepstakes check. I could make a new friend or get an idea for a book or a song or a nonprofit that might change the lives of millions.

The thing is you never know. But when I blithely accept my brain's first explanation, I get re-runs *(Hangover Part III's)* of yesterday.

Today, I wake to a world that's completely unrecognizable.

I use this lesson as today's mantra and apply it immediately anytime I feel disturbed. I am resolute that—no matter how bad any event or person might look—"there is always another way to look at this."

So, yea, the first *Hangover* was kinda fun. But I'd rather see Bradley Cooper, Zach Galifianakis, and especially me starring in a whole new film.

PEACE: THE ALL-PURPOSE ELIXIR

I began to think of children not as immature adults,
but of adults as atrophied children.

— KEITH JOHNSTONE

Today's mantra is an all-purpose elixir. I use it at all times, in all situations.

No matter what happens, no matter how bad things look, I remind myself that "I could see peace instead of this."

I'm in no way beholden to see peace. There's no pressure to give up my perception. But I *am* asked to raise peace as a possibility. No matter how remote it might seem, it helps to admit that "I COULD see peace instead of what I'm currently seeing."

The Course tells me I see nothing that is really alive or really joyous. Rather, I see a dull and gray substitute to what's really there. With spontaneity educated right out of me, I only see what I think ought to be there. My perceptions are frozen. They're locked in stone like King Arthur's sword.

I like to trick my mind out of its habitual patterns by practicing an improv technique popularized by Keith Johnstone, a pioneer in improv theater.

For five minutes, three times today, I look around the room and shout out the wrong name for everything my eyes light upon. For example, I call the TV a pancake, the couch a steel guitar.

This not-so-silly exercise allows me to transcend the world and to entertain the slight possibility that maybe, just maybe, "I could see peace instead of this."

THE BULL IN
THE CHINA SHOP

What is "out there" depends on what you choose to look for.

— FRED ALAN WOLF

One of the most infuriating dilemmas in science is that the moment researchers attempt to measure atomic and subatomic systems, they literally morph into something else. Like shapeshifters, they mutate once a human being gets involved. It's almost like they read our minds and, out of courtesy, politely turn into whatever configuration we're expecting.

You want a wave? Here, have a wave. You prefer particles. Voila! particles!

It's my consciousness—my expectations—that forms what's there for me to see. And once that formation solidifies, other possibilities vanish. They're rendered nonexistent.

In other words, it's literally impossible to "see" the true nature of reality.

Lesson 35 describes it like this. I surround myself with the environment I want. These objects, these people, these circumstances seem to be "out there." They seem to exist completely independent of me and what I think. But they're not.

I am literally part and parcel of all I perceive. Nothing exists independently of my observations. Everything I see, all alleged "separate objects" are linked to my mind in surprising and mysterious ways.

Today, in three 5-minute practice periods, I stop to look at how I'm perceiving the world. And I concede that I'm the one setting everything into motion.

BLAST EVERYONE
WITH LOVE TODAY

Call everyone to your table of kindness.

— MAJAYA

One of the things I love most about the Course is I can do it anywhere. The trick is to not get hung up on doing it right, on having to meet every fool deadline.

I once practiced this particular lesson (My holiness envelops everything I see) while on travel assignment in Quebec, Canada. Rather than review and analyze the sled dogs, my ski partners, the trekkers who led me on wolf-watching and ice-fishing expeditions, I made a conscious decision to envelop everything I experienced in love and holiness.

I used my pretend love laser to blast everything with hope and peace and love.

Here's why I stick with the Course year after year:

1. It requires no effort on my part. In fact, the more I give up to the Dude, the more effective it becomes.

2. It can be practiced anywhere. I've worked the Course lessons on airplanes, in an African safari tent, and in a Filipino hot springs.

3. When I started following the big, fat book in earnest, my life began to change. When I asked the Voice for assistance, all sorts of miracles were orchestrated on my behalf.

So let's review. I don't have to do anything. It's geographically flexible. Miracles appear before my eyes.

Today, in four 3- to 5-minute practice periods, I ramp up my love mojo. Instead of obsessing about the cardboard cutouts my brain pumps out, I actively connect with an attitude of love. Rather than confine and reduce all I behold, I merge with each situation, every person and rest in pure, unencumbered presence.

NON-STOP
DRESS REHEARSAL

I'm thinking about naming my first son Emmy so I can say I've got one. I want Emmy, Oscar, and Tony—and my daughter Grammy.

— NOAH WYLE

Alessia Cara, the 21-year-old Canadian pop singer who in 2018 won the Grammy for Best New Artist, is living proof of one of my top ten maxims: "We animate into our lives whatever we put our attention upon."

The night of her big win, when she strode to the stage to accept her award, she said, "Holy cow. I'm shaking. I've been pretend-winning Grammys since I was a kid, like in my shower."

So what I want to know is what are you rehearsing? In your head. In your shower. In your everyday thoughts.

If you can't answer right away, just look around. Look at where you are. Look at what you have.

That, my friend, is what you've been rehearsing.

In ACIM Lesson 37, I rehearse a statement that upgrades every single thing in my life: My holiness blesses the world. I'm asked for four 3- to 5-minute practice periods reflecting on this thought.

Until I fully realize that I am holy, completely 100 percent whole, I will still believe in (and therefore experience) sacrifice. Until I learn to bless the world, to see through eyes of gratitude, a "payment" will be involved. Either from myself ("I need to try harder") or from someone else ("It's not fair what that creep did to me").

And here's the real kicker. From the perception of problem (even the tiniest complaint), I will continue to see loss. And I will have no idea that my lack of gratitude, my lack of blessing, my lack of wholeness is the cause.

My purpose, the Course tells me, is to see the world through my holiness. To see it through the beauty Cara sings about in her hit "Scars to Your Beautiful."

CALLING ALL SUPERHEROES

We can change the world if we start trusting our own superpowers.

— NINA HAGEN

Baby Huey, a popular cartoon character when I was growing up, is a naïve, oversized duckling in diapers. Because he has the mentality of a baby, but the size and strength of a sumo wrestler, he inadvertently knocks things over and constantly causes problems. He has no idea of his superhuman strength. That's us, in a nutshell.

Our consciousness has the size and strength of a sumo wrestler, but because we don't know it, we squander our abilities and often make a mess of things.

Lesson 38 (There's nothing my holiness cannot do) speaks to the size and strength of our abilities.

If you really get this one, if you incorporate it into your everyday thinking, you've mastered the Course. It's the reason the law of attraction works. It's the reason there's never reason to despair. It's why J.C. could heal the sick, raise the dead, and walk on water.

The only reason the world "stays" the way it is now is because we use our superpowers to stare at things we don't like. We run the data we downloaded from our culture instead of generating the brilliance we're capable of.

Every atom, every molecule, every energy wave of your being pulses with the creative life force.

So allow me to paraphrase from the actual lesson itself:

- Holiness is your superpower.

- It reverses all laws of this world.

- It allows you to remove all pain, end all sorrow, and solve all problems.

- It gives you dominion over all things.

Ready to don your cape and step out of the phone booth?

THE RUMBLE IN THE JUNGLE INSIDE MY HEAD

*If you sucked all the thoughts out of
your head, you'd find nothing but peace.*

— JILL WHALEN

The ego is a shapeshifter constantly working to throw me off guard. It tries to convince me it's big and scary and powerful and that it can get me at any time.

Lesson 39 (My holiness is my salvation) provides a simple tool to overcome the ego's default position of bracing for disaster. It tells me, in no uncertain terms, that my badass holiness will vanquish the ego's every ruse.

Because the ego deals in untruth and rumor, it has to conceal itself to be effective.

That's why, whenever I have the presence of mind to do so, I separate myself from the ego's voice by simply observing it. I think about it in third person. That way I'm not tempted to take the ego's lies as my identity.

I'm asked today to close my eyes for five minutes (in the morning and evening and whenever it's convenient) so I can seek out the ego's many guises: uneasiness, depression, anger, fear, worry, attack, insecurity.

And to know that whatever complex form these thoughts seem to take, they're all the same: an attempt to keep me in hell. They're unloving and, therefore, NOT TRUE.

PURPLE LIGHT

*Nothing prepared me for being this awesome. It's kind of a shock
to wake up every morning and be bathed in this purple light.*

— BILL MURRAY

It has come to my attention there are people out there who think it's
important to struggle, to fight, to fix all the problems.

But what if the only reason we think we're in trouble is because our
thoughts and energy are vibrating at a frequency that doesn't match
the Bigger Thing?

Lesson 40 (I am blessed as a Child of the Universe) reveals the purple light Bill Murray is talking about. It's what all of us are entitled to—
being blessed, being happy, being peaceful, being loving and loved.

Anything that doesn't line up with that frequency is an illusion,
a mirage that we created and we can change. Simply by picking a different door.

As the Course also says, "The separated ones have invented many
cures for what they perceive to be the 'ills of the world.' But the one
thing they do not do is question the reality of the problem."

Today, four or five times an hour, I will question the reality of
all my so-called problems and bask in the sheer deliciousness of the
purple light.

GET OUT! ESCAPING THE LITTLE HOUSE OF HORRORS

Love has befriended me so completely it has turned to ash and freed me of every concept and image my mind has ever known.

— HAFIZ

I'm a sucker for a good quote—probably because I'm a writer and adore words and ideas. I rarely write anything (except travel articles) without leading off with a quote.

ACIM Lesson 41 (The Divine Buzz goes with me wherever I go) is chock full of worthy words of wisdom for my collection.

For example, "Leave appearances. Approach reality."

What appears to be (in the news, in my litany of dislikes, fears, and problems) is a hologram of my beliefs. As long as I continue to "invent cures" for my personal house of horrors, they will continue to star in my reality. But the minute I question their validity, they will literally disappear.

This is SO difficult to believe because, like all humans, I've invested my entire life in the idea of problems. I think it's my mission to eradicate things I do not like.

But what if they're not even real?

Today, instead of believing in what the Course calls "the heavy cloud of appearances," I will celebrate the fact that the Divine Buzz (the Source of all Joy) goes with me wherever I go. One practice period is all that's required.

And I will know that anything that might look like a problem is just me making up a story that will go "poof" the minute I withdraw my belief.

The problem, as this lesson stresses, is not real.

IT'S ALL A GIFT

*My favorite moments shoot certainty full of holes. They barge
in unaccounted and track mud all over the carpets, grab me
by my shirt, drag me out into the street and say, in effect,
"Wake up you fool and open your eyes. There is more.*

— NATE STANIFORTH

Lesson 42 is an RSO (rip that sucker out) that I've chosen to replace
with these four lines from today's lesson:

My passage through time and space is not at random.
I cannot fail in my efforts to achieve the goal of the course.
It's a gift and I don't have to do anything.
I can receive this gift anytime, anywhere, in any circumstance.

When I ask to see things differently, as the Course suggests, I turn
the light on all thoughts that cause me pain and, like cockroaches,
those thoughts begin to scatter.

Nothing—my anger, guilt, frustration, even death—makes me any
less worthy of the gift. My thoughts (what the Course calls the ego) try
to tell me I'm not worthy, that it's not okay to feel certain things.

But today, I vow to separate myself from my thoughts (just a little).
The trick is to simply observe them, not adopt them as my identity.

As I learn to be gentle with myself (often the hardest thing to do), I
find there's no need to "find my happier self" or to "cut the anger from
my psyche." The Truth about myself can't be changed by my judgments, my opinions, my belief that something's not okay.

For today, as often as I can, I will breathe and know that whatever
train of thoughts plows through my head is all okay.

SUPER GOD TO THE RESCUE!

It didn't really come up that much, the need to yodel.

— ELIZABETH BERG

When George Eastman introduced the first commercially available camera in 1888, he had a goal. He wanted to make photography "an everyday affair." Or as his company Eastman-Kodak later rephrased it, to make it as "convenient as a pencil." Their marketing slogan was: "You push the button, we do the rest."

That's sorta how I see A Course in Miracles. I don't have to understand it. I don't even have to like what it says. I just have to push the button.

Lesson 43 (God is my Source. I cannot see apart from Him) is another RSO. It's one of those lessons I don't like all that much. It's preachy and strikes me as not much fun.

So here's what I do when I feel grumpy about one of the lessons.

First, I flip through the text and find one of the lines I've underlined, one that I DO like. For example, today I opened to:

Only you can deprive yourself of anything.
The laws of happiness were created for you.
Lack does not exist in the kingdom of God.

Secondly, I replace the word *God*, which, as I mentioned earlier, has more baggage than the Chicago airport, with one of my trusty synonyms.

Next, I turn my day over to the Holy S (aka the Voice). Relying on an unseen badass that happens to be holy is much more desirable than turning it over to the vicious brute that some churches pontificate about.

And here's the clincher. In the end, none of it's up to me. I just have to push the button.

GO TOWARD THE LIGHT

There's more joy than I knew.

— MARY KARR

I'm not psychic, but I'm pretty sure that 100 years from now (hopefully sooner), future generations are going to look back at our belief in separation and limits and wonder, "What were they thinking? How could they have been so misinformed?"

They'll scratch their heads at our refusal to live in the light, to celebrate our joy in much the same way we look back at the Roman Circuses.

"Are you kidding me?" we think. "How could thousands of people sit around drinking wine and being entertained by lions ripping gladiators apart?"

They'll consider it a laughable curiosity that we treated ourselves this way, that we chose to suffer when right on the other side of the veil is everything we could possibly want.

Lesson 44 (The Dude is the light in which I see) basically tells me it's far more radical to live in light than to live in despair.

The side effect of despair and limitation is I live at half throttle. By not delighting in my inherent gifts, I actually live out the outdated Roman Circus–like notion that I am weak and incapable of creating my life.

Future generations will also consider it freakishly odd that we felt so guilty and didn't have the fun and joy to which we are entitled. They won't understand why we didn't relish in our creative powers. They'll puzzle, "They had this amazing gift and they left it sitting in the corner, unwrapped."

For what it's worth, future generations, I'm doing my part (in three 3- to 5-minute practice periods) to proclaim my light and spend my day in unadulterated wonderment.

LIKE HOUSEBREAKING A PUPPY

We all long for love. Everything else is just killing time.

— KENNY LOGGINS

Training my mind to think with Source is like housebreaking a puppy.

I keep taking it back outside and showing it a different reality. Until, one day, it finally realizes, *Wow, there's a whole big world out there. And it's a lot more fun to pee on trees and bushes and fire hydrants than on Pam's ratty old house slippers.*

On a daily basis I instruct my mind to look for beauty. Encourage it to seek out the bigger picture, to focus on the love. My mind is an incorrigible slacker, keeps wanting to return to familiar old ruts. Keeps listening to the spin doctor that looks at the world as a potentially scary place. Insists on focusing on the "information" from my five senses, from the news media, from the default setting that says, "Be careful. Worry. Don't even think about learning to trust."

So I just keep taking it back outside, directing it to focus on what I know to be Truth. That everybody in the world really loves each other and that kindness is always the correct answer.

When I choose kindness and generosity in whatever situation I find myself, to whomever happens to be in front of me, it opens a crack to see a whole different reality.

That tiny twist—a smile, offering a hand, even just being generous in thought—changes the inner landscape. It reminds me, "Here's how the world could be."

Generosity doesn't fit the narrative, not in a me-me-me world. And that's the very thing that shakes up the old story, the dominant paradigm.

And anytime that puppy starts heading toward those slippers, I simply pick it up and take it back outside.

THE F-WORD FOR BEGINNERS

Leave your fear at the train station.

— PAUL SELIG

According to *A Course in Miracles,* forgiveness (the F word) is an always-available get-out-of-jail-free card. It's the answer to damn near everything.

The problem is we don't really understand what it means.

Forgiveness doesn't tell me to overlook something someone did to me. The F word, according to the Course, means it's impossible for anyone to DO something to me. For me to think, even for a brief moment, that I understand the world from the tiny bits of my perception is an epic fail.

All I can see, all I will ever see, is what the viewfinder of my limited perception shows me. If my perception is fixed, nothing can come between the goal that it has chosen.

Let's say I choose the perception that so-and-so is a misogynistic asshole. If that perception stays fixed (meaning, I refuse to forgive), nothing—not a miracle, not a sign, not an evidential slap in the face—allows any other reality to manifest.

Likewise, if my perception is convinced that money is hard to come by, the world's unlimited abundance cannot get through my blockade. It's right there, eager to unfold in my life, but my perception has put up orange cones.

Forgiveness means knowing my perception is forever tiny and incomplete. Forgiveness is to defy the lie that something is wrong, that life blows, that so-and-so is a horrible, evil person.

The best feature of forgiveness is that it relieves me of having to make judgments. Knowing I can't and don't understand "the whole" relieves me of having to decide what's good and bad, decisions I'm incapable of making. It literally sets me free.

Today, I use my get-out-of-jail-free card during three 5-minute practice periods. I close my eyes, think of all the douchebags I have yet to forgive, and repeat this phrase: "Source is the Love in which I forgive."

I'M SORRY, WHAT?

I've given God a big bag to fill. Because when you give him a small bag, it's like, "You can do that yourself. Why'd you bother me?"

— YVONNE ORJI

The same Voice that hired Bill Thetford and Helen Schucman to write the Course told Yvonne Orji, the Nigerian American comedian who plays Issa Rea's friend Molly on HBO's *Insecure,* to take up comedy.

Like Helen, she rolled her eyes.

Comedy? I just finished a master's degree in public health. I don't do funny. I'm an immigrant. My parents expect me to be a doctor or a lawyer, maybe a pharmacist.

But by then, Yvonne had enough experience to trust what Lesson 47 (The Dude is the strength in which I trust) promises: "His voice will tell you exactly what to do. In all situations."

So she wrote a five-minute comedy bit to use as her talent in a beauty pageant. That led to her animated stand-up work that led to the starring role on Insecure that led to a contract for a new book, *Bamboozled by Jesus: How God Tricked Me Into the Life of My Dreams.*

As she says, "The Holy Spirit sensed my doubt because right after he told me to do stand-up, I got a download from Heaven. . . . I grabbed a pen and paper, and I wrote everything I heard as He dictated plans for my life."

Over the years, Yvonne has developed a very intimate relationship with the Voice. By trusting its advice, she found exactly what this lesson promises: a place in her mind with deep peace, a place that knows nothing is impossible.

As she says, "Y'all, this comedy thing was His idea. And the reason I am so good and so happy is because I know how God works. I have seen His M.O. so many times. I can be like, 'But I thought this was it? God be like, 'Oh, that's what you thought? I got the goods for you.'"

Today, I'm asked to pick up my own goods in four 5-minute practice periods. I'm asked to close my eyes, look at my fears and dismiss each one.

A COURSE IN MIRACLES
EXPLAINED IN 11 WORDS

Your being by nature is joy.

— MOOJI

While it seems really dense and bogged down in words, *A Course in Miracles* can be summarized like this:

The universe has my back and everything's going to be okay.

Everything else is just a big ruse.

By practicing the lessons, I begin to "get it" that joy is my natural state. I begin to realize that fun is my guiding light and feeling good is my purpose. I even go so far to recognize that joy is why I'm here.

Lesson 48 (There is nothing to fear) simply states a fact. Today's practice periods should be short, simple and frequent. Make the "nothing to fear" mantra a running commentary.

And know that when you allow your natural hum of joy to emerge, your beautiful broadcast literally uplifts the world. Sharing it is an important public service.

THING 1 AND THING 2

To fight the Empire is to be infected by its derangement.

— PHILIP K. DICK

Dr. Seuss's Thing 1 and Thing 2 wear red jumpsuits and blue afros. My Thing 1 and Thing 2 are voices that compete in my head with opposing narratives.

Thing 1 is my creative voice. It says things like, "Dance, sing loudly, high five that stranger on the bridge." It's the part of my mind that Lesson 49 (Source speaks to me all through the day) assures me is in constant communication—even when I'm not aware of it.

Thing 2 is my monitor voice. It urges caution, measures what I could lose, teaches me to be a consumer. It conditions me to focus on my safety, to wriggle into a constrictive mold so people I don't even know will say, "good job."

Thing 2 is what the Course calls the ego. It lives in the past, worries about the future, is obsessed with lack. Basically, it's a grievance machine. It's happiest when pretending to be me.

Today, I make note of Thing 2's disorganized and distracted narrative. Instead of fighting it, I simply notice. I choose to identify instead with the part of my mind (Thing 1) where stillness and peace forever reign. This lesson promises I can easily listen to Thing 1 without interrupting my regular activities in any way.

Instead of saying things like "I am anxious" or "This Course makes no sense," I will stop four times today (for five minutes) and remind myself: "Thing 2 might be anxious" and "Thing 2 might believe the Course makes no sense," but Thing 1 is right here, safe, unencumbered and unaffected in any way.

MANNA, UMBRELLAS, AND PENNIES FROM HEAVEN

Our bodies resonate with the love and power of creative cosmic rhythms dancing through every cell in our beautiful beingness.

— RAMON RAVENSWOOD

Anyone who hangs out with Tom Cruise for more than an hour or so notices people constantly bring him things—freeze-dried organic blueberries, for example, or a baseball hat to block the sun or a green juice. Every hour or so, his personal chef or one of his assistants shows up with some new item he simply can't live without.

These "gifts" seemingly show up out of nowhere. If it starts raining—poof—an umbrella miraculously appears. Whatever he needs—a culinary pick-me-up or a costume change or a yellow vase for a bouquet of roses—shows up, almost magically.

He doesn't even have to ask.

In the case of the *Top Gun* star, it's his crew that works the magic. But it's also a fitting metaphor for Lesson 50: I am sustained by the love of Source.

What I've noticed is that once I rid myself of the old "life sucks" paradigm, once I get it that the universe has my back, really cool things begin magically appearing in my life.

I call it manna—gifts from the universe—that literally falls from the sky whenever I let go of the idea that I need to be fearful, that I need to worry.

My dear friend, Annola, laminated a sign that when laid on the dashboard of my car, reflects this sentiment on the front window: "Everything always works out for me."

It's my motto and today I repeat again and again, "I am sustained. I am sustained. I am sustained."

Boom!

Review I

When they said sit down, I stood up.

— BRUCE SPRINGSTEEN

Lessons 51 to 60 are reviews, reminding me of the 50 lessons I've allegedly mastered.

I'm asked to spend two minutes in the morning and another two minutes before I nod off to ZZZZ-land thinking about miracles. Considering it takes more time to microwave a Hot Pocket, that's not a preposterous ask.

The key is to get these concepts stuck in my head like, say, "Who Let the Dogs Out?" or Britney Spears's "Baby One More Time."

My goal is to inadvertently find myself humming these concepts, tapping them, and especially applying them whenever I'm distressed or believing something's wrong. Meditating on these ideas in the morning is cool and all, but I want their replacement to be automatic.

Here's how I want it to work:

"We will, we will . . ."

I hope you're thinking, "rock you."

Queen's hit "We Will Rock You" is so catchy, so familiar, that those four simple words "We will, we will . . ." trigger my auditory cortex, and I can't help but immediately fill in the rest of the line.

That's my goal, the involuntary application of these principles. The very second a troubling thought crops up, ka-boom! a miracle pops in to replace it.

And speaking of music, it's such a potent force that, instead of another recitation of the principles, I've chosen a song for each of the following 10 reviews. Play it on YouTube (it's easy enough to find a link) while brushing your teeth each morning. Apply anytime your asshat tries to point out that whatever it is you're looking for is somewhere else, hiding around the next bend.

Each review also comes with a miracle story that defies what we think we know, a story that suggests "maybe there's something bigger going on."

Because conventional wisdom deems miracles too good to be true, too pie-in-the sky, we Course students need to hear (over and over again) that miracles are normal, that they happen ALL the time. In this review, I hereby invoke the four-minute-mile rule, the one that says that if one person did it, the rest of us can do it, too.

IT'S ALL A MIRAGE

I do not believe in miracles, I rely on them.

— YOGI BHAJAN

The need-to-know: Nothing is as it appears.

From the jukebox: "I Feel Good" by James Brown.

The "We will, we will . . .": Life doesn't give a sh*t about me.

The ". . . rock you": James Brown was born into extreme poverty, was abandoned by his mother before sixth grade, lived much of his childhood in his aunt's brothel, and, when he was 16, was sent to a juvenile detention center for stealing a three-piece suit from a car.

Doesn't sound like much of a miraculous life. But if it wasn't for the detention center, the Godfather of Soul, the most sampled artist of all time, would have never met Bobby Byrd, who not only secured his early release from the detention center, but adopted him into his large family, invited him to sing lead for his R&B vocal group, and launched his career as one of the most influential musical artists of all time.

As Brown once said, "If I hadn't stolen that suit, I'd have never found my 'family.'"

It's a good reminder that nothing is as it appears on the surface. Let me remind myself today (over and over) that I am incapable of accurately judging anything.

PAST? WHAT PAST?

The aim of life is to live, and to live means to be aware,
joyously, drunkenly, serenely, divinely, aware.

— HENRY MILLER

The need-to-know: The world I see is a picture of the past.

From the jukebox: "Happy" by Pharrell Williams.

The "We will, we will . . .": I have to work my ass off to make things happen.

The ". . . rock you": World travel plays a starring role on many a vision board. "Common knowledge" (aka the past) insists the best way to accomplish that goal is get a job, accumulate enough money and vacation time to visit, say, Cape Town or Belize or the Cook Islands, all places I've visited in the last few years.

I, on the other hand, had no expectations one way or another. I knew I had a burning desire to travel, but I had nary a clue how to make that happen. What I did have was the wherewithal to acknowledge I had no clue. It was abundantly clear to me that if I was going to jet around the world, my only option was to give it up to the universe.

I let it go completely, trusting the universe was a heck of a lot smarter and more abundant than me.

Instead of following the "accepted path" of slaving away and accumulating money and vacation time, I now travel for free. The universe led me into travel writing, an occupation I'm not even sure I knew existed when I first made the declaration that I wanted to be a world traveler.

Money? Who needs money?

MIRROR, MIRROR
ON THE WALL

God had come to seem like Miles Davis, some nasty genius scowling out from under his hat, scornful of my mere being and on the verge of waving me off the stage for the crap job I was doing.

— MARY KARR

The need-to-know: The world I see reflects my thoughts. If I see suffering and loss, I'm not allowing my real thoughts.

From the jukebox: "Celebrate" by Kool & the Gang.

The "We will, we will . . .": The world is chaotic and we're all destined to wither and die.

The ". . . rock you": When Mike Pauletich was 42, he was diagnosed with early onset Parkinson's. Doctors told him that within a decade he'd be unable to walk, stand, or feed himself.

Seven years later, with the disease in full swing, he agreed to participate in an experimental new drug treatment that injected a chemical called neutrurin into his brain through two holes in his skull, one in each hemisphere.

Almost immediately, his shaking disappeared, his mobility improved, and his speech became markedly clearer. Before long, he was heli-skiing and running marathons. He even climbed Yosemite's Half Dome.

His doctor was astonished. By April 2013, however, she learned the experimental Parkinson's trials had failed. The neutrurin injections worked no better than the placebo sham surgery where fake "divots" were drilled into patients' skulls.

Pauletich's doctor almost hated to tell him. She looked into his records and was even more blown away to discover he had undergone the sham surgery. Neutrurin had never been delivered.

Instead, he got a miracle. He replaced meaningless thoughts with ultimate truth. He gave up the insane belief that he was a body, that he could suffer. Meaningful beliefs (his Divine perfection) restored him to Truth.

BIG, BAD THINKING PROBLEM

I have an insane belief in my own ability to manifest things.

— JIM CARREY

The need-to-know: Thoughts have power. (Or as the Course describes it, there's no such thing as an idle thought.)

From the jukebox: "Don't Worry, Be Happy" by Bobby McFerrin.

The "We will, we will . . .": My thoughts have no bearing on physical reality.

The ". . . rock you": One of the key reasons I accept all invitations to present workshops (what I call play shops) is because I meet the most amazing people. I hear the most miraculous stories.

In Seattle, one year, I met a woman who used the principles in *E-Squared* (which, like this book, was adapted from the Course) to win one of HGTV's Dream Homes. Another got front row tickets to a U2 concert, even though it was sold out.

At a workshop in Austin, one of the participants told me about the time she casually mentioned, "My lawn is out of control. I just wish someone would come over and mow it."

Not 15 minutes later, she heard a lawnmower outside revving its engine. She looked out her window to see one guy mowing her lawn, another with a weed-eater. She had no idea who they were. There was no sign on their truck, no notice of why they appeared. She never saw them again. But they did a fabulous job executing the very thing she had just requested.

Isn't it a fun possibility (and a guaranteed fact according to the Course) that everything (healing, every need) could be that incredibly easy?

MIRACLE 101

The people who know God well—mystics, hermits, those who risk everything—always meet a lover, not a dictator.

— RICHARD ROHR

The need-to-know: True reality presents a world of peace and safety and joy.

From the jukebox: "Better When I'm Dancing" by Meghan Trainor.

The "We will, we will . . .": Life's a sh*t show.

The ". . . rock you": Six local plumbers were lined up outside my friend Bonita's rental apartment. They were shaking their heads, ruing the fact that the serious clog in Apartment 5A's waterline could not be fixed for less than $8,000. And that was if they were lucky while digging up the drainage pipe.

One after another, the local plumbers unanimously agreed there was no other solution. Eight grand was the rock bottom bid. Bonita might have bought it except that she hadn't budgeted $8,000 for that month's repair bills.

Bonita decided to ponder it for one more day. She decided to let the Dude reveal an answer. She decided to do what most of us forget to do—she asked for a miracle.

Next morning at a meeting in Kansas City, Bonita asked colleagues for suggestions. One plumber's name came up repeatedly.

"Why not?" she shrugged. "So what if he charges extra to drive from out of town?"

She explained her situation, told him what his fellow plumbers had all concluded.

"I can do it for less," he said. "In fact, I'm so sure I won't charge you travel time."

He walked into the apartment and within an hour, the $8,000 problem was fixed.

Bonita's bill? Two hundred dollars.

So despite what all the "local, stuck-in-the-old-reality plumbers" say, it pays to know there's always a different reality once you get out of town.

SNIDELY WHIPLASH IS ONLY A CARTOON

There's no such thing as a moustache-twirling bad guy.

— LIN-MANUEL MIRANDA

The need-to-know: The truth remains unchanged, and everything I want and need is right there behind my fearful self-image.

From the jukebox: "Imagine" by John Lennon.

The "We will, we will . . .": I am at the mercy of the world I see.

The ". . . rock you": Michelle is the single mom of two little boys. After reading my book *E-Squared*, she encouraged her boys to focus on what they wanted each night when they went to bed. When her oldest was six, he announced he wanted a turtle.

"I couldn't back down from what I always told them, and I didn't want to put any doubt in his mind," she told me. "But what was I going to say when he didn't get this turtle after I'd been harping about this asking and believing thing?"

She kissed him goodnight, but, "as I turned my back, I immediately started worrying. How would I explain when this didn't happen!"

"At around 10:30 P.M., there was a knock at my door. It scared me silly! I cautiously went to the door and peered through the window. It threw me off when I saw my girlfriend's cousin's husband standing there.

"He didn't have a very good reputation and we never talked to each other, but curiosity won over and I slowly opened the door.

"Very sheepishly, he stammered and finally just blurted out, 'Sorry if I startled you, but I work maintenance for the county golf course. I just found this turtle and while driving home, something told me that maybe your boys would want this.'

"I was dumbfounded! We were not on his route home. He had to go out of his way.

"My son," the next morning when she showed him, "was not at all surprised. His attitude was 'Of course, I got a turtle. That's what I asked for.' But to me it was mind-blowing and proof that we should always have the faith of a child."

OPRAH IS IN THE HOUSE

Don't fight forces; use them.

— BUCKMINSTER FULLER

The need-to-know: My thoughts, which are the opposite of truth, are make-believe. All I have to do is recognize this, and I am free.

From the jukebox: "It's a Wonderful World" by Louis Armstrong.

The "We will, we will . . .": But that's impossible!

The ". . . rock you": Cathy had her heart set on a fairy-tale wedding. She wanted it held at the Carmel Mission, she wanted the reception to be at the Pebble Beach Golf Resort on the Monterrey Peninsula, and she wanted someone famous to attend. After trying to convince her to elope instead, her hubby-to-be finally relented, even though he worried that the biggest day of her life would end in disappointment.

First, the Carmel Mission was only available to members (which they weren't), the Pebble Beach function space was booked four years in advance, and, while her husband-to-be could try, he didn't really have access to anyone famous.

"Let's just take a month and fly to Tahiti or Paris. Or both," he suggested.

It all seemed rather impossible. Except she talked her way into the Carmel Mission, she happened on to a cancellation at Pebble Beach, and her husband, through a friend of a friend, booked George Michael (this was in 2014) to play at her wedding. At the last minute, however, the former Wham! singer canceled.

"Two out of three's not bad," the groom shrugged.

Except the night of the reception, the groom was called over by the caterer. "Hey, Bob," he said, "Oprah wants to come in and congratulate you and Cathy."

"Quit pulling my leg," he said.

"No, really. She's here for a golf tournament in honor of the seventy-fifth anniversary of the publication of John Steinbeck's *The Grapes of Wrath*. We told her the club wasn't open because of the wedding. So she and a friend want to know if they can come in and say hi!"

Let's just say Cathy got not just one celebrity, but two. Her friend was none other than Clint Eastwood.

ON MY SIDE

I wandered everywhere, through cities and countries
wide. And everywhere I went, the world was on my side.

— ROMAN PAYNE

The need-to-know: As I release false ideas about myself, I recognize it is impossible to suffer loss or deprivation or pain.

From the jukebox: "Dancing Queen" by ABBA.

The "We will, we will . . .": Poor me. If it's not one thing, it's a hundred others.

The ". . . rock you": Twenty years ago, Ley was diagnosed with bipolar disorder. Here's her story:

"I had suffered the problems that come with the bipolar label for all my life. After being diagnosed, I set out to discover all there was to know, so I could be informed about my condition. I read countless books, read websites, pamphlets, talked to others with bipolar. I wanted to understand why I was the way I was. I wanted to heal, and thought lots of information was the best way to do this.

"Today, I see that all that reading, all those years poring over information about the disease was totally counterproductive. All it did was to teach me 'how to be bipolar.' As time went by, I began to develop even more of the symptoms I was reading about. My life became unbearable. I suffered major anxiety, deep depression, panic attacks, eating disorders, body dysmorphia, low self-esteem, OCD, agoraphobia. I didn't leave my house for two years. I suffered countless problems in all my relationships. I gave up on life and basically closed down completely. I had no hope of ever recovering and wanted to die. This was the ego's story.

"Today, since studying *A Course in Miracles*, I am symptom-free! I am happy, healthy, in love with life, and extremely grateful for all that ACIM (and God, of course) has done for me. My only desire in life is to be able to share this wonderful system of healing with others. To show people that there is a way out of the seeming nightmare, to give hope that what the Course insists can happen DOES happen! I am living proof. All it takes to exchange the nightmare for a beautiful dream is a little willingness to see things a different way. God will do the rest!"

UNDER HOUSE ARREST

*I have neither the time nor the patience to wait for
the media and mainstream science to catch up.*

— EDWARD E. CLOSE

The need-to-know: Everything always works out for me.

From the jukebox: "Living in the Moment" by Jason Mraz.

The "We will, we will . . .": It's a frightening world out there. I'd better protect myself.

The ". . . rock you": Elizabeth Gilbert didn't mention this story in *Eat Pray Love,* but when she was in Indonesia, going through her horrible divorce, suffering with intense depression, she decided to treat herself to a silent retreat. She booked a beachside hut on a tiny island off the coast of Lombok. It was very poor, not your typical tourist destination.

Her plan was to spend 10 days without talking. Not a challenge since no one spoke English anyway. Her daily routine included walking completely around the island. A young Muslim woman who lived on the other side, in the fishing village, noticed her and acknowledged her each morning by placing her hand on her heart and smiling.

One day, Liz came down with a horrendous case of food poisoning. She was really sick, really dehydrated, and terrified. This was before cell phones. When she didn't show up for her daily walk, the woman from the village somehow sensed she was in trouble. She left her village, walked to the other side of the island, and knocked on the door of every hut until she found Liz. When she saw her condition, she hurried away to retrieve fresh food and fresh water. Liz started crying and fell into her arms. This complete stranger rocked her as if she were her own child. Neither woman exchanged names. Liz has no idea who she was, but she says her immense kindness will, for her, always represent the face of Islam.

PUT IT TO THE TEST

Evade every influence that keeps you frozen in the past.

— ROB BREZSNY

The need-to-know: Fear is a nothing burger.

From the jukebox: "Shower the People with Love" by James Taylor.

The "We will, we will . . .": God is a big scary monster who sits on a throne waiting to catch me doing something "naughty, naughty."

The ". . . rock you": When Paramahansa Yogananda was 15, he was sent to the Indian city of Brindaban with nary a rupee. He had been yammering about wanting to quit school and devote his life to God. His brother, Ananta, a stolid accountant, pulled a fast one on him.

"Okay," he challenged. "You wanna do God's work, fine. But forget your inheritance. Why don't we put your vaunted philosophy to a test in the tangible world. I'll buy you a one-way ticket to Brindaban. It's where Lord Krishna first displayed his glories. Take no money. No food. You can't beg. Let God provide your food and return trip home.

"You're not allowed to reveal your predicament to anyone. If you return before midnight without breaking these rules, I'll give you my blessing and even become your first initiate."

Ananta undoubtedly smirked as he sent off his penniless brother to the strange city he'd never visited, but not before searching for a hidden stash.

"Shouldn't we take a couple of rupees as a safeguard?" pleaded the friend who agreed to accompany him. "At least then we can telegraph home if we need to."

Paramahansa rebuked his friend, refused to proceed if he took a "safeguard."

As the train rumbled toward the holy city, the friend started whining. "I'm really getting hungry. Why did you talk me into this?"

Right before the last stop, two men stepped into their compartment and began joking with the young boys. As the train pulled to a stop, they linked arms with Paramahansa and his friend and led them into a horse cab.

Long story short, they ended up at an ashram, taking the place of a couple of princes who, last minute, had to cancel their lunch plans. They were not only served a 30-course meal while being fanned by a hostess, but they visited Madanamohana Temple and other Krishna shrines, were given train tickets back to Agra, and fed a dinner of the finest Indian sweetmeats.

Was Ananta ever surprised when, at a few minutes before midnight, the young yogi walked into his home with piles of rupee notes and bursting with stories. His brother, as promised, insisted on receiving spiritual initiation that very evening.

I AM THE LIGHT, BABY

It's all vapor, really—our entire lives the tiniest
blips in the ever-expanding universe.

— LISA GUNGOR

We did it! Made it through the first 50 lessons (and the 10-lesson review) where we learned the world is nothing like we thought. It's actually malleable and responds to what we believe and think and say. We're the artists, the creators, the only ones to hold accountable if, for some reason, our world doesn't appear like we think it should.

Lesson 61 is a biggie. Get this one lesson (I am the light of the world), get it deep in your bones and boom, everything changes!

Not only are you light (underneath the wah-wah-wah of the hamster wheel of thought), but being light is why you're here. It's your raison d'être.

From here on out:

Instead of detailing the number of minutes and number of times to review each lesson, I suggest deciding for yourself. The ultimate goal is to apply the sentiment anytime the asshat appears in your mind with some unsolicited comment: *I'm thirsty. I want a smoothie. Wonder how many calories are in whey powder? Jim thinks smoothies are nothing but sugar. I should probably call my sister. Why does my knee hurt? Smoothie.*

If you're an overachiever or just someone who likes rules, I've added the suggested practice times from the original workbook at the bottom of each page. The first number is the recommended number of minutes, the second is the number of times per day.

For example, 5/2 (as Lesson 61 requests) is five minutes in the morning and five minutes in the evening. As always, apply as needed.

THE TOUR DE FORCE
LESS MENTIONED

*Let us step into the night and pursue
that flighty temptress, adventure.*

— J. K. ROWLING

I get why people sour on *A Course in Miracles*. Its marketing and branding team sucks.

The real bennies of this life-changing program are rarely if ever mentioned. It comes off as something you HAVE to do, something that requires work. Nobody bothers to mention the excitement. The adventure. The fun.

It's like when Coors beer translated their "Turn It Loose" slogan into Spanish. Their global branding team failed to double-check the Spanish translation—a colloquial term for diarrhea. When Gerber started marketing baby food in Africa, researchers neglected to uncover that, in Ethiopia, where many consumers can't read, labels show the contents. Darn those cute Gerber babies!

The Course, of course, doesn't have branding experts or marketing gurus, so I'm not sure how we got so led astray.

But I do feel indebted to mention this one tiny reason I continue to practice it day after day.

When you surrender long-standing beliefs about yourself, about the world, about what is and isn't possible, you literally embark on a magnificent adventure. You discover things you've never experienced before. Things you never thought possible.

You unearth depths of your own being that have yet to be activated. You uncover revelations that change every aspect of your life. Each day when you open the book and follow its simple instructions (and it's not even hard or time-consuming), you find trails, roads, and byways you had no idea existed.

Truly, the gift of the Course is so much better than any new Jaguar. Or big house. I approach it as a daily, ongoing, epic adventure.

5/2/Apply as needed.

MY NEW JOB TITLE: DEPLOYER OF MIRACLES

What we have chosen to see often costs us true vision.

— A COURSE IN MIRACLES

"Soooooo," it always begins, at a cocktail party or a gathering of strangers. "What do you do?"

Most of us have a suitable answer we can pull out of our pocketbooks. Usually it's a job—I'm an accountant or a teacher. Or maybe a zookeeper.

I, too, have that pat answer at the ready. It's simple enough to tell people what I do during a few hours of every day. I write.

But every now and then when I'm feeling mischievous or wanting to start an unusual conversation, I'll say something like, "I'm a miracle deployer."

Deploy, according to the dictionary, is to position into readiness, to bring into action, to distribute strategically.

And that's what happens when we talk about anything—be it miracles or woe is me! We deploy it into action.

Lesson 63 (The light of the world brings peace to every mind through my forgiveness) basically says that when I give up my old story (that's what forgiveness is), I'm left with nothing but peace and joy. I'm like a helium balloon—destined to rise once I trim back the ego's bollocks that keep it down.

Rather, I affirm as often as I can today that my only role is to be happy, to spread molecules of merriment, and to let peace radiate out from me to every mind.

5/2/Apply as needed.

LET'S TALK ABOUT LOVE, BAY-BEE

You can suffer—but only from false beliefs.

— MICHELE LONGO-O'DONNELL

Forgiveness (the function I'm asked not to forget today) means withdrawing my conviction from the notion there's a "problem" that needs to be solved.

Once I pluck a particular problem out of the gajillion possibilities in the quantum field, I collapse that wave. I turn it into material form. I make it real.

The world, we know now, is made up of waves that we collapse (by looking for them) and then whip the bejesus out of ourselves for creating them.

My function is to "be the light." And it's much easier to fulfill that function when I focus on the gajillion possibilities rather than zero in on one problem, one collapsed wave.

This lesson tells me it's all very simple—although it begs the question why the Course uses so many words to tout simplicity.

Every decision I make leads to either unhappiness *(This problem is real. I believe in it with all my heart)* or happiness *(Absolutely anything is possible once I return to the field of gajillion possibilities)*. I prefer #2.

10–15/1 (That's 10 to 15 minutes, one time, ideally early in the morning.)

A THOUGHT-TWISTER THAT
SLOWS DOWN LOVE AND JOY

The unleashed power of the atom has changed everything except our modes of thinking. We shall require a substantially new manner of thinking if humanity is to survive.

— ALBERT EINSTEIN

Merriam-Webster just announced the addition of 850 new words to their dictionary. My favorite, coined by a writer of *The Simpsons,* is *embiggen* (to make bigger or more expansive).

That's what I think *A Course in Miracles* does. It embiggens my happiness.

Lesson 65 (My only function is the one my Source gave me) encourages me to be single-minded in my pursuit of joy, to make this my one and only goal.

I know a lot of people get hung up on the wording, but this lesson is very simple. It's also very radical.

To believe that happiness, joy, and fun is why we are here is a completely foreign concept to most people. As I said, it's so radical that most people can't even wrap their heads around it.

Which is why the Course suggests I set aside a time every day to reflect on the importance of my mission.

10–15/1/Apply as needed.

A MOST UNLIKELY
LOVE AFFAIR

Reclaim your land with love.

— JACK KORNFIELD

I've mentioned the asshat before.

The voice that tells me I'm not good enough, the one that points out my flaws, the one that rolls its eyes and says, "Who are you to talk about *A Course in Miracles?*"

Today's lesson tells me I've indulged this voice long enough. There's no need to fight it or kick it in the shins.

I simply point out the truth: My purpose is to be happy.

I might as well sit back with my double latte and the quiet assurance, as this lesson promises me, that "My happiness and my function are one."

It's not "I'll be happy WHEN I fulfill my purpose." That's the asshat putting in its two cents.

It's "My purpose and my happiness are identical. They're one and the same."

And since resisting the asshat or engaging it in senseless arguments doesn't make me happy or change anything, I officially declare my love, even for the scared little asshat.

Who knows? I might even send flowers.

10–15/1/Apply as needed.

BEEP-BEEP

A better world is sitting, literally, right in front of us.

— TOM SHADYAC

The energetic world, the world you can't see, touch, taste, or smell, is the foundation on which all else rests. It's the building block—the supreme cheese—that forms everything. Scientists discovered this matrix of energy (they call it the field) about a century ago, but because it's so mind-blowing and opens up so many new doors, few of us have yet fully employed its power.

Most of us, 100 years later, are still focused on the material world, which is a little like rooting for Wile E. Coyote. Despite all his elaborate schemes and complex contraptions, that sorry ole coyote is never going to catch the Roadrunner. And our stubbornness (*beep-beep!*) in believing that the cut-and-dried, machinelike world is the be-all and end-all keeps us in spiritual diapers.

The spiritual world, the world that most of us can't see, connects us to an unlimited, enormous consciousness with no edges, no boundaries, and no limits to what it can create.

Everything in the nonphysical world is cooperative, user-friendly, and win-win. In fact, the real world, without the blinders, is nothing like you think. It's nothing like the movie set you manufactured to serve as your "reality."

Lesson 67 (Love created me like itself) tells us that no matter how it may appear to the naked eye, life in its pure, unaltered form (without a "life sucks and then you die" consciousness laid over it) is a bubbling cauldron of possibility, composed of perfect love.

Because our minds have become so preoccupied with false self-images, we need to remind ourselves as frequently as possible today of the following truths:

Love created me loving. Holiness created me holy. Kindness created me kind. Helpfulness created me helpful. Perfection created me perfect.

It's especially useful to realize that it's not just your tiny, solitary voice saying these things. You've got the whole of creation seconding the motion.

10–15/1/Repeat twice an hour.

LAY THAT SUCKER DOWN

Love is both how you become a person and why.

— JOHN GREEN

Grievances clog up the pipes and keep me from fully knowing my badass self.

Let's use comedian Patton Oswalt for demonstration purposes. A few months ago, he tweeted out a cheeky poem about Trump's wall. A conservative war vet from Alabama took exception and came back with this response: "I just realized why I was so happy you died in *Blade Trinity.*"

Minutes later, the vet posted a follow-up jab. "And you shoot basketball like the sawed-off little man you are."

Witty Oswalt could have continued on with the fiery exchange. But instead he took Lesson 68 (Love holds no grievances) to heart. He was determined to see his former "enemy" as a friend. He decided to let his grievances go.

His next tweet: "Aw, man. This dude just attacked me on Twitter, but then I looked at his timeline and he's in a LOT of trouble healthwise. I'd be pissed off too. He's been dealt some shitty cards—let's deal him some good ones. Click and donate—just like I'm about to do."

Not only did he donate $2,000 to the vet's GoFundMe page, but he encouraged his four million followers to do the same.

Thanks to Oswalt, the vet's campaign to treat his sepsis and diabetic ketoacidosis raised $15,000 in a couple of hours, three times its original goal.

But most importantly, the vet, too, gave up his grievances. "These generous outpourings of love and support have given me a whole new perspective. I'm not a man who cries, but I am truly humbled."

Oswalt, of course, had to second his new friend's tweet, "This is why compassion and forgiveness are always best."

15/1/Apply as needed.

THE SOMEONE IN MY HEAD
THAT'S NOT ME

*The running commentary that dominates my field
of consciousness is kind of an asshole.*

— DAN HARRIS

Pink Floyd's *Dark Side of the Moon* opens with the voice of the band's long-time roadie, Chris Adamson, saying, "I've been mad for f**king years—absolutely years." It's one of dozens of spoken voices heard throughout the album.

My favorite lyric from this perennial classic is "There's someone in my head and it's not me."

It's also the theme of Lesson 69: My grievances hide the light of the world in me.

My grievances are the voice in my head that's not me. The Course calls it my ego.

It keeps me busy with silly details, fears, and other inane nothingness obscuring my true identity as light and love.

Today, I say begone to that "someone in my head." I devote myself to finding the light within.

In my longer practice period, I'm asked to close my eyes and let go of all content that normally occupies my consciousness.

"Very quietly," I'm asked to "think of my mind as a vast circle, surrounded by a layer of heavy, dark clouds."

Even though the clouds seem like the only reality, I settle down in perfect stillness and devote myself to moving beyond the clouds, moving beyond the "someone in my head that's not me."

As I let the power of the universe work in me (And it will. It wants to), I watch as the light in my mind, just like the cover of the *Dark Side of the Moon* album, passes through a prism to form the same impenetrable, colorful truth.

15/1/Apply as needed.

SPIRITUAL DRANO

*I can't understand why people are frightened
of new ideas. I'm frightened of the old ones.*

— JOHN CAGE

Lesson 70 (Salvation comes from me) says guilt is an invention of my mind. This "faulty invention" constructs a worldview based on problems, on fear, on protecting myself from all the things that *could* go wrong. It leads me to separate myself from the whole and to believe that this, this limited viewfinder filled with individual beings, is what I have to work with. I use my enormous, inexhaustible consciousness to scope out escape routes. Every moment wasted on worst-case scenarios undermines my ability to create the true and the beautiful. Every moment spent worrying erects a block between me and all the signs and opportunities and, yes, blatant love that is here for the sole purpose of my enjoyment. I flip the map of Truth with "facts" from my negative orientation. When negativity emerges (and it *will*, because groupthink, no matter how altered and off-base it may be, is powerful), I feel validated. I smirk and think, *See, told you so.*

But as I learn in the Course, the going "life sucks and then you die" paradigm is a fictional story, a made-up pack of lies we humans have been telling ourselves for the last . . . I don't know . . . 40,000 years?

We train ourselves from a very early age to put on a pair of gray-colored glasses and look at the world through the lens of defeat and pain. We get brownie points for finding problems. Expecting the good in life sounds dangerously like "not facing up to reality." There is a bias against too much optimism and happiness.

Even therapists, who purport to brighten our lives, encourage us to dig up old baggage and peek at creaky skeletons lurking in our subconscious closets. They pat us on the back for noticing where we are stuck, for paying attention to how we are suffering.

But it's not any more true than all those zombie movies that are popular right now. It's a huge relief to endorse today's idea that nothing outside myself can hurt or disturb or upset me in any way. Twice a day, for 10 minutes or so, I will stop and remind myself that it is me and only me that's in charge of my universe.

10/2/Apply as needed.

A WHOLE NEW
INSTRUCTION MANUAL

None but ourselves can free our minds.

— BOB MARLEY

Not long after he returned from India, spiritual guru Ram Dass was speaking in New York. Decked out in a flowing white robe and beads, he was confronted by a woman in the audience who stood up and asked, "Why are you dressed like that? Aren't you Jewish?'

Without missing a beat, he answered: "Only on my parents' side."

All of us are SO MUCH MORE than the genetic makeup of our bodies, the heredity of our families. We are literally God in drag.

Lesson 71 (Only Love's plan for salvation will work) tells me that trying to be anything else is crazy ridiculous.

The ego's plan (if only this were different, I'd be okay) is like following a map of Peoria to navigate the streets of London. Or like using a do-it-yourself bookshelf manual to fix my vacuum cleaner. Source's plan is to know that everything IS OKAY! To celebrate that fact with full frontal abandon.

This lesson also has one of my all-time favorite passages:

What would you have me do?
Where would you have me go?
What would you have me say, and to whom?

The answers I get from this practice are the only instruction manual I could ever need.

10-15/2/Apply as needed.

MONEY IS EVERYWHERE

*Happiness comes from many sources, but none of
these sources involve car or purse upgrades.*

— MR. MONEY MUSTACHE

Once, at an executive women's retreat in Orlando, I met a brilliant CPA named Christi. I feel compelled to mention that I wasn't at this weekend retreat because I'm an executive woman. I work in my pajamas. I was there because I was invited to give a two-hour presentation which, you'll be happy to hear, I didn't give in my PJs.

But this story isn't about me.

It's about Christi, who is brilliant, not just because she helps clients with taxes and financial planning and all that other left-brain rigamarole, but because she helps them really understand money. Not in the way most of us understand money, but in the way money really is.

She considers it her duty to make sure they know that money is energy and that those numbers on their balance sheets and tax forms are a direct result of their thoughts and beliefs. She loves to tell her clients that money is unlimited and that it's only their thoughts and beliefs that could ever keep it away.

So while Christi's mission is to maximize and optimize finances, mine is to maximize and optimize joy. That's why, as I often say, my goal is to become the Warren Buffet of Happiness.

And that's what *A Course in Miracles* does. It helps me realize that the way I see myself and the world is upside down. It teaches me that living a wonderful, fulfilling life has nothing to do with finances and everything to do with how I see the world.

Lesson 72 encourages me to give up pitiful illusions, to reach in and grab the absolute peace that abides within. It's there within everyone, hidden under my thoughts and lunatic beliefs, hidden under worry and stress and belief that money (or really anything at all) is limited. Limitation is a false construct that I cemented in with my thoughts. It can be changed at any time.

Today, I notice that, like Christi preaches, money (and abundance of all kinds) is everywhere.

1/hourly (Every hour, spend a minute reminding yourself that your upside-down perception is ruinous to your peace of mind.)

73

THE EGO IS NOT MY AMIGO

Being mad at your mother
just doesn't pay the bills.

— WHITNEY CUMMINGS

The part that stands out in Lesson 73 (I will there be light) is how **easy** it is to pass the barrier of grievances that stand between me and my happiness. It's worth repeating. It's easy.

Because it's a wordy lesson, one of those RSOs that rub me the wrong way, I plucked out two major points:

1. What I see in the world mirrors what is within. All bad guys are middlemen employed by the ego to traffic in grievances.

2. Even though they seem ferocious and real, they're figments. They're not really there.

The ego, it's a relief to discover, makes nothing that is real (I repeat this line often), so it's actually easy to find the light. It's easy to find the light. It's easy to find the light.

10–15/2/Apply as needed.

EFFORT IS OVERRATED

"Excellent!" I cried.
"Elementary," said he.

— SIR ARTHUR CONAN DOYLE

If you really want to change your life, ditch the struggle, throw overboard the idea that you have to do more, try harder.

Lesson 74 (There is no will but Love) encourages me to give up conflict and rest in a deep sense of joy and increased alertness. It tells me this peaceful, joyful way of being is my natural state. It assures me that anytime I perceive a problem, I'm at odds with how Source sees me.

I spend the first few moments of the longer periods scouring my mind for secret beliefs in scum and villainy and then, after dismissing each one, I sink into deep fathomless peace.

I'm also asked to watch my mind today and quickly deal with any thought of conflict. Should one arise, I'm instructed to tell myself immediately:

There is no will but Love. This conflict thought is meaningless.

Because our beliefs are so powerful, literally sculpting our lives on a moment-by-moment basis, we must play Whac-a-Mole with any thought that's less than peaceful.

I like to use my Staples "Easy" button. This three-inch red button, when pressed, repeats, "That was easy." I take it all to my playshops˙ and tell everyone I know that it's one of my favorite mantras and most treasured beliefs.

Today, I say good riddance to every conflict. If one comes up, I simply hit my button, remind myself it's not real, and whack it with the words "smooth" and "easy."

10–15/2/Apply as needed.

˙What I call workshops.

THE WORLD AS YOU'VE NEVER SEEN IT BEFORE

"Suppose a tree fell when we were underneath it,"
Piglet said. "Suppose it didn't," said Pooh.

—A. A. MILNE

When John Lennon and Yoko Ono launched their "War is Over" campaign, a deejay asked them, "Isn't that ridiculous? The soldiers, the Vietnamese? How can you tell them the war is over?"

John, as always, had the perfect answer.

"People need to remember that they've got the power—not the government or leaders or teachers."

His belief that we've got to imagine it first was early law of attraction. Who knew John Lennon was one of its first practitioners?

Lesson 75 (The light has come) is a campaign similar to Lennon's inspiring campaign.

He and Yoko plastered the message "If you want it, war is over" on billboards all over the world—11 cities from Tokyo to Berlin to New York. They also distributed leaflets and ran full-page newspaper ads.

Yoko re-launched the campaign in 2018.

As she said, "When we drop small pebbles, it immediately affects the ocean of the whole wide world. We'll keep doing it. Together. We change and the world changes."

So today, I celebrate personal change. I celebrate that the light has come. I celebrate the beginning of true vision, a happy vision, a vision that replaces the other world I created by believing it was real.

As the Course reminds me, in my thoughts and beliefs lies all power. And therefore:

I will dwell not upon the past today.

I will see the world, bathed in light, as I've never seen it before.

And I will remember what John said, "I—all of us—have the power."

10–15/2/Apply as needed.

CRAZY MAD BELIEFS

*It's not what you don't know that kills you, it's
what you know for sure that just ain't true.*

— MARK TWAIN

If you're a parent, your kids have undoubtedly accused you of TMI. It stands for "too much information."

Lesson 76 (I am under no laws but Truth) tells me that not only have I picked up TMI, but that most of it is TMFI (too much false information).

Today, I examine the strange and twisted laws to which I feel bound. The Course calls it insanity to believe I must obey "laws" of medicine, of economics, of health. To think I would starve without stacks of green paper strips and piles of metal discs is the height of madness.

These ridiculous laws play a big role in how I experience life. They're like the kitchen junk drawer filled with a bunch of forgotten items: dried-up magic markers, rusty scissors, old birthday cards from people I don't even remember, and keys that probably used to open something, although I'm not sure what.

This lesson offers freedom. It asks me to clean out the junk drawer, to examine the mad beliefs that run my life.

The list of laws that hold me prisoner is long indeed. I need eight hours of sleep, money comes from working hard, it's dangerous to talk to strangers.

That's why today I repeat (in my head, not out loud) over and over and especially when confronted with one of those preposterous laws: That's not true, and no one can make me believe it.

10–15/2/Apply as needed.

REALITY IS A MENTAL CONSTRUCT— MAKE YOURS JOYFUL

We are powerfully imprisoned by the terms in which we have been conducted to think.

— BUCKMINSTER FULLER

When you were born, you were powerfully connected to a rich, deep world, a world of magic and enchantment. You could do anything.

But then your parents got ahold of you.

It's wrong to speak your mind, crazy to talk to the angels, ridiculous to think you could be a painter.

Why did you believe them?

Lesson 77 (I am entitled to miracles) says I am not here to "get by." I am here to create the good, the beautiful, and the holy. I am here to dance, to spread love, to give birth to the very best that's inside me.

Those dysfunctional families everyone loves to go on and on about? We can heal them.

The poverty? The homelessness? The greed that pervades our culture? We can change it.

We have that kind of power. But we have forgotten. We've squandered our power on meaningless things. We've bartered it for security.

We've wasted it by not trusting it.

Miracles are my birthright, my destiny. Just like I can talk, clap, and drive to the nearest QuikTrip, I am capable of performing miracles.

This is a guarantee, ensured in my creation, implicit in the laws of the universe.

10–15/2/Apply as needed.

TURNING MR. HYDE
BACK INTO DR. JEKYLL

People show up in our lives as opportunities to reach out in love.
In spite of what we see, there is fullness and glory. Our job is to
call it forth, to strengthen it, to honor it, to pray for it to rise.

—MICHELE LONGO-O'DONNELL

You may have heard about Dr. Hew Len. He's a former psychologist assigned to the special ward at the Hawaii State Hospital, a notorious clinic for the criminally insane.

It was so bad that Hew Len's predecessors left in despair (often in less than a month) after making zero inroads in the lives of the seriously disturbed murderers, rapists, and you know, the type of dates we hope not to encounter on say, Tinder or Match.com.

Hew Len was different. He rarely left his office. In fact, not once did he meet with any of the inmates, preferring instead to retrieve their files one-by-one and practice the ancient Hawaiian art of ho'oponopono.

Basically, as he explains it, he was healing the part of himself that created such atrocities. It's pointless, he says, trying to heal others. All he can do is heal himself.

Little by little, nurses started noticing changes. Inmates required less shackling, less drugs. Somebody began tending the gardens, repairing the tennis courts. The atmosphere changed SO MUCH that prisoners, one by one, were eventually released. After four years, Hawaii's clinic for the mentally insane was shuttered forever.

Although Lesson 78 (Let miracles replace all grievances) doesn't actually prescribe ho'oponopono, it reflects Hew Len's belief that anything that happens TO me is my responsibility.

Anything I perceive, any person I don't like is my creation and thus my responsibility. One hundred percent. No exceptions.

It sounds crazy. But it worked for Hew Len and it's the only thing that can ever heal my life. I must first heal my perceptions. The world is a projection of my mind, and today's lesson asks me to choose just one lucky individual and use him or her to heal the planet. It asks me to turn a single Mr. Hyde back into a Dr. Jekyll.

All it requires is saying these shockingly simple phrases: I'm sorry. Please forgive me. I love you. Thank you.

10–15/2/Apply as needed.

IMPORTANT NEWS FLASH: THERE IS ONLY ONE PROBLEM

*For things to reveal themselves, we need to be ready
to abandon our views about them.*

— THICH NHAT HANH

On Prince's debut studio album, *For You*, he produced, arranged, composed, and performed every single track. He played the electric guitar, the acoustic guitar, the bass, the electric piano, the acoustic piano, the clavinet, the drum, the bongos, the congas, the finger cymbals, the wind chimes, the orchestral bells, the woodblocks, and 14 other instruments.

Released when the Purple One was only 20, this album is a good metaphor for Lesson 79: Let me recognize the problem so it may be solved.

It says that, despite many wily manifestations and clever guitar licks, all problems are being played by the same player. Every "sad song" is being sung by the exact same issue: faulty perception.

The only problem I could ever have is a distorted perception.

So today I think of Prince's album and remind myself, again and again, that all problems were created by a single performer: my flawed perception.

10–15/2/Apply as needed.

WITHOUT PERCEPTUAL DISTORTION, LIFE IS BLISS, JOY, AND CONTINUING MIRACLES

We have to challenge the status quo to allow for a better future.

— SAMUEL MOCKBEE

Harper's Magazine recently listed mistaken reports of animals in distress compiled by an animal rescue shelter on the island of Guernsey.

A sick seal on a beach ended up being a duvet.

A dead cat was a hand puppet.

A gull hanging from a fence was a carrier bag.

An injured bird was a blond wig.

A stray pug was a frog.

I laughed at what the magazine cleverly headlined "Faux Paws" because these mistaken distress calls are so quintessentially human. Over and over, I think there's something to worry about, something to report, something I need to fix.

But in reality, my problems are nothing but perceptual distortions.

A Course in Miracles is very clear. My view of the world is mostly illusion. Once my demented perceptions are removed, truth shows up, truth that makes me indescribably happy. Lesson 80 asks me to recognize my problems have been solved.

10–15/2/Apply as needed.

Boom!

Review II

*I've found that if you tuck one part of your pant
leg into your sock, people expect less of you.*

— GARY SCHWARTZ

Time for another review.

You may think you've mastered this stuff, but, believe me, you need to hear it again and again. We all do.

In this review, spend the first couple of minutes pondering the "need to know." Then close your eyes and listen. The Voice will take it from there.

Keep in mind that the Voice, although subtle, is like the Bruce Springsteen fan in the movie *Blinded by the Light*.

It will do anything for you. It loves you. Remarkable things will happen.

Speaking of remarkable things, this review, like the first one, encourages you to dance, whoop, and holler. Music and its jubilant cousins allow you to bypass logic loops in your brain. It allows you to stop thinking long enough so miracles can become your mother tongue.

TRIP THE LIGHT FANTASTIC

I used to think the human brain was the most wonderful organ in the body. But then I realized who was telling me this.

— EMO PHILIPS

The need-to-know: My true identity is light of the world.

From the jukebox: "I Am Light" by India Arie.

The "We will, we will . . .": But that wanker said . . .

The ". . . rock you": When Taz's dog Izzy was a puppy, she ran full speed ahead to every single canine she saw, wagging her tail, eager to make a new buddy. There were no exceptions to her joy and exuberance.

This is how we would be too (running to every other member of the human race in joyful glee) if we hadn't condensed reality into our very limited perception.

Every person has immense light and love inside them (no exceptions) and the only reason we cannot see it is because of the lens we laid over it. We covered it up with our beliefs and expectations, with facts that we just KNOW are true.

Nothing is as it appears. All we see with the limited five senses is a hologram of our beliefs and expectations. And it's flawed, and it gets us in trouble.

Daryl Davis is doing his part to bridge the divide. He's a black musician who attended early primary school overseas. When his parents moved back to the United States, like most of the boys in his sixth-grade class, he joined the Boy Scouts. One day, while marching with his troop, people started throwing rocks and sticks at him.

His first thought was, "They must not like Boy Scouts."

At that point, his parents sat him down and had the race talk.

He was stunned.

"How could they not like me?" he thought. "They don't even know me."

Since that time, he has taken on the hobby of getting to know white supremacists and, instead of yelling at them or berating them, he sits down and asks questions. He genuinely wants to know what they think.

As he says about engaging his "enemies," "when you are actively learning about someone else, you are passively teaching them about yourself."

Some black activists have labeled his methods non compos mentis, but as he likes to say, "I've got dozens of retired hoods and robes in my closet. How many do you have?"

10–15/2/Apply as needed.

HALLELUJAH ANYWAY

*Memory of joy and liberation can become
a navigational tool, an identity, a gift.*

— REBECCA SOLNIT

The need-to-know: When I let go of everything I believe, perfect days unfurl before me.

From the jukebox: "Walking on Sunshine" by Katrina and the Waves.

The "We will, we will . . .": But it's just so unfair . . .

The ". . . rock you": It's a cinch to be grateful when the sails of life are blowing your way. But what about those times when things "appear" not to be working out?

My tack? Say "hallelujah!" anyway.

My friend Gail told me about a girlfriends' outing. One of the friends, on the day of, woke to find her daughter running a fever.

She called Gail whimpering about her bad luck. Gail responded in the way she responds to everything: "That's fabulous!"

"No, you didn't hear me," her girlfriend said. "I'm not going to be able to go today."

Again, Gail said, "That's fabulous!"

She reminded her that she'd been needing some free time to sift through paperwork and that this so-called setback provided the perfect opportunity.

Her friend thanked Gail for the reminder, and not only did she end up having a delightful day with her daughter, but while cruising the Internet, came across the very house she'd been lusting after for three years. This dream house was way more than she could afford, but on this day, while dealing with the disappointment of thwarted plans, she saw that "her house" had gone into foreclosure and was selling for one-quarter the price.

As Gail said, "She now has a contract on her dream home."

10–15/2/Apply as needed.

DID YOU LOOK IN THE DRIVEWAY?

Feel at home in the universe, enjoy its innumerable marvels.
Be active in it, contribute to it, participate in the healing.
This is where Reality is.

— RICHARD ROHR

The need-to-know: I have but one purpose and that is to be happy.

From the jukebox: "Girls Just Want to Have Fun" by Cyndi Lauper.

The "We will, we will . . .": SHI*T, F**K, D*MN!!!

The ". . . rock you": Jean (not her real name) was doing the Dude Abides experiment from *E-Squared*. The idea is to ask for a blessing, a sign that you are loved by the universe. Although I encourage people to refrain from making specific requests, "Jean," who studied geology in college and loved rocks, thought to herself, *Wouldn't it be cool if my blessing was a crystal agate?*

The next day she came home and sitting in her driveway was the biggest crystal agate she had ever seen.

Another reader, Siobhan, was recounting a long list of undesirable circumstances in her life when her friend stopped her. "Well, what exactly do you need?"

And with that question, she got it. Enough complaining.

"I need a vacuum cleaner."

Her friend laughed and said, "Better make room for a new vacuum cleaner."

The next week, instead of recounting her woes, she was brimming with good news. She was listing all the many manifestations that had shown up.

"Oh and I forgot to tell you," she suddenly remembered. "I went home last Sunday and there, in my driveway, was a vacuum cleaner."

Moral of this story? Pay attention to your driveway.

10–15/2/Apply as needed.

NAMASTE, MY ASS!

I used to be Snow White, but I drifted.

— MAE WEST

The need-to-know: I cannot suffer. I cannot experience loss. I cannot die.

From the jukebox: "I Gotta Feeling" by Black Eyed Peas.

The "We will, we will . . ." Easy for you to say . . .

The ". . . rock you": Dr. Michael Shermer, a professor and public intellectual who writes a monthly column for *Scientific American,* is so wary of all things "supernatural" that in 1992, he started a quarterly journal with the stated aim of debunking fads and cultural influences on science. It's even called *Skeptic magazine.* The avowed atheist once debated the existence of God with Deepak Chopra on *Nightline.*

Which is why I love the following story so darned much.

In the summer of 2014, Michael Schermer married Jennifer Graf from Cologne, Germany. During the shipping of her belongings to his home in California, boxes were damaged, heirlooms lost.

An old transistor radio that belonged to Jennifer's beloved grandfather, Walter, successfully made the journey. Walter had been Jennifer's only father figure and had died when she was 16.

Michael, knowing how much it would mean, attempted to resurrect the radio after decades of silence. He changed the batteries, searched for loose connections, and even tried what he called "percussive maintenance"—smacking it against a hard surface. He finally gave up, and Jennifer stuck it in the back of a drawer in their bedroom.

On the day they exchanged rings and said their vows in front of his family, Jennifer, 6,000 miles from home, was feeling nostalgic, wishing her grandfather could be there to give her away.

After the ceremony, she motioned to Michael, said she needed to speak to him. Alone.

"There's music coming from the bedroom," she whispered.

Since they didn't have a music system in the bedroom, they searched for errant laptops and iPhones. They even checked the back door to see if their neighbors had unexpectedly scheduled a party.

Michael wrote in *Scientific American:* "[Suddenly] Jennifer shot me a look I haven't seen since the supernatural thriller *The Exorcist.*"

"That can't be what I think it is, can it?" she said.

They opened the desk drawer and, sure enough, her grandfather's transistor was playing a romantic love song.

The radio continued to play throughout their wedding day. They finally fell asleep to classical music emanating from Walter's radio. It stopped working the next day and has remained mute ever since.

And while famous skeptic Michael Schermer said he'd never have believed such a story if he heard it from someone else, he admitted that "the eerie conjunction of these deeply evocative events" rocked him back on his feet and shook his skepticism to its core.

And that's what I'd call a miracle. That a longtime upholder of scientific orthodoxy was willing to publicly share a revelation that contradicts his aggressively argued position of many years. To actually suggest that science may not be the only road to truth, after all. That it might not offer the definitive and complete view of reality.

As Schermer says, "We should not shut the doors of perception when they may be opened to us to marvel in the mysterious."

10–15/2/Apply as needed.

FAULT IN YOUR STARS

The fault you perceive in another isn't even there.
It is a total misinterpretation, a projection by a mind
conditioned to see enemies and make itself right.

— ECKHART TOLLE

The need-to-know: Grievances show me things that aren't there.

From the jukebox: "Once a Day" by Michael Franti.

The "We will, we will . . .": But those other people . . . they're so scary . . .

The ". . . rock you": When Matthew Lester was 25, he joined the anti-Islam group Britain First. He'd heard dangerous Muslims were infiltrating his country. He wanted to do something to help. But within a few months of joining the far-right group, he concluded that instead of tackling problems, Britain First was exacerbating them. Its grievances, as this lesson emphasizes, were showing evils that did not exist.

After admitting on Twitter, "I've been an unwitting twat," Lester showed up at the Crayford mosque in southeast London. He was astonished at all the kindness and love he was shown. From there, he embarked on a month-long pilgrimage of penitence by visiting mosques all over London. He even apologized for letting his grievances show him faults that weren't there.

10–15/2/Apply as needed.

MIRACLE, FIND ME NOW!

You are a Deity in jeans and a t-shirt, and within you dwells the infinite wisdom of the ages and the sacred creative force of All that is, will be and ever was.

— ANTHON ST. MAARTEN

The need-to-know: I choose to look deeper and perceive only light.

From the jukebox: "Wake Me Up Before You Go-Go" by Wham.

The "We will, we will . . .": But it's just so hard . . .

The ". . . rock you." Many years ago, I had the opportunity to interview SARK for a profile in an inflight magazine.

You've probably seen her "How to Be an Artist" poster. Stay loose. Learn to watch snails, etc. It was a perennial favorite (along with Farrah Fawcett in the red bathing suit) in college dorm rooms back in the '80s. I still have a copy framed and hanging in my guest bathroom.

She told me about her commitment to being an artist even when she had to eat catsup sandwiches, even when she had to scrounge lunch by sitting in hotel lobbies with a sign, "Take an artist to lunch."

Back in the catsup sandwich days, when cash wasn't yet flowing, she started using this affirmation: "Miracle, find me now." She'd repeat it again and again. One day, when feeling rather desperate to pay rent, she began her favorite mantra in earnest. She was walking down the street in San Francisco, where she lives, and six $100 bills floated down to her out of nowhere.

10–15/2/Apply as needed.

YOUR NEW BEST FRIENDS

Joy is the ultimate act of defiance.

— BONO

The need-to-know: I am supersonic light.

From the jukebox: "Don't Stop Me Now" by Queen.

The "We will, we will . . .": But they (him, her, those people) are wrong. And I'm right.

The ". . . rock you": My friend Annola was visiting a small Kansas town with her boyfriend. She's African-American, he's white, and the local yokels weren't sure what to think of this unusual combination. They didn't exactly tell them to leave, but they made it clear they weren't happy with their presence.

Annola told her guy, "Don't worry. I can fix this."

So she got very clear in her mind, began focusing on love, on Truth, on the unshakable fact that we all really love each other. And before long, the "haters" dropped away, the judgers disappeared, and everyone in the little town became this biracial couple's new best friends.

Speaking of Annola, here's another mind-blowing story about the multidimensional reality of the quantum field. In the Field of Infinite Potentiality (the FP, as I often call it), we exist in countless dimensions, but because we're focused on this one material dimension, we miss a lot of blessings, miracles, signs, and possibilities.

A few months ago, Annola sold one of her extra bread pans at a garage sale. It was longer than most and she had plenty, so she decided to let it go. Last week, she was making a particular recipe and thought to herself, "Hmm, too bad I sold that pan. It would work perfectly for this recipe." She opened the cabinet and there, nested in the frying pan she uses on a near-daily basis, was the extra-long bread pan that she'd sold but needed to draw back into her life.

10–15/2/Apply as needed.

GOOSEBUMPS: THE SKIN CONDITION, NOT THE NOVEL

We create the illusions we need to go on.
And one day, when they no longer dazzle or comfort,
we tear them down, brick by glittering brick."

— LIBBA BRAY

The need-to-know: I am free. I am under no laws but my own.

From the jukebox: "Best Day of My Life" by American Authors.

The "We will, we will . . .": But it's really hard to write a book, be a comedian, make it as an artist . . .

The ". . . rock you": Today's lesson is the perfect statement of our freedom. We can listen to consensus reality. Make up laws. Give them power. But as Lesson 88 reminds us, consensus reality is dead wrong.

Comedian Hasan Minhaj grew up in a small university town, was a nerd, a smart kid. He studied political science in college. But after seeing Chris Rock's standup show "Never Scared," he got goosebumps. It was the big one, the thing he wanted to do.

He started making YouTube videos with the photoshopped body of Conan O'Brien. He put that vision in his mind. He started moving in that direction.

Today, you'll find plenty of YouTube videos of the nerdy immigrant kid from the small college town—only now they're of his one-man comedy show, or his Netflix series, or his stint as emcee of the White House Correspondent's Dinner.

As the Course tells us, anything's possible. Once we let go of consensus reality.

What gives you goosebumps, my friends?

10–15/2/Apply as needed.

REWRITE, TAKE II

One of the greatest paradoxes of your physical senses is that your eyes actually show you what you believe, not what you see.

— MIKE DOOLEY

The need-to-know: I am entitled to miracles.

From the jukebox: "Ain't No Stoppin' Us Now," by McFadden & Whitehead.

The "We will, we will . . .": But they say . . .

The ". . . rock you": *A Course in Miracles* makes no bones. Thoughts become things. There is no exception to this rule. The reason we don't fully recognize this unalterable reality is because our thoughts bounce around like pinballs. I want this. Wait! No. I want that. Oh, but if I get that, this might happen? It's got to be maddening.

In the "No such thing as an idle thought" department, consider Samin Nosrat who won a 2018 James Beard Award and is featured in a popular Netflix documentary. She's often referred to as "the next Julia Child."

Eleven years ago, when she was not yet 30, she bought a sketchbook from an art supply store. She labeled it "Manifestation Journal." In it, she listed things she envisioned for her life, both small and large.

"What's pretty bananas," she says, "sometimes I'll misplace the journal. I'll forget about it for six months or so. When I find it, it's almost word for word what has happened in my life. It's really mind-blowing to look at how specific goals come to life when you plant a seed."

The journal covers everything from small, candid "notes to self" (chin hairs under control) to creative ideas (Bay leaf pinata) to life-altering dreams (Go to Italy. Start writing first book), all of which have come true.

She also leaves lists above her desk: interviews she'd like to do, projects she'd like to take on, people she'd like to collaborate with.

"I sort of just stopped being embarrassed at some point about having what seemed like wildly unachievable dreams. I had to stop being afraid that someone would judge me and be like, 'What is this?'"

"What is this" is proof that, as the Course says, "Your mind creates your future."

10–15/2/Apply as needed.

NO PROBLEMO!

This idea that there is a problem . . .
that's the wild hair in the ass of humanity.

— ADYASHANTI

The need-to-know: It is impossible to have a problem that has not already been solved.

From the jukebox: "Beautiful World" by Colin Hay.

The "We will, we will . . .": Everything's going wrong.

The ". . . rock you": If you've been hanging out at the party disguised as this book, you already know my favorite practice in all the world is gratitude. I practice it nonstop.

I notice that when I don't, when I start thinking something's wrong, that some person doesn't love me enough or that I'm not worthy of this or that, my thoughts take a big dip toward darkness.

Lesson 90 (the last in the review) lays it all out. The only problem I can ever have is forgetting to be grateful. The Course calls it a grievance.

As I become more aware of each tiny grievance, those subtle messages that still run very quietly in the background, and return to gratitude, I get closer to that truth I always talk about: the biggest secret in the world is we all really love each other.

Last night, while dancing on the roof with my beautiful friends at a spiritual community in Ajijic, Mexico, I looked out over the stunning Lake Chapala landscape and realized I was so in love, so happy, so who I really AM.

And that's why I get up every morning, make my intention for an extraordinarily epic day, and continuously count my blessings. Grievances don't stand a chance.

10–15/2/Apply as needed.

GLORIOUSLY CRAZY

A little nonsense now and then is relished by the wisest men.

— ROALD DAHL

April Fools' Day was right up there on my list of favorite holidays. What a blast putting sugar in the salt shaker, adding food coloring to the milk, running into my parents' bedroom screaming, "Becki [my sister] just fell down the stairs and broke her leg. April Fools!"

ACIM 91 (Miracles are seen in light) isn't fooling when it tells me miracles are happening all around me, all the time. It insists the only reason I don't see them is because I engage instead in such foolish practices as worry, feeling unworthy, trying to be cool.

These silly ideas are what the Course calls darkness, which is nothing but a ridiculous April Fools' joke. They give the ego a great excuse to discourage me from trying to feel my strength, to dissuade me from seeing all the ongoing miracles.

So basically, the joke's on me. Miracles are within easy reach once I quit pretending I'm weak, once I quit obscuring the light.

Today's idea, like the dozens of pranks I played as a kid, needs frequent repeating. Because once I get it that "weakness" is but an April Fools' folly, miracles will leap like lords into my awareness.

10–15/2/Apply as needed.

LOOK PAST APPEARANCES

Man's concept of his world built on the experience of the five
senses is no longer adequate and in many cases no longer valid.

— SHAFICA KARAGULLA

The planet you call home is spinning at a rate of roughly 930 miles per hour. It's orbiting the sun at an astonishing 66,486 miles per hour. But unless you just polished off a few pitchers of beer, you probably aren't aware of any such movement. That's one tiny example of how we distort reality.

Very early on—say, sometime around birth—our minds establish a pattern of perception and then proceed to filter out everything else. In other words, we only "experience" things that jibe with our very limited perception.

In *E-Squared*, I mentioned the girl from the Philippines who said it was weeks, if not months, after arriving in the United States before she noticed that some Americans had red hair, including people she knew and dealt with on a regular basis. Red hair was inconsistent with what she had been conditioned to see and expect. So for months, she was subjectively blind to red hair, seeing it as the brunette of her culture.

Our brains are designed to be efficient, not accurate. So we take the 400 billion bits of information that are offered each second and we begin screening. We begin narrowing.

I'll take that bit of information over there, and let's see—this one fits nicely with my ongoing soap opera about the opposite sex.

Lesson 92 tells me all concepts and judgments, all things I take for granted are distortions and that TRUE seeing only comes through light. It says I'd roll over laughing if I really understood the mental derangement that passes for thought.

When I see through my eyes (which basically report a carbon copy of my beliefs), I see weakness, lack, and division.

But there is another way of seeing. Through the strength of light.

Today, I'm grateful that as I give up the "hologram" I see with my eyes, I begin to see the radiance, the brilliance, and the love that shows up in light.

20/2/Apply as needed.

THE BROADER PERSPECTIVE

*When you're a mother, there's a love with your kids
that's beyond Earth and time and space.*

— BEYONCE

Say what you want about Facebook, but, since my daughter's untimely death, I treasure the memories that occasionally pop up—us in a Stockholm photo booth or riding horses at the Egyptian pyramids or hiking in Machu Picchu.

It delights me to see the two of us clowning around, being goofy, abiding, as Lesson 93 suggests, in light and joy and peace.

Taz and I had a lot of silly rituals. Our favorite character on the TV show *Gilmore Girls* was the eccentric Kirk Gleason who, over the course of seven seasons, worked as everything from a bath mat salesman to a termite exterminator to a parachute jumper. We regularly sent each other pictures of Kirk, in all his glory. We called it "The Daily Kirk."

On the first of every month, whichever of us proclaimed "Hedgehog" first was guaranteed a lucky month. It started when she was in grade school, but even in college we'd text each other the simple phrase. Since she stayed up late, she always prevailed at 12:01 on the dot. When she lived in Europe, 12:01 came several hours before I even qualified for our little game.

Even now, Taz sends hedgehogs from the other side. On May 1, it came in the form of a news clip about British rocker Peter Doherty who was temporarily hospitalized after being stabbed with a . . . hedgehog spike.

On June 1, the word "hedgehog" came in as a text message . . . from (don't ask me how?) Taz's phone.

July 1, I was at the toy store buying a birthday gift for my friend's grandbaby. I asked the clerk about the hottest new toys for one-year-olds. Without hesitating, she led me straight to a stacking hedgehog pull toy.

As Julia Roberts once told an interviewer who asked if she regretted not having an adult relationship with her father, who died early of throat cancer, "Are you kidding me? He's with me all the time."

Taz, too, is still with me all the time, albeit in a different form. She now has the broader perspective where every moment is light and joy and peace.

5/every hour

LIES MY EGO TELLS ME

The world isn't dangerous . . . unless you step directly into a volcano or cover yourself in raw meat and traipse across the Serengeti, you should be okay.

— GERALDINE DeRUITER

I'm currently compiling a playbook of the ego's many manifestations. Here are just a few:

1. The ego encourages me to find my identity in a psychology manual. The Course assures me I will never find a single clue to my true reality in a psychology book. The *Diagnostic and Statistical Manual of Mental Disorders* (DSM) and other psychological "theories" are basically a rogue's gallery of the ego. As long as I insist on staring at symptoms, I will never contact the deep interiority that exists within me.

2. The ego tells me security, money, and more, more, more is the holy grail. A recent *New Yorker* cartoon showed a forlorn caveman, dressed like Fred Flintstone, sitting in a cave with a half-dozen giant boulders. He says to his partner: "I thought getting bigger rocks would make me happier, but I guess I was wrong." One of the ego's craftiest ploys is to make me believe that material things—fancy houses, expensive purses, etc.—is what's missing in my life.

3. The ego encourages me to look for the flaw in the tapestry. Amazing miracles happen around me, nonstop. I completely overlook them because, too often, I'm focused on problems. When Moses used his staff to part the Red Sea, I'm sure a follower or two complained about mud in their sandals. This gigantic sea was literally separating into two, leading them to the Promised Land, and they were focused on gunk between their toes.

To put it bluntly, the ego is a destructive force that rises up pretty much every time I close in on the land of milk and honey.

But here's the good news. Nary a single one of the ego's stories is true. And since I'm the one who created the ego (in a misguided attempt to protect myself), I can let it go at any time. I can connect with the true part of my Self—my sea-parting magnificence, the unwounded part of me that the ego will never be able to touch.

Lesson 94 (I am as the Dude created me) encourages me to go deeper, to go beyond my paltry little list of attributes. This lesson is repeated over and over and over again throughout the Course. And today, I'm asked to repeat it over and over, every hour.

So I'll repeat my one-note Samba. I am as the Dude created me.

5/every hour

DITCH THE COMMANDMENTS. JOIN THE PARTY.

Every day brings a chance for you to draw in a breath, kick off your shoes, and dance.

— OPRAH WINFREY

More than 15 million people in more than 180 countries Zumba every week.

Why?

Because it's easy and it's fun.

The ultimate goal of any Zumba class is to feel what creator Beto Perez calls the FEJ: freeing, electrifying joy. That's what happens when you dance uninhibited to hip-hop, samba, salsa, merengue, and mambo.

You may be wondering what Zumba has to do with Lesson 95: I am one Self, united with my Creator.

Zumba went from obscure dance class in Cali, Colombia, to world-wide phenomena for one simple reason. A marketing genius transformed it from have-to (I've got to go exercise) into I-cannot-WAIT-to. Perez insisted it had to be something his mother could do (in other words, simple), and it had to be enjoyable enough to reap true behavioral change.

Unlike Zumba, God has a major PR problem. It's the last place most people would turn to find freeing and electrifying joy. Church, crucifixes, penance. I mean, who needs it?

So I propose a new way of looking at God. Not only have I updated its name, but I tell anybody who will listen that the real God (not the God invented by man, fabricated for the sake of control) is the coolest, the most fun, the most direct path to FEJ I've ever found.

Or to quote Beto once again, "Magic happens when your inhibitions (or old school beliefs) go out the window. And if you happen to get lost, just shake your booty."

5/every hour

DIVINE INTOXICATION

There are two basic motivating forces: fear and love.
When we are afraid, we pull back from life. When
we are in love, we open to all that life has to offer.

— JOHN LENNON

Remember when you were in grade school picking teams for say, kickball or Red Rover?

Even if you weren't the team captain, you knew exactly who you wanted on your team.

Every single third-grader knew which players were the fastest, the most daring, the one most likely to succeed in breaking through the meaty arms of the classroom bully brigade.

Still today I get to choose who's on my team, who leads the executive committee in my mind. Only now it boils down to two team players.

The ego, the PR person for fear and limits.

Or love.

Lesson 96 says there's no middle ground. There's no maybe. The ego and love are incompatible. They can't be reconciled. So it's time to decide.

One choice leads to lack, limitations, more of the same.

The other leads to Divine Intoxication.

5/every hour

TAKE THE GIFT, DAMMIT

Accepting the idea there were going to be no problems
was a greater adjustment than one might think.

— GLENDA GREEN

The standard paradigm goes something like this: life is hard, requires a constant influx of dinero, and, if I'm lucky (knock on wood) and nothing goes wrong, I might be able to enjoy my final years with a brief retirement.

The Course says it's all utter nonsense. And that my search for legal tender, convenience, and even spiritual enlightenment is a big fat waste of time.

Do you really think you're here "to create a brand"? To market Doritos or buy inflatable swimming pools? Do you really think tracking your market share, your 401(k), your days until the weekend, is a valuable pursuit?

Lesson 97 encourages us to enjoy spirit's gift. The gift that's already here. The gift that requires not one iota of effort from you or me.

Picture the dude as Oprah:

You get a gift. And you get a gift. And you get a . . .

You get this gift even if you f**k up. Even if you never get off your couch. Even if you're constantly devising evil plans to get back at your college adversary.

It's life, baby, and it's here, coursing through your veins, and there's nothing you can do to stop it.

So forget your feeble fears, your efforts to amass fortunes, to collect things.

Forget you even have a body. Just rest in the vibrancy of spirit that lives and moves and animates your oh-so-holy self.

5/every hour

TODAY, I SIDE WITH TRUTH

Nothing outside can give you salvation. . . .
You have to light your own lamp. You have to
know the miniature universe that you yourself are.

— BANANI RAY

One of the main tools in the ego's arsenal is telling me that my salvation (doing the daily lesson) is a huge burden, a time-sucking sacrifice, a cumbersome chore.

Maybe it mentioned that to you, too.

It goes something like this:

You've got much better things to do than to stop every hour to take a stand for salvation.

And besides, salvation is for boring church types.

Why bother taking a stand for ACIM? That's for losers, not to mention you're already way too busy.

So today, as I willingly play my part in the grand scheme of salvation, I remember the following:

Salvation = joy and love and fun.

Salvation means all the important stuff is already taken care of. The sun comes up every morning and I don't have to do a thing. It warms the soil, turns seeds into food, and provides light for me to go out and have a good time. My heart beats without me having to remind it. My body heals itself every time I scrape my knee. And it also heals everything else when I don't focus on the problem and block the flow.

The big stuff, all the important stuff, goes on seamlessly without me having to do a darned thing.

5/every hour

I NEED DO NOTHING

We are making hay when we should be making whoopee;
we are raising tomatoes when we should be raising Cain.

— A N N I E D I L L A R D

Like all of us, Kenya Barris, creator of *Black-ish,* a wildly popular, Emmy-winning comedy, was led to believe that if he wanted the goodies—success, acclaim, God's blessings, etc.—he must abide by a list of "good people" rules.

And he tried. He really did. Until finally, the weight of all the demands became too much to bear.

Well, guess what?

Even though he broke all "the rules," even though he left the conventional path, the blessings kept right on coming. His career took off. *Black-ish* was nominated for Emmys and People's Choice awards. He couldn't keep up with all the acclaim.

He called it a stunning realization. Grace comes because grace comes. He did not have to earn it.

That's why my favorite mantra is this: I need do nothing.

The Course says it like this: "It would be far more profitable now to merely concentrate on this (I need do nothing) than to consider what you should do. It is the ultimate release that everyone will one day find in his own way at his own time."

The Course says we can save time by using but this one practice. I need do nothing, it says, is a statement of allegiance, a truly undivided loyalty.

Lesson 99 says it's my one and only function.

Because here's the thing. We are already good people. We are already given God's grace. We do not have to earn anything. It's given to all of us. It's our natural state.

Once we surrender the "good people" rules.

5/every hour

THE ENLIGHTENMENT FAST TRACK

*Re-examine all you have been told in school
or church or in any book.*

— WALT WHITMAN

A reader emailed me this morning to regretfully admit that, alas, she was unable to faithfully execute the hourly reminders requested in the Course workbook.

I had to chuckle because a) in 25 years of doing the Course, I have never once successfully completed the task myself, and b) the only reason I'm asked to do that is because my mind is like a pinball machine. And I need help.

I have shown great aptitude at proving over and over again that, despite my best intentions, my efforts are futile. They simply don't work.

But there is, the Course assures me, a better way.

The better way is a four-letter word: HELP!!!

In Lesson 100, I learn the following:

1. The Dude's will for me is perfect happiness.

2. My joy is essential to the healing of the world.

3. And the Dude itself is incomplete without my joy.

So anytime I don't feel perfect happiness, I have to stop and realize that I made a decision that differs from my Source.

And since that decision was my best effort (again proof of my futile efforts), I just have to offer that magical four-letter plea: HELP!

5/every hour

GOD ONLY MAKES 10S

*Enlightenment is not a mountaintop you claw
your way to. It is a reality you experience.*

— ALAN COHEN

The Dude's will for me is perfect happiness. I'm supposed to repeat this mantra every hour.

Perfect, of course, means 100 percent. Never stopping. All the time. From sunup to sundown. And even when I sleep. It's SO radical and SO outside my range of experience that how can I even wrap my mind around it? 24/7? How can that be?

So today, in order to hook into just a wee bit of willingness (all I'm ever asked to contribute), I wrote myself a mantra, a little ditty that I plan to repeat A LOT. Quietly, inside my head, since I prefer not to be institutionalized.

Like the irresistible catchiness of Applebee's "I want my baby back, baby back . . ." I hope to get this mantra lodged in my head:

Epic. Awesome. Forever fine.
Happiness, fun, and joy are mine.

5/every hour

OLD BELIEFS ARE GOIN' DOWN

And to the tiger in the zoo, Madeline just said, "pooh, pooh!"

— LUDWIG BEMELMAN

NPR recently ran a report about Madeline, Ludwig Bemelman's plucky heroine who, you may remember, lives "in an old house in Paris, covered in vines." I read all the Madeline books to my daughter when she was young. We both loved them.

Being reminded of Madeline's courageous "pooh, pooh!" to the tiger in the zoo made me smile because that's exactly what Lesson 102 (I share the Dude's will for my happiness) tells me to say to old belief systems that so insistently wave their hands in the back of the classroom, those beliefs that are on constant alert, looking for ways to sabotage my happiness.

The old beliefs are stubborn. They claim to be working on my behalf. They adamantly insist they're keeping things in control so I can be happy. That tired old belief system is relentless, telling me there's always some violation, some person out there who is messing up, who is doing it wrong. Of course, it's never me.

So today, as I channel Madeline and brush aside the scary tiger and all my other judgments, I realize there's no reason to delay, no reason to limit, no reason to wait an instant longer for the endless peace and joy and miracles to which I'm entitled.

5/every hour

WHAT THE HOLY BIGWIGS
FAILED TO MENTION

*In our true blissful essence . . . everything is alright forever and
forever and forever.*

— JACK KEROUAC

Lesson 103 (God, being love, is also happiness) is another attempt to
set the record straight. It tells us joy is our natural state. It tells us perfect happiness is our birthright.

The God most of us believe in is an invention of man, a Divine
National Security Agency fabricated for the sake of convenience. We
accept this human-made God as an indisputable fact. But it makes no
sense. If God is love, if God is perfect, and if God is all the other benefi-
cent descriptions we ascribe to him, why would he toss anyone into a
lion's den?

And pardon me for being impudent, but why would anyone in
their right mind want to hook up with a capricious and unjust god
who gets his jollies from punishing them?

Far as I'm concerned, one of the best descriptions of the Dude is
outrageousness. I mean look at J.C. He was walking on water (when
he wasn't turning it into vino) and multiplying material objects (fish,
loaves, etc.).

That's pretty outrageous. And that's what he meant when he urged
us to follow him (not, as I often point out, to worship him). We're
meant to be outrageous. Bold. Dazzling.

Society has tried for years to rope us in, to keep us in line. But that's
what we're undoing, lesson by lesson with this Course.

We are not here to play it safe. We are here to be the light. To shine
our brilliance. To risk. To love. To spread our joy.

5/every hour

TODAY, I CHOOSE TO BE FREE

Dance first. Think later. It's the natural order.

— SAMUEL BECKETT

The rules we pick up here on planet Earth revolve around the following themes: Stop. Don't. Be Careful.

In the Course, we learn just the opposite:

Go for it.
Of course, you can.
Throw caution to the wind.

Lesson 104 (I seek what belong to me in truth) assures me of the blissful freedom that comes from giving up judgment, especially the below-the-surface, quiet doctrines instilled by our culture. Those times we listen, nod our heads, but secretly think, "You're wrong, you know."

Today, I commit to living south of my neck, in my heart. Whatever happens, whatever anyone says, irrespective of my internal response, I will embrace it and willingly give 100 percent.

Living sans judgment, as this lesson proves, comes with a rarely experienced sense of freedom, connection, and community, a palpable interaction with all that is.

My judgments, I find, are nothing but a strategy waged by the separate self so it can stay protected in its lonely silo. Letting go of all defenses comes with a risk, but when I give up "I'm right," when I validate every moment and every person, a great dissolving takes place.

I discover the connection that is already here. The oneness that existed before time, the oneness that will be here long after time.

5/every hour

GETTING TO CARNEGIE HALL

We can only be said to be alive in those moments
when our hearts are conscious of our treasures.

— THORNTON WILDER

Some mornings when I'm running to pickleball (no need to be impressed; it's a mere one block away), I repeat over and over in my head, "Thank you, God. Thank you, God. Thank you, God."

And I feel so joyful, so lucky. I've found that the more I focus on my blessings, the more blessings knock on my door. It's like Halloween night when a parade of adorable ballerinas, princesses, and miniature zombies show up to delight me. (And all I have to do is provide a bowl of candy.)

Lesson 105 (The Dude's peace and joy are mine) says everything we give—joy, love, creativity—expands. Creates growth. Generates more.

People often ask me, "How is it possible to be so joyful when the 'what you see' looms so large in your mind?"

And all I can say is it's the same as the answer to the old joke, "How do you get to Carnegie Hall?"

Practice, practice, practice.

5/every hour

SILENCE THE THUNDER
OF THE MEANINGLESS

I know a lot of miserable Academy Award winners.

— JOSH RADNOR

The ego offers an unrelenting litany of unconscious, unexamined assumptions. Be more. Do more. Get more.

Lesson 106 says, "Don't accept its petty gifts. Don't buy its shallow notions of happiness."

For 20-some years, Nipun Mehta has proven this lesson's maxim—that it's impossible to give without also receiving. He has defied every cultural norm. Instead of accumulating, he gives. Instead of fearing, he trusts. Instead of achieving more, more, more, he seeks out connection, brotherhood, generosity.

"It's a much lighter way to be," says the former Silicon Valley software engineer who started ServiceSpace in 1999. "We were a bunch of 20-somethings who just wanted to give."

Starting with small experiments in generosity, they eventually created a free restaurant (Karma Kitchen), an active online organization that encourages small acts of kindness (KindSpring), and Laddership Circles that create transformational economies based on the spirit of gift.

To this day, even though their Awaken Circles have spread to living rooms across the globe, they refuse to monetize.

Rather than live in the accepted culture of scarcity and fear, Nipun, his family, and friends have created a strong cocoon of generosity.

"We've created a deep connection and a collective energy. Even when the giving act is entirely invisible, an unmistakable transformation takes place," Nipun says. "It's always unclear who is the biggest beneficiary."

So today, take it from Nipun. Be still. Listen for truth.

It's your pilot light. And it will change everything.

5/every hour

GET SPIRITUALLY DRESSED FOR THE DAY

*Be hopeful, be brave, and rejoice in having
a bit of untamable strangeness in your heart.*

— NEIL GAIMAN

When it's not plugged in . . .

> . . . a TV can't transmit Netflix.
> . . . a toaster can't brown bagels.
> . . . an iPhone can't recharge.

Likewise, when I don't consciously plug myself in each morning to the field of infinite potentiality, to love, to the primal and intimate union with all life, I'm unable to perform as my highest self.

Esther Hicks compared it to vacuuming my bedroom without attaching the cord. It may look like I'm working my way across the room, getting into those stubborn corners, applying the crevice nozzle. But if my cord isn't properly attached to a power source, I might as well be taking a nap.

But . . . oh, when I do plug in!

Today's lesson (Truth will correct all errors in my mind) reminds me that suffering, death, and pain are self-made concepts. They will vanish as soon as I plug in, as soon as I ask for help, as soon as I rely instead on her majesty, the Dude.

5/every hour

DO YOU COLLABORATE WITH THE UNIVERSE OR MAKE IT YOUR ENEMY?

I have no purpose for today except to look upon a liberated world.

— A COURSE IN MIRACLES

Ask any physicist. We live in an interactive universe. Physical forces respond to how we think, what we expect, how we behave. That's what this lesson means by "To give and receive are one in truth."

Most of us, instead of collaborating with this awesome force that spins worlds and expands galaxies, wage war against it. We literally put up our dukes and dare it to fight when it just likes to say, "Chill, dude. Have a lemonade."

So if you're wondering whether you're engaged in the most effective collaboration with the universe, here's a guide:

Collaborators high-five their riches. They know they're heirs to incredible wealth.

Combatants says things like "Riches? You've got to be kidding me. Can't you see I'm struggling here?"

Collaborators inhabit every moment. They gobble up "the now."

Combatants live everywhere but in the moment. They're buried in their phones, in yesterday's disgruntlements, in tomorrow's worries.

Collaborators zero in on possibilities. They know nothing's set in stone, that change is exciting. They celebrate the myriad prospects in every situation.

Combatants cuss. They're mad as hell and they're not going to take it anymore. They build a monument to their woe is me!

So to summarize, my fellow collaborators, today we're going to high-five our riches, inhabit every moment, and zero in on the infinite number of possibilities the universe dishes up today and every day.

5/every hour

I CAN DO ALL THINGS

What we think is so is only a reflection of our deepest
fear holding us to the shackles of limiting belief.

— GLENDA GREEN

Stephen Curry is one of the greatest shooters in NBA history. He has played on four All-NBA teams, was voted MVP twice, and recently signed the first $200 million contract in the NBA.

The fact that the celebrity point guard is a dwarfish six feet three inches, tiny compared to his fellow teammates, makes it even more remarkable that among his fortes is excelling during the clutch.

You see, Stephen has an edge, a secret sauce that, while available to all of us, few of us ever use. He employs Lesson 109 (I rest in God), getting his mojo from a higher source.

He doesn't depend on his own strength, his own skills, his own training. Rather, he invokes the power of love, what I often call Radiant X. Every time he takes a shot (or really does anything that matters), he invokes his mantra: "I can do all things."

This mantra that he put on T-shirts refers to his favorite Bible verse, Philippians 4:13. His "Curry One" basketball shoes even come with a lace loop scripted 4:13.

While I'm not a big verse reciter, I gotta admit, "I can do all things through that which strengtheneth me" is worth adding to my brain's portfolio.

5/every hour

THAT TIME I FAILED
TO TAKE THE RED PILL

When I don't stop daily to inventory all the
gazillion things going right in my life, the crazy
voice in my head tries to make me its bitch.

— FROM MY BOOK *THANK & GROW RICH*

On this limited physical plane, life sometimes sucks. But as the Course teaches me (over and over), these thoughts and perceptions are NOT real. A much higher Truth prevails. I am a multidimensional being, and this higher truth is forever available IF and WHEN I choose to hook up.

Some days, I get hijacked and instead of starting my morning with my Course workbook lesson or my AA 2.0 program, I use life drama (it's always there if that's what I choose to look for) as an excuse not to take the red pill.

I no longer beat myself up. Eventually, I even feel gratitude that each time I forego my daily maintenance, I find Exhibit A in just how powerful the Course really is.

It's like an exercise program. You don't do it for a week, look in the mirror, and say, "Hey, good-looking. You did it. Guess you can quit now."

I pretty much have to open that workbook every morning. It's not like it's really asking too much. How hard is it to read a five-minute lesson? If I was asked to take a pill for some horrible illness, I'd ingest it with religious fervor.

Lesson 110 is repeated more than any other lesson: I am as the Dude created me.

I can pretend to be a dysfunctional, unbalanced woman with all sorts of agendas and vendettas, or I can remain as the Dude created me: an eternal spirit bringing peace to all the world. The power in this one phrase (not to mention the power of getting up each morning and committing to a higher truth) undoes the past, redeems the world.

Like Neo in *The Matrix*, I have a choice. The blue pill (where I remain unaware) or the red pill where I discover reality without the preprogrammed script.

5/every hour

Boom!

Review III

You're here and you're breathing and you get to take
part in the ongoing creation of the world.

— ROB BELL

This review (Lessons 111 through 120) is all about the bennies. Radiant X wants to show off, to prove to you just how much there is to gain by working this Course.

In return for a very small ask—five minutes, twice a day—Radiant X will completely rewire your thoughts.

The trick (and this is where the asshat doth protest) is to use the lessons each time your peace is threatened. Again, make it automatic. "We will, we will . . . rock you." Use the lessons as a mantra.

Rather than a different jukebox selection for each day of this review, I suggest repeating this one: "Dance to the Music" by Sly and the Family Stone. Or pick your own favorite.

So, first thing in the morning, devote five minutes to the lesson and then right before sleeping, give it another five. Apply, as needed.

Piddly request. Ginormous outcome.

111

WHY I SUBSCRIBE TO
THE PREMIUM CHANNELS

Standing on the corner of awesome and bombdiggity.

— SHARED BY A READER ON MY TWITTER FEED

For morning and evening review.

Need-to-know 1: Miracles are natural.

Need-to-know 2: Miracles are effortless.

The skinny: While much of the world subscribes to the default frequency, the one that out-pictures the world we watch on the news, I commit to an amplified frequency.

Instead of operating from the culturally agreed-upon channel that radios in limitations, lack, and division, I tune in to the premium channel that broadcasts a fuller, more beautiful, more accurate picture.

This, I find, is reality.

THE DUDE ABIDES

*Memory and identity are burdens from the past that
prevent us from living freely in the present.*

—NAVAL RAVIKANT

For morning and evening review.

Need-to-know 1: Light and joy and peace abide in me.

Need-to-know 2: I am as the Dude created me.

The skinny: The aim of *A Course in Miracles* is to disengage from consensus reality, to practice operating from a full spectrum of frequencies.

We're born with the whole enchilada, but well-meaning grown-ups encourage us to wave good-bye to our imaginary friends, to detach from our mystical connection.

With practice and daily attention, we can reconnect with the full spectrum and start to notice that miracles are everyday affairs, as common as the morning sunrise.

FLYING FRIENDLY SKIES

Stagger onward rejoicing.

— W. H. AUDEN

For morning and evening review.

Need-to-know 1: Serenity and perfect peace are mine.

Need-to-know 2: I am one with everything.

The skinny: Please accept this gift of three more "well, duh!" stories from my in-box, all of which happened in airports.

1. "Since I was five, I've loved astronauts and space flight. I always dreamed of someday meeting an astronaut. While "playing" with the experiments in *E-Cubed,*[*] my wife gifted me with a book by astronaut Chris Hadfield. I read it in tears, thinking, "This guy and I could have been brothers."

    Well, guess who he meets a few days later at the airport? The one and only . . . Commander Chris Hadfield.

2. Mary Kay was in the Minneapolis airport, and she couldn't get the song "Tears of a Clown" out of her mind. Before she boarded her next flight, she bumped into Smokey Robinson, whom she'd always adored and hoped to meet. He even gave her a big hug.

3. The last airport/miracle story started with a joke. A friend said he's always wanted to meet a porn star. Only half serious (or maybe not), he just "happened" to be seated next to a real live porn star on the plane. She even showed him her website.

---

[*] Another *Course in Miracles* adaption.

114

IT'S ALL JUST A BIG MISUNDERSTANDING

Thoughts are the ultimate buzzkill.

— JAMES TWYMAN

For morning and evening review.

Need-to-know 1: I am spirit.

Need-to-know 2: My body cannot contain me.

The skinny: All problems boil down to a single misunderstanding: We view the world from a different perspective than our Source.

Lesson 114 is another attempt to correct the misunderstanding.

When you get it that you are spirit and have no limitations, the following three truths become evident:

1. There is nothing you could ever do, nothing that could ever happen that can separate you from your Source.

2. You are loved beyond anything you could ever imagine. The word "love," purloined by a culture that knows nothing of the sort, is a paltry substitute for this deep, abiding connection.

3. Because of your inalienable connection to this bigger thing that cannot be named, you have the power to create worlds. In fact, that is why you are here.

YABBA-DABBA-DON'T

*Everything is ecstasy, inside. We just don't
know it because of our thinking-minds.*

— JACK KEROUAC

For morning and evening review.

Need-to-know 1: My only purpose is to be free.

Need-to-know 2: No one's free until everybody's free.

The skinny: Like all card-carrying members of the self-help community, I often rely on my limited mind to fix my problems.

I sometimes lecture myself:

"Be less stressed."
"Think positive thoughts."
"Quit seeing yourself as a loser."

The Course tells me my egoic mind, which created those concepts in the first place, isn't capable of "fixing" anything.

The best it can do is re-run catalogued lessons from the past. Re-run fear, old patterns, whiny judgments. It cuts itself into pieces and pits them one part against another.

Today, I short-circuit my limited mind by identifying with my timeless self, my energetic self, my holy self, who's already online with every good thing.

ON BEHALF OF LOVE

Love intentionally, extravagantly, unconditionally.
The broken world waits in darkness for the light that is you.

— L. R. KNOST

For morning and evening review.

Need-to-know 1: The Dude's will for me is perfect happiness.

Need-to-know 2: That perfect happiness is all I want.

The skinny: Don't fret. Don't stress. Don't work so hard.

When I worry and wonder and work to find peace and serenity and whatever else I desire, I send out vibes of "Eeks!"

Vibes of "Eeks!" are diametrically opposed to my perfect happiness.

I can strive, fret, and send "eeks!" out into the atmosphere. Or I can rest in knowing that Source, as we speak, is lining up everything I could possibly want or need.

THE MATERIAL WORLD:
IT'S A TEMP JOB

The Ego and Love are never on the same kickball team.

— DEBBY HANDRICH

For morning and evening review.

Need-to-know 1: Everything but love is make-believe.

Need-to-know 2: Love = happiness and joy.

The skinny: All apparent problems are temporary, ephemeral. Any situation that keeps me from feeling connected and ready to break out in dance (say, the political situation or societal divisions) is a game of charades.

It only seems rock solid because I keep staring at it, pointing at it, pronouncing it to be true. It will only "be true" as long as I continue to stare and point.

CHANGE THE PLOT POINTS

*The only person you are fighting is yourself and your
stubbornness to engage in new circumstances.*

— JON KRAKAUER

For morning and evening review.

Need-to-know 1: I gladly exchange my pretend world for peace and joy.

Need-to-know 2: Shhh! There's a mighty voice broadcasting a completely different story.

The skinny: A group of cells, about the size of a gumdrop, hang out at the base of your brain stem. This control center, known as the reticular activating system (RAS) sorts and evaluates incoming data. It sends what it thinks is urgent to the active part of the brain and steers the nonurgent stuff to the back. But while it's organizing, it's also interpreting, drawing inferences, and filtering out anything that doesn't jibe with your story.

The good news is you can change your story. You can exchange the plot points the RAS is currently sending to the active part of your brain to the plot points we're promised in these lessons. It's as straightforward as five minutes in the morning and five minutes before sleep.

I INVOKE MY
SUPERPOWER OF LOVE

God says yes, we can have what we want, because love wins.

— ROB BELL

For morning and evening review.

Need-to-know 1: I am mistaken when I believe I can be hurt in any way.

Need-to-know 2: I use my get-out-of-jail-free card to invoke the power of love.

The skinny: When my daughter, an avid Harry Potter fan, was in grade school, she and her friend Kylie ran around waving their pretend wands, casting spells and shouting phrases such as "Ascendio" and "Obliviate."

While I don't have a wand, I do believe in invoking the power of love. It works better than any potion or charm taught at Hogwarts.

The Course, boiled down to its essence, says, "I have one function and it's the only thing that'll ever make me happy."

Choose love. Choose love.

Any time love's opposite rears its illusory head, I reach for my wand of love and know NOTHING can ever defeat it.

That's the guarantee of the Course. Love always wins.

DELETING ALL MAD IDEAS

The universe looks less like a machine
and more like one big thought.

— SIR JAMES JEANS

For morning and evening review.

Need-to-know 1: I chill in Truth.

Need-to-know 2: I am as the Dude created me.

The skinny: I lay aside my faith in the alternate reality of limitation, sickness, doom, and gloom. I let go of all perceptual adjustments I "made up" to justify my beliefs. I joyously release any idea that interferes with love and happiness, light and peace.

Today, I chill.

NOT FORGIVENESS AGAIN

Anything will give up its secrets if you love it enough.

— GEORGE WASHINGTON CARVER

We give the dying one simple instruction. Walk toward the light.

Lesson 121 (Forgiveness is the key to happiness) offers the same piece of advice. Only it urges us to do it today. Do it now. Don't wait.

Admittedly, it uses slightly different verbiage.

But get this in your noggin.

All it really means is "walk toward the light."

In whatever situation you find yourself, walk toward the light.

Don't get stopped by appearances, by judgments, by your conviction that what's happening is wrong, that that bastard is evil. Just keep moving toward the light.

Today we pick someone who isn't our favorite. As the Course says, someone's already popped into your mind. That person will do.

Don't make this hard. Try on this mantra.

Forgiveness is surprisingly easy.

Don't focus on what happened in the past. Simply call that person up in your mind (that's where they are anyway) and notice the light in him. Or her.

If you look and listen carefully, you can't help but see it. If you open yourself up to now, the light (in this alleged dimwit) becomes so apparent that you will marvel, "How did I miss this before?"

That light is all you really want. It's the key to happiness. It's the answer to every alleged "problem" and "devastation" you think you have.

Don't wait for your deathbed. Walk toward the light today.

15/1

SINK INTO HAPPINESS

Magic is becoming the new norm.

— BENTINHO M. ASSARO

It's open window season where I live, which means some of my best teachers wake me up each morning with their chorus of joy.

These teachers (most people call them birds) are riffing on the day, blaring songs that will never be sung in that exact arrangement again. They're not reading self-help literature or wondering how to heal their childhood wounds.

Likewise, the sun rose this morning with a brand-new palette of colors. It painted a one-of-a-kind vista unique to my GPS coordinate on this big stone hurtling through space. It's not mad at the president or worrying about nuclear war.

The natural world is my best teacher.

Those cardinals and tree frogs trilling advertisement for mates? The squirrels using my fence as a tightrope? They're my mentors when it comes to Lesson 122: Clear your mind of all dead thoughts.

The mother fox parading her kits alongside the road is not obsessing about work or whether or not her butt looks big.

Worry, anxiety, fear, wondering whether or not your butt looks big—all dead thoughts.

Being glued to a smartphone or a box with 292 channels—dead thoughts.

Forgiveness (which this lesson promises will give me everything I want) is simply letting go of all dead thoughts (and that's anything that's not happening right this very now).

Today, I step outside, listen to the soundtrack of nature, check out the new episode playing every hour in my backyard. I'm going to follow my mentors in the natural world who neither toil nor sow, neither worry nor fret.

Dead thoughts be gone.

15/2

YOU CAN'T MAKE AN ELEPHANT PURR AND OTHER REASONS TO GIVE UP RESISTANCE

Don't surrender all your joy for an idea you used to have about yourself that isn't true anymore.

— CHERYL STRAYED

A Course in Miracles is about developing a different operating system, about hooking into a broadband frequency through which blessings can freely flow.

According to Lesson 123 (I thank the Dude for its gifts), it's a day to celebrate how far I've come, a day to give up resistance. To resist life is as futile as trying to make an elephant purr. It only makes me miserable.

I can try and try, but fighting, fixing, focusing on what's wrong is like driving the wrong way down a one-way street.

But I CAN turn around. I can move with the flow of the universe. I do this by taking my attention off everything I think sucks. All those problems I think need fixing. All those issues I have with so-and-so. Or with my job. Or with my body.

When I step into the stream of gratitude, when I start noticing the gazillion things that are going right, those annoying problems have a way of fixing themselves. They literally dissolve.

Without any input on my part.

15/2

JOY TOO DEEP TO COMPREHEND

God is my boo.

— MAYA ANGELOU

My eyes, as remarkable as they are, can only see one percent of the visible light spectrum. To be scientific, human eyeballs only perceive wavelengths between 10^{-4} and 10^{-6} of the electromagnetic spectrum.

Radio waves, infrared waves, X-rays, terahertz waves, for example, are beyond my eyes' capabilities.

So for me to think I see "reality" with my wavelength-challenged eyeballs is ridiculous.

Lesson 124 (Let me remember I am one with everything) encourages me to experience the world from a higher, largely invisible frequency.

This frequency, the underlying foundation of who I am, literally changes energy fields. As I learn to "see" only the loving and the lovable, everything I touch is blessed and healed.

Today, I celebrate that I'm safe, protected, and can fail at nothing. I celebrate that my anxieties are meaningless, and that power and strength will prevail in all my undertakings.

I find, as this lesson promises, joy too deep to comprehend.

15/2

INVINCIBLE MARIO, HERE I COME!

We were trying to create something that had never been done before.

— KOJI KONDI, CO-CREATOR OF SUPER MARIO BROS.

If I remain eye-to-eye with a problem, I will continue to fight it. If I stubbornly refuse to budge from the level of my alleged difficulty, we (the difficulty and me) will continue knocking the living daylights out of each other.

In Lesson 125 (In quiet I receive), I learn to resolve my issues with a different approach.

Instead of staring down my issues, I channel Nintendo's Super Mario, who completes his mission by jumping to higher levels. When I duck into secret coin rooms and other "quiet places," I'm able to confront my "stuff" from an elevated perspective.

When I recognize my true nature (love, the highest level possible), my opponents are less daunting. Why would I want to duke it out? From the highest level, solutions, answers, and revelations show up. And I discover they were within me all the time.

10/3

REPAIRING THE GLITCH

It takes a special kind of mind to break away from the norm,
to know or to believe that what everybody accepts is not right.

— WANGARI MAATHAI

Lesson 126 (All that I give is given to myself) teaches me that the need to maximize self-interest is nothing but a long-standing glitch. It calls out the myth of separation and proves that everything I give boomerangs right back to me.

It may seem like I am separate from you, that my attitudes and beliefs have no bearing on your behavior, that my thoughts have no effect on you. But that's old-school conditioning.

Today, I bravely leave that washed-out old paradigm in the dust.

Instead, I send a message of trust out into the world. No matter how it appears, I will trust that you're not really an a-hole. I will trust that, like me, you care about life and want only to be courageous, generous, and kind.

I divest myself of the you-versus-me paradigm, recognizing it's not what makes me (or anybody else) happy.

As I follow my heart, freely offer my gifts, and take interest in others' well-being, I enter a different realm. I find a world restored to unity.

15/2

DON'T LET THE PAST
ASSAULT YOUR NOW

We lean forward to the next crazy venture beneath the skies.

— JACK KEROUAC

Kum Back, a bootleg album released in a plain white jacket in January 1970, demonstrates why I go through the lessons in the Course workbook every year.

The album is an early version of *Let it Be.* Sourced from a multi-track tape recording of the Beatles at Twickenham Film Studios, this unauthorized bootleg features Paul McCartney singing out of tune, John Lennon botching lyrics, and more than one poorly conceived guitar lick.

The point is the Beatles, the bestselling band in history, were far from perfect. They had to practice. By the time Beatlemania swept the globe, the music-bending group had honed their skills for three entire years at tiny clubs in Hamburg.

My brain has been running the bootleg album—the inferior album of limitation—most of my life. Letting go of my old story takes practice.

That's why I flex my muscles every morning by devoting my day to peace, to joy, to seeing love in everything. That's why today I will repeat Lesson 127 (Love is a law without an opposite) over and over.

Daily practice is how I free my mind, how I surrender all limitations in which I've placed my faith.

My *Let it Be* masterpiece awaits, as I escape limitation and all ill-conceived guitar licks that hold on to the past.

15/2

MORE THAN A RANDOM CONFIGURATION OF MOLECULES

Until we know the assumptions in which we are drenched,
we cannot know ourselves.

— ADRIENNE RICH

After Derek DelGaudio was named Magician of the Year, an interviewer asked how he first got interested in magic. Was it a particular magician? Or a particular trick or a—

He stopped the interviewer right there. "It was never anything I saw. My imagination was captured by what I couldn't see."

And there you have the operative sentiment of Lesson 128 (The world I see holds nothing that I want). What I SEE is just my version of a bunch of random molecules. I'm not really Pam. Pam is a made-up story, a fairy tale.

My brain (like all human brains) takes in sounds and light and crafts a story that matches my beliefs and expectations. This lesson teaches me it's not real.

Like DelGaudio said, the juice is what we *can't* see. When we strip away the labels, the boxes, the random configuration of molecules, we find our essence.

We find the world we DO want. We find the intoxicating, invigorating ecstasy of who we really are.

10/3

THE GAMEBOARD OF AWARENESS AND CONSCIOUSNESS

*Authentic spirituality is not some little flicker or
buzz of knowingness, but a vast fire of liberation
providing both heat and light for what must be done.*

— ROBERT AUGUSTUS MASTERS

Our beliefs shape and mold the reality that plays out in our lives. These beliefs, both conscious and unconscious, drive our feelings, our actions, and our inner commentary.

For example, if your belief game piece is currently stuck on the square of victim consciousness ("Things happen TO me," "Life sucks and then you die" are a few standards on this square), you can affirm and intend all you want, but your belief, the guy driving the bus of your reality, ends up with the last word.

When you spend most of your waking hours on that game board square (it's extremely popular), your channels are plugged. All good waiting to be bestowed can't get through.

Lesson 129 (Beyond this world there is a world I want) reminds me there are more squares on the game board of consciousness, squares of greater joy, fulfillment, and satisfaction.

There are squares where losing is impossible, where love endures forever, where hate cannot exist and vengeance has no meaning.

Today, I unbind my mind from all things that keep me prisoner. I value them not and they disappear.

10/3

BE RECKLESSLY GENEROUS AND RELENTLESSLY KIND

All right is almost always where we eventually land,
even if we f*ck up entirely along the way.

— CHERYL STRAYED

When a quarter lands on the floor, I either get "heads" or "tails." I can't have it both ways. ACIM 130 (It is impossible to see two worlds) asks me to decide.

Letting the Divine Buzz handle the details doesn't mean sitting around polishing my nails and refusing to pick up the phone when, say, Oprah calls. It means a rigorous practice of connecting with the big guy and asking It to line up my schedule, allowing It to make sure I meet the folks and make the connections that best align with my mission. It always involves love. Expansion. Joy.

I devoted my life to the Divine Buzz many years ago. I appointed it the CEO of my career and, so far, it hasn't let me down. It's enabled me to write 20 books and create a life without "a real job" for more than 30 years.

It has enabled me to make a living on my wit and my craft.

The only thing keeping anyone apart from this power is their own walls and judgments.

Judgment, I'm relieved to find out, is not my function. My only job is to choose the Divine side of the coin.

5/6

FAILURE IS NOT AN OPTION

What keeps the world in chains but your beliefs?

— A COURSE IN MIRACLES

Every town has one. The mumbling guy on the street. The woman in all black who frequents coffee shops carrying a three-foot cross. Those intriguing characters who always make you wonder. In Lawrence, Kansas, where I live, we have a whole contingency of such characters.

Dennis, who typically wears a Spiderman outfit, never leaves home without his "daughter" Cheryl, a plastic doll he either carries or pushes in a stroller. Over the years, Cheryl has "grown up" from a baby doll to a bigger doll until now she's the size of a storefront mannequin which, in truth, she actually is.

Pranksters kidnapped Cheryl the other day and the local police force, taking it quite seriously, put out an APB, which thankfully resulted in an immediate recovery. Dennis and Cheryl are local celebrities. Dennis even has his own Facebook fan page.

The point I'm trying to make is that Dennis is no different from the rest of us. His world, although a slight deviation from what's considered normal, is very real to him. Just as the world we've made up in our minds is very real to us. But both—Dennis's world and the world we "see" and believe in with such a tenacious grip—are fiction. Neither constitutes Reality.

Reality, according to physicists who study these things, is that we are all connected. We are all one.

We only "see" a separate, divided, ugly world because we imagine it to be that way. Illusions are as strong in their effects as is truth.

Because we continue to repeat and believe in the world we see on the six o'clock news, we continue to see the all-hell-breaking-loose world of destruction and limits. Because dodging minefields is our source of vision, we continue to see a world of doom. Through our rote insistence on fear, we have created a fearful world.

But it's no more real than the world of Dennis.

In Lesson 131 (No one can fail who seeks the truth), I release all dismal thoughts and meaningless laments and slip effortlessly into the light, the love, the truth.

10/3

LIFE DOESN'T SUCK, SH*T DOESN'T HAPPEN, AND THE GLASS IS 100 PERCENT FULL

His gifts are sure, eternal, changeless, limitless, forever giving out,
extending love and adding to your never-ending joy.

— A COURSE IN MIRACLES

The quote at the top of this entry is a mighty big claim. And far removed from what most of us believe.

To get it, to really believe I'm meant to be happy is the first step to enlightenment. Any other choice (and make no mistake, it is a choice) is a fool's errand.

And that's why Lesson 132 asks me to "loose the world from all I thought it was." Current scientific theory alleges we're born into a world quite separate from ourselves, a world impervious to what we think.

But once again, this lesson reminds me there is no world apart from what I wish. So I can either enslave the world with my fears, doubts, and miseries or I can choose what this lesson calls my ultimate release.

I can continue to believe in the world as it appears now or I can believe in my eternal state. I can settle for "what is" or I can create something new. I can continue to interfere with Truth or I can step aside and let my natural joy rush in.

It's a simple matter of deciding where to shine my spotlight.

15/2

THUMBS UP? THUMBS DOWN?

When the brain gets involved, it starts a spreadsheet.

— PETE HOLMES

The human brain likes to solve, understand, decide, debate, **argue, in**fluence, opine, and whine. It rarely shuts up. It gets its jollies **by mak**ing everything complicated.

Even Facebook's simple thumbs-up sign now comes with **a selec**tion of six emojis.

In today's lesson (I will not value what is valueless), I **abandon all** complication. I make one simple decision: to value only the **valuable.** To make all decisions based on benefits to me. Theories **matter not.**

Despite Facebook's six emojis and the brain's unending **dicing and** splicing, I recognize there are only two alternatives: fear **(which dis**guises itself in a million costumes) or love.

I recognize that if fear shows up in one of its endless **costumes, it** doesn't mean there's an actual problem. It just means there's a **problem** in perception.

Ergo:

Fear (or costumed problem): I can't pay my bills.
Truth: I have a perceptual problem.

Fear (or costumed problem): I can't see eye to eye with **my boss.**
Truth: I have a perceptual problem.

Fear (or costumed problem): I am overweight and **unattractive to** the opposite sex.
Truth: I have a perceptual problem.

Today, I acknowledge I have been mistaken. Not 99.9 percent **of the** time. But 100 percent of the time. And I remind myself in **each of my** two 15-minutes sessions that, despite prevailing sentiment, it is **impos**sible to ask too much from life.

15/2

IT'S NOT WHAT YOU THINK

Sin does not exist. And it is this that true perception sees.

— A COURSE IN MIRACLES

ACIM is radical, countercultural. It calls to question the very fundaments of reality.

When I negate the inexhaustible substance in which I live, I end up with a small, oftentimes-scary reality. Because I identify so deeply with this limited reality, it seems very real. It seems as if I have no choice. I certainly don't recognize that it's my doing.

Lesson 134 asks me to rescript my entire understanding of the world, of other people, of forgiveness. Starting with these key beliefs:

No one can upset me.
No one can make me mad.
No one can hurt me.

To believe other people are apart from me and can behave in ways that have no bearing on my thoughts or that my behaviors have none on theirs is complete folly. We're all on the same volleyball team.

Furthermore, any asshole or problem that appears to threaten me is a golden opportunity. It's a chance to shine light into an area in which I (oh yay!) get to evolve.

There's no need to slay dragons or erect heavy walls of protection or don useless armor.

I simply have to admit, "I don't understand this."

I simply recognize that I'm perceiving this douche, this complication in a way that cannot be true.

I ask for help.

And walk free from the chains of misery and fear.

15/2

MY SECRET WEAPON

Hate, in the long run, is about as nourishing as cyanide.

— KURT VONNEGUT

Lesson 135 (If I defend myself I am attacked) is one of my favorite lessons. I use it ALL the time.

It comes in handy whenever I'm tempted to play victim. It's the perfect antidote when I notice myself feeling offended by something someone says. It's particularly useful when I forget the truth about myself.

Because anytime I defend myself, I take on a role that's not really me.

To defend myself is to pretend I can be hurt. It's to make believe that my perception, the hologram that proves itself over and over again to be incomplete, is somehow more accurate than the truth I'm learning here in the Course.

If I defend myself in any way, I forget that I am a beloved child of the Universe. I forget that everything is FOR me. Nothing is against me.

I forget that every single thing that happens, every single person who pushes my buttons is a gift.

This lesson doesn't suggest overlooking something someone did to me. It says it's impossible for anyone to DO something to me.

If my perception stays fixed (which it will once I start defending myself), nothing—not a miracle, not a sign, not an evidential slap in the face—can allow any other truth to manifest. All I can see, all I will ever see, is what the viewfinder of my limited perception shows me.

Instead of attacking back when my viewfinder shows my fellow humanoids spouting inanities, misinformation, and what looks like hate, I use this lesson to remember: they're simply replaying old tapes and desperately need my love.

Radical actions such as choosing not to attack, to justify, to see the "crime" upsets the going cultural position. It creates a resonant field that goes out into the ethers making our world a little sweeter, a little safer, a little more beautiful.

15/2

TAKING MY BRAIN OFF-LINE

"Everybody everywhere has his own movie going, his own scenario. Everybody is acting his movie out like mad, only most people don't know they're trapped by their little script."

— TOM WOLFE

Defenses are secret magic wands I wave when truth threatens my beliefs.

Lesson 136 (Sickness is a defense against the truth) says sickness doesn't happen TO me. Rather it's an insane, albeit effective device I use for self-deception. It seems unassailable because it "appears" to separate me ("I've got the flu. You don't.") from the whole.

Bodily conditions seem beyond my control. This lesson says, "Think again."

Sickness is not a thing that happens to me. It's a choice. Because the ego wants me to think I'm in constant danger, it uses the body as a storyline, as a means to an end, as a subtle and effective way to generate fear.

This lesson assures me that who I am remains unsullied despite my pitiful and futile attempts to alter it with defenses and ridiculous complaints.

There's a great scene in *The Matrix* where Neo finally realizes the truth of who he is. He finally recognizes the matrix as an illusion. At that moment, as he claims his power, the cascade of bullets from agents Smith and Jones's guns literally drop to the floor. They cannot hurt him. He is free from fear. He is free from his ego.

15/2

HOW THE GRINCH STOLE REALITY

*We can conjure up new worlds with
our imagination and creativity.*

— ROBERT RODRIGUEZ

It's a dog-eat-dog world. Or that's what we're told.

Lesson 137 (When I am healed, I am not healed alone) aims to prove the story of separation is like my old cheerleading uniform. Way too tight, way too restrictive. I should have thrown it out 30 years ago.

Me against you is an antiquated story, long disproven by quantum physics. Today, I rewrite the story with a simple flick of the old consciousness. It starts with this phrase:

Every person is my ally.

I commit to invoking this powerful phrase in every interaction:

With the barista at the coffee shop, "We're all in this together."

With the UPS driver delivering my latest Amazon package, "We're all in this together."

With my stepdad who goes on and on and on and . . . "We're all in this together."

This approach is especially effective in the arena where most interactions take place. In my head.

That so-and-so . . . *Oh yeah! We're all in this together.*

When we approach each person (especially the Grinches in our lives) with this attitude, it becomes easier to recognize that "we are one and that anything that happens to you also happens to me."

10/2

FEEL THE BEAUTIFUL

There is nothing more truly artistic than to love people.

— VINCENT VAN GOGH

Robert Holden, a fellow Hay House author and *A Course in Miracles* teacher from Great Britain, loves to tell stories about his daughter Bo.

One day, when she was four, he found her out in the garden, gazing up at the sky. She was smiling with great joy.

"Hey, sweetheart," he said, interrupting her reverie.

"Hi, Dad!" she answered back.

"Whatcha doing?"

"Just laying here. Feeling beautiful."

Lesson 138 (Heaven is the decision I must make) reminds me that truth cannot be learned, only recognized. I will lay aside this insanely complicated world and like Bo, I will look at the sky, smile, and feel beautiful.

Hope you'll join me.

5/2

NEVER FORGET THERE'S
AN OFF BUTTON

*Man's chief delusion is his conviction that there are
causes other than his own state of consciousness.*

— NEVILLE GODDARD

NASA astronauts take an oath. They commit to their spaceship no matter what the weather, no matter how far off path it goes.

That's what Lesson 139 (I will accept atonement for myself) asks me to do. To commit to love. No matter what the weather. No matter how far off appearances go.

I can either buy into the world and its endless list of choices. Or I can trust in the one decision that takes the spaceship home. I can trust in love, love that ensures I am wholly loved, wholly lovable, and wholly loving.

Wholly, by the way, means 100 percent. No exceptions.

Everything else (my body, my woes, my countless decisions and plans) is a virus in my consciousness.

Long ago, my brain established a false sense of perception. The brain's left cerebral hemisphere, where the faulty interpretations and major fabrications start, plucks out a story and creates an image to match. This false perception judges, distorts, and causes unnecessary emotional distress.

Suffice it to say, this spin doctor in the brain is not my best resource.

I realize it is EXTREMELY difficult to believe that news events, our bodies, our beliefs are made up. They seem so real. This lesson says the magnitude of self-deception is on a scale so vast that it's nearly impossible to conceive.

In this lesson, I commit to reach for a higher truth. I commit to love no matter what. I commit to guide my spaceship—no matter what the weather, no matter what the appearances, no matter what my brain tells me.

Choosing love is not difficult. It's just very, very different from the way we were taught.

5/2

PLASTERING OVER TRUTH

There are three things extremely hard—steel,
a diamond, and to know one's self.

— BENJAMIN FRANKLIN

Inscribed on the entry of the Oracle at Delphi are the words "Know Thyself." According to legend, the seven sages of ancient Greece left this wise maxim at the Temple of Apollo as a foundation for western civilization.

Never mind that they've been co-opted by everyone from Plato and Socrates to Carl Linnaeus, the *Matrix* movies and Miz Cracker on the tenth season of *RuPaul's Drag Race*.

But what does it really mean? According to Lesson 140 (Only salvation can be said to cure), to really know myself is to go deep, beyond the chatter of my mind, beyond the thoughts that run like warnings on the bottom of a pharmaceutical ad.

To know myself is to fully get the truth of who I am. Invincible consciousness. I'm either awake or asleep. There is nothing in between. Although the ego tells me that's a line of bullshit, I refuse to listen.

No longer do I judge by size, seeming gravity, or anything related to form. Today, I lay all interfering thoughts aside. I affirm that nothing can hurt me.

Nothing can affect my invincibility. That's what it means to Know Thyself.

5/Every hour

Boom!

Review IV

God wants us to put this stuff down now. He wants us to wear the world like a loose garment. And be of good cheer.

— MARY KARR

Okay, sports fans, it's time for another review. Lessons 141 through 150 reinforce previous lessons, encouraging us to clear all thoughts of self-deception.

Only love is real.

Begin each day of the 10 days with the above mantra. This sets the stage for an extraordinarily epic day. Then simply repeat the two "need to knows" for each lesson.

Five minutes in the morning. Another five minutes at night. Again, may I remind you it takes longer to listen to Led Zeppelin's "Stairway to Heaven." An incredible bargain for a priceless gift.

The only other ask during the next 10 days is this: anytime your ego starts in on an alternate reality (*This is so unfair, That punkass is asking for it,* etc.) simply stop, recognize it's a red herring, and bop it on the head with your mantra.

Only love is real.

Oh, and your selection from the jukebox?

"Love Is All Around" by The Troggs.

THE MAIN THING IS TO KEEP THE MAIN THING THE MAIN THING

The foundation for knowledge is "I don't know."

— CHARLES EISENSTEIN

Only love is real.

Need-to-know 1: Forgiveness is the key to happiness.

Need-to-know 2: Forgiveness offers everything I want.

The skinny: Forgiveness is not about letting old so-and-so off the hook. It's a get-out-of-jail-free card, offering instant release from the world of illusion.

Let me guess. There's probably a corner somewhere in your house of illusions with beliefs about your body, how it operates, what it needs, what it's capable of.

The dusty basement in your illusions is cluttered with beliefs from your culture, beliefs about what is socially acceptable, ideas about your gender, your race, your need to be liked.

And if your family is anything like my family, it probably left a few boxes to trip over, as well.

Today, I remember all illusions are subterfuge and I will consciously apply my trusty get-out-of-jail-free card. Forgiveness, like Batman's Batmobile, Popeye's spinach, and Superman's phone booth, works every time.

SUBVERT THE
DOMINANT PARADIGM

You can never change things by fighting the existing reality.
To change something, build a new model that
makes the existing model obsolete.

— BUCKMINSTER FULLER

Only love is real.

Need-to-know 1: I am heir to a gazillion blessings.

Need-to-know 2: I am one with my Source.

The skinny: Despite the $500 billion advertising machine's incessant propaganda, the world is wildly abundant. Today, rather than focus on the marketer's drumbeat of limitation, I focus on the world's unending largesse. I focus on the bounteous gifts spread out before me.

Renee Jain, a coach of positive psychology, says most Westerners have a negativity bias where "bad stuff" outweighs the good 3:1.

I prefer a lineup like this:

Life is freaking awesome.
The universe is bounteous and forever generous.
Something amazing is bound to happen to me today.

Today, I say thank you for all the blessings barreling my way, all the abundance, the joy, the peace of mind I count on day after day.

SMALL SIGN, GINORMOUS IMPLICATIONS

Facts, my dear Sancho, are the enemy of truth.

— MIGUEL DE CERVANTES

Only love is real.

Need-to-know 1: In quiet, I claim my gifts.

Need-to-know 2: All that I give boomerangs back to me.

The skinny: The brain, as cool as it is, mainly serves as a reducing valve. It takes the overwhelming flood of information available and filters it down to a trickle. It's efficient for survival, I suppose, but it screens out most of life's wonderment.

That's why I've made it my mission to point out miracles, signs, and blessings that our rational, utilitarian minds screen out.

In June 2018, while driving the winding roads to my dad's memorial in the Great Smoky Mountains, I nearly flattened a turtle. Thankfully, I managed to swerve just in time.

When I was growing up in small towns, my dad often took me for "Oh, look at that" drives out in the country. We frequently spotted horned toads and box turtles, and 70 percent of the time, we stopped, picked them up, and took them home for pets.

In fact, my turtle Pokey, after three weeks of winning the Saturday night Turtle Races in Ellsworth, Kansas, held in the IGA parking lot, had to be retired. Race officials deemed it unfair to other contestants.

Keep in mind, I haven't run across a turtle in probably 30 years. But on the way to Dad's memorial, smack dab in the middle of the road, just like I remembered, was a box turtle.

Most people would shrug, call it a coincidence, but you and I know better.

JUST BEYOND THE STORY

Yesterday and tomorrow are just wounds and stories.

— MICHAEL GUNGOR

Only love is real.

Need-to-know 1: THIS is all there is.

Need-to-know 2: My illusions hold nothing I want.

The skinny: By relying on an inventory learned from my family, my culture, and my past, I miss the teeming energy available in the atomic now. There is great substance within each present moment, just waiting to explode with goodness and magic and blessings. But by reapplying old, often inappropriate "cultural paradigms," I miss the magic—I completely overlook all the life-empowering data that's trying to stream to me from my inner, nonphysical self. This traps me in a web of defensive, limiting perceptions.

Anytime I'm not in the present moment, that tape loop kicks in and old constrictions and perceptual habits take over, infecting my thinking, my actions, and my beliefs. They're also a son of a bitch when attempting to be happy or manifest my dreams.

None of these habits of thought are true, but because they're buried for the most part, living in my subconscious like rats in the cellar, they subtly play out in my life experience anytime I'm not "in the now." My friend Jay calls them BS—belief systems full of that other kind of BS. Unfortunately, these are the programs I often use to explain, identify, and cope with my life. They run most of the time even when I'm affirming and intending other things.

They always feature moi as a separate identity and a separate body that, by their very nature, are slated for the chopping block. Can we agree these masks and costumes are not our fullest, most eternal selves?

WHITTLING DOWN THE VAST, INTERCONNECTED MYSTERY

Behold infinity and all that you see shall be given to you.

— GLENDA GREEN

Only love is real.

Need-to-know 1: Underneath it all, there's eternity.

Need-to-know 2: It's either heads or tails. You can't have both.

The skinny: The Course gives me the following criteria for deciding what's real:

1. Will it last forever? If not, it's a perceptual problem. What fades and dies was never really there and has nothing to offer.

2. Does it involve loss of any kind—to you or someone else? If so, it's a perceptual problem. Anything you take from someone else or perceive they take from you is an illusion.

3. What purpose does it serve? If it's related to bodily concerns, has a price tag, has eminence as valued by the world, it's a perceptual problem. Adios, amigo.

4. Does it invoke guilt of any kind? Again, nothing but a perceptual problem.

SWIMMING WILDLY, JOYOUSLY, IN THE NOW

*I am kind of paranoid in reverse. I suspect
people of plotting to make me happy.*

— J. D. SALINGER

Only love is real.

Need-to-know 1: Failure is not an option.

Need-to-know 2: I give up all masks and costumes.

The skinny: The world I see is my personal interpretation. But as the Course reminds me, "perception is learned, selective, unstable, and inaccurate."

Robbin, from my possibility posse, told a wonderful story that speaks to this truth.

She and her daughter were on the turnpike and noticed a bumper sticker on a big truck ahead of them. You've seen the bumper stickers with mom, dad, the two kids, and the pet, right? Well, this bumper sticker said, "Meet my family" and portrayed a series of guns, from pistol on up to gigantic artillery cannons. Robbin and Kitty looked at each other, rolled their eyes, and, like I would have done, made a judgment.

Robbin pulled up to the toll booth behind the truck and reached for her wallet to pay her fare.

The toll booth operator stopped her. "Put your money away. The truck in front of you paid your toll."

So today, let us look past our perceptions and judgments and lean toward one another and cherish all magnetic nudges toward inclusion.

JOY IS MY MISSION; SOURCE IS MY CEO

Stop giving your inner critic leadership positions.

— SARK

Only love is real.

Need-to-know 1: I no longer value the parody I've made of eternal creation.

Need-to-know 2: My get-out-of-jail-free card resolves all problems.

The skinny: Sheldon and Penny from *The Big Bang Theory* provide a perfect example of the Course maxim that "perception is learned, selective, unstable, and inaccurate." In other words, perception is in the eye of the beholder. Take Penny's tattoo. In one episode, Sheldon asks Penny, "Why do you have the Chinese character for soup tattooed on your right buttock?"

Penny answers back, "It's not soup. It's courage."

It's impossible to look at anything or anyone without seeing our own personal interpretation. Is it soup? Is it courage? Only forgiveness supplies the correct answer.

STOP TALKING SMACK

Some people have a way with words,
and other people . . . oh, uh, not have way.

— STEVE MARTIN

Only love is real.

Need-to-know 1: No harm, no foul.

Need-to-know 2: Sick, no more.

The skinny: Just curious, my friends?
What are these phrases still doing in your head?

"Something needs to be fixed."
"This is not good enough."
"I don't have enough."

Visualize all you want. Affirm until the cows come home. But as long as your vocabulary is toxic, as long as you fail to get up each morning and realize how bloody blessed you are—to be alive, to have these 24 hours—all your efforts will be futile.

Most of us are smart enough not to re-watch our least favorite movies when they debut on Netflix, so why do we insist on running repeats of the least favorite events in our life?

PROUD TO BE MAYOR
OF CRAZY TOWN

You can spend your whole life building a wall
of facts between you and anything real.

— CHUCK PALAHNIUK

Only love is real.

Need-to-know 1: My good is everyone's good. And vice versa.

Need-to-know 2: Choose joy, choose joy.

The skinny: In 1909, Guglielmo Marconi, the Italian inventor who pioneered long-distance radio transmission, won the Nobel Prize for sending vibratory radio waves 2,000 miles across the Atlantic Ocean.

But when he first suggested that frequencies of energy can be transmitted without wires, people thought he was nuts. He was referred to an insane asylum when he wrote to the Italian Ministry of Posts and Telegraphs explaining wireless telegraphy.

"Everyone knows that's impossible," detractors scoffed at the crazy experiments he conducted in his parents' attic.

So, yes, believing our thoughts, dreams, and beliefs are being transmitted out into the universe, shaping our destiny, is probably not going to be popular with everyone. Some go so far as to call me delusional.

But that's fine by me.

I'd rather be appointed Mayor of Crazy Town than habitually focus on what's not working, on what can't happen.

I believe I can sit here in my Kansas home and, with my powerful, radio-transmitting thoughts, create joy, peace, and insane happiness for everyone.

MAYBE THE INVISIBLE WORLD REALLY ISN'T

Carry something beautiful in your heart.

— BLAISE PASCAL

Only love is real.

Need-to-know 1: I accept my freedom now and forever.

Need-to-know 2: I am because we are.

The skinny: I have walked by Chicago's Tribune Tower at least 40 times during my many trips to the Windy City, probably more. But it wasn't until a walking tour (and only after my guide pointed it out) that I noticed the more than 150 stones and artifacts imbedded in its façade. There are fragments from the Taj Mahal, the Berlin Wall, the Dome of St. Peter's Cathedral. There are stones from the Sydney Opera House, the Great Pyramids, and the Great Wall of China.

It was fun to connect with all these worldwide landmarks without leaving downtown Chicago, but the biggest impact was my shock at never having noticed them before. Really?

Just another reminder that the Course is absolutely correct: I see only what I decide to see.

THE OPTICAL ILLUSION KNOWN AS YOUR LIFE

Everything is a prop to help us love more.

— SUE MORTER

We've all been fooled by optical illusions—M. C. Escher's descending stairs, for example, or the human skull that, upon closer examination, shows a woman staring into her vanity mirror.

Optical illusions are so common you'd think we'd be more skeptical of the tricks routinely played on us by our eyes.

Lesson 151 (All things are echoes of universal truth) tells us that our senses are not reliable witnesses. Over and over again, they distort reality. They show us "images" that are not there.

Which begs the question: Why do we so implicitly believe all that our senses report? Where did we get the ridiculous notion we should depend on these perceptual "deceivers" to judge ourselves, others, and the world around us?

As this lesson says, it's not that the act of judging is being yanked away. It's that our human bodies lack the proper "equipment" to adequately judge. As the old saying goes, "Fool me once, shame on you. Fool me twice, shame on me."

Instead of being fooled twice, I gain access to a more reliable connection. When I give my thoughts over to love, the optical illusion of pain, suffering, and loss disappears. It literally evaporates.

No longer fooled, we learn to trust that, no matter how it may look, everything is a prop for love.

15/2

ALL IN

The second I decide something is done, it's done.
I just have to wait for all y'all to see it.

— WILL SMITH

Lesson 152 (The power of decision is my own) reassures me that I create my own reality. It asks me to "accept no opposite and no exception, for to do so is to contradict the truth entirely."

It says my creative power remains unchangeable, that all transitory states are by definition false. It says the minute I make any intention, it's real, it's a viable creation.

But until I "make no exceptions, accept no opposites," my intention stays on an invisible vibrational plane. Until I catch up vibrationally, I'm unable to see and enjoy my fabulous creations.

I'm a master at the first part of the equation. Making intentions. But the second part, where I get out of my own way and allow love and joy and the new Tesla into my sphere of awareness, presents a thornier dilemma.

For right now, I forget my intentions. I focus instead on every brilliant, juicy, delicious thought I can. Thoughts that remotely resemble my intention and everything that doesn't. When joy is the dominant emotion, I'm able to pull dreams out of thin air like magicians pull rabbits out of hats.

5/every hour

BLAST OPEN YOUR HEART

We mistake punishment for justice, fighting for action.

— CHARLES EISENSTEIN

I call Lesson 153 (In my defenselessness my safety lies) the Ph.D. program. It lies 180 degrees from everything my culture teaches. I am deeply conditioned by concepts of good and evil, perpetrators and victims. I must conquer the patriarchy, push back on corporate greed, punish the evildoers.

In this lesson, I learn that viewing the world through this simplistic lens is to perpetuate the problem. By adding my blows to the humiliation of the bad guy, I wreak the very devastation I claim to be against.

"But I can't just let them get away with it!" my ego rails.

Here's what I'm asked to do instead. Recognize that my "enemies," the "villains" I so deplore, are fragments of a senseless dream. They're but tiny pieces of the whole.

Once I get my ruler out to measure, once I look closer, I see they're optical illusions. I notice the "other" is actually me. To attack is to deny my own safety.

Breaking engrained cultural habits of separation takes practice. I have to disrupt the old story from within my heart. I must put away the toys of guilt, set aside the practice of conquest and control.

As this lesson reminds me, I will not see the light until I offer it to all my brothers.

So today, I invest in the story of oneness. Instead of defensiveness, I will remember, "I am a mirror of you, you are a mirror of me. In your shoes, my brother, I would do as you do."

15/2/hourly

A LOVING GIFT OF
FREEDOM TO THE WORLD

There's no such thing as a moment that isn't rich with treasures.

— E S T H E R   H I C K S

Say what?

Lesson 154 (I am among the ministers of Source) has to be a mistake, right? How am I, this perpetually insecure human being, supposed to offer assistance or a message of hope to others? I sometimes have trouble getting out of bed.

This lesson says that voice is the ego (aka Mr. Asshat) swaying to his old familiar beat.

Rather than join in like I used to do, the Course tells me to call on my holy spokesperson. It knows my appointed role, and it knows how to fulfill it.

I like to think of Hobson, the hilarious butler who took care of Dudley Moore in the 1981 movie *Arthur*.

Deftly performed by John Gielgud, Hobson loved his irresponsible charge with an open heart, no matter what ridiculous, immature thing he did. All Arthur had to do was ring a little silver bell.

The Course tells me that my own personal Hobson (aka the Holy Spirit) will always, without fail, be available. Always. Always. Always.

So whenever I notice my mind settling into a problem state or forgetting to be grateful or worrying about anything at all, I just stop, think of Hobson, and ring the silver bell.

15/2/hourly

REWRITING THE LAWS
THAT RUN MY LIFE

It's the inner world that needs adjusting, tweaking and plucking when the outer world fails to please.

— MIKE DOOLEY

As a travel writer, I often end up confronting customs and laws different from my own.

In Singapore, for example, it's illegal to hug in public. In Cannes, you can be arrested for wearing a Jerry Lewis mask. I've also heard of some pretty weird laws in my own country. In Devon, Texas, I'm told, it's illegal to make furniture in the nude. Darn that, Devon, Texas.

We might get a chuckle out of these (and let me just add that I don't plan to pack my Jerry Lewis mask on my next trip to Cannes), but more than these "laws," I am also at the mercy of arbitrary laws I've imposed in my own head. Laws such as "life is a struggle," "I have to do everything myself," "It's me against the world."

Lesson 155 (I will step back and let Hobson lead the way) reminds me that the world is an illusion. When I consult my own personal Hobson, I'm led away from loss, sacrifice, and deprivation, I'm ushered away from all the "laws" I activate with my beliefs.

Here's what Hobson promises:

1. The world is limitless, abundant, and strangely accommodating.

2. Everything always works out for me.

3. By following my heart, I lead a life of purpose and meaning and big-ass joy.

4. The more love I give, the more I receive.

5. Actually, the more of anything I give, the more I receive.

15/2/hourly

NOTHING MORE DECEPTIVE THAN OBVIOUS FACTS

Really, weren't these facts just placeholders
until the long view could really assert itself?

— DAVID LEVITHAN

I'm a journalist, trained, degreed, the whole nine yards. I started my illustrious journalism career at *The Kansas City Star,* the same newspaper where Ernest Hemingway and Walt Disney started their road to fame.

The last few years I've begun to alter my beliefs about "the facts" I'm sworn by my profession to seek.

I'm not so sure that "just the facts, ma'am" is helpful anymore. In fact, these so-called facts create a negative energetic momentum I no longer care to perpetuate.

The "facts" I now choose to report are that happiness is my birthright, that love is the only reality.

Lesson 156 (I walk with the Dude in perfect holiness) says the only reason "journalistic facts" look otherwise is because I waste my focus on foolishness, on senseless whims.

In lightness and in laughter, the quaint absurdity of "journalistic facts" disappears. As I claim my rightful place as light of the world, I see that "journalistic facts" were a silly dream.

Today, I let doubting cease. I shine with the glory of my perfect, holy, universal light.

15/2/hourly

I'M MELTING!!!!!

You are the universe doing what the universe does, just as light is what the sun does or a wave is what the ocean does.

— MICHAEL GUNGOR

Lesson 157 (Into Presence would I enter now) sounds complicated. Where is this holy place? And how do I gain admittance?

Presence is impossible to translate into words. Byron Katie calls it "first generation" truth. Seeing life without filters, without all the baggage and myths I lay upon it.

That's why I'm encouraged to spend the day in silence and in trust. To walk away from imaginary constructs that have colored my thoughts, feelings, and fundamental experience of reality.

There's no need to think the right thoughts, understand the right concepts. I simply allow myself to feel the joy of life, to let myself melt into the cosmos.

15/2/hourly

IDENTITY IS PROVISIONAL

Everyone is involved, whether they like it or not,
in the construction of their world.

— JOHN O'DONOHUE

The conceit of our culture is that each of us is a separate individual, fist fighting for our life, karate chopping our way through our 70 or 80 or 25 years on the planet.

We reduce big issues down to separate entities. We blame that guy over there. It's him (or her) causing all the problems. If only they'd shape up.

But each individual, each germ, each problem is part of the big soup, connected to all.

And as long as narcissism and selfishness and other problems exist, we must recognize that each of us is a piece of minestrone or a chopped onion contributing to the broth. By casting blame on "the other," we actually co-sponsor the problem. We're in on the conspiracy.

The Course teaches me to think of myself as a verb, as a wave of the ocean temporarily doing this or that. I am not a body, but rather a continually changing wave contributing to the whole.

Lesson 158 (Today I learn to give as I receive) asks me to repudiate the version of myself or anybody else as a separate collection of static molecules. I'm asked to behold a light beyond the body, beyond what can be touched.

I greet each person as the Light he or she is—no matter what form, no matter what mistakes. As I bestow the store of miracles that are mine to give, I re-engineer a new reality that's expansive, unlimited, and inclusive of everyone.

15/2/hourly

LET THE UNIVERSE HAGGLE WITH THE DETAILS

The instant it is welcome it is there.

— A COURSE IN MIRACLES

Lesson 159 (I give the miracles I have received) assures me I have a treasure house of riches, an unlimited trove of gifts ready to contribute to my happiness. It says there's no limit to the miracles I can distribute—no sickness unhealed, no lack unsatisfied, no need unmet.

My ego, true to form, takes exception. It constantly rides my ass, warns me to be careful, to hoard, to save my treasure. It advises me to make sure I have plenty first. Only then can I afford to give it away. But not too much.

This lesson urges the exact opposite approach. It goes so far as to say the *only* way to claim my gifts is by giving them away. That's how I recognize I have them. That's how I find proof.

The gift economy, a philosophy more than a financial practice, is to refuse to believe in scarcity and fear. Instead of always trying to "get more," a gift economy is for those looking for ways to give. It's so radical most people can't even understand it.

I pitched a story about the gift economy to my editor at *People* magazine. She loves heroes, good news, and heart-warming human interest stories. But even though I gave her three specific examples of people working solely in the gift economy, she couldn't understand it. "But how does it work?" she kept repeating.

It works, although I could never explain this spiritual belief to her, because once you give up your incessant fear and belief that it's a dog-eat-dog, every-man-for-himself world, abundance can't help but show up in your life. As this lesson proves, it's the reality of the human condition.

15/2/hourly

WHAT THE BANANAS!

*Infinite Intelligence is ever ready to carry out
man's smallest or greatest demands.*

— FLORENCE SCOVEL SHINN

I have inadvertently become a PR person for the universe.

The perks, as you can imagine, are many, but the best thing about this job is that my "employer"—if you want to call this universal love energy my "boss"—doesn't ask that I pimp some useless product or lower my standards or pretend to believe in something I don't see proof of every single day.

The universe is not trying to sell anything. All it wants to do is give. And give. And give some more.

My job as one of its many "press agents" is to let the world know that we are loved unconditionally—always, without exception, no matter what.

I'm in charge, if you will, of publicizing the fact that the universe is trying like bloody hell to interact with me and you and everybody else.

As Lesson 160 (I am at home. Fear is the stranger here) tells me, the universe wants nothing more than to bless me, to guide me, to help me create the most exciting version of myself possible.

And here's the cool part. Not one thing is required of me for this to happen. I don't have to earn its favor. Or send in a coupon. I just have to release the "reality" I read about in the news. I just have to make space in my consciousness for the universe to get in.

I just have to quit fighting life and let it be.

The old reality is as passé as the bump (it's a dance, for those of you who missed the disco days), it's defective and it's causing us to miss the most freakin' amazing things.

15/2/hourly

MI CARA* ES SU CARA

I may not be totally open, but at least I'm ajar.

— SARAH SILVERMAN

Lesson 161 (Give me your blessing, my holy bro) reminds me, yet again, I see what I wish to see. The world in my viewfinder is not random. It's carefully designed by my frightened little ego to assure its survival. By showing me a partial world, a world of discretely curated fragments, the ego gets away with its horror story.

Today, I walk out of the theater of the macabre as I make another attempt to go beyond, to reach the light. If I really want this (again, this is not random), it is within my reach to see beyond the ego, beyond the body.

Here are instructions straight from the Course:

I pick one brother (or sister) and see him in my mind. I picture her face, his hands, her familiar gestures. Now, I ask him (this is all done in the mind, by the way) for the blessing of seeing him as he really is.

This simple act of love, looking fully at another human's face, imagining living inside and seeing what's really there, is one of the most radical practices on earth. In an instant, I realize I am not alone.

15/2

---

* Face in español.

DEAR DEPRESSION—
KISS MY BEAUTIFUL,
TRUTH-PROCLAIMING ASS

It gives its strength to everyone who asks, in limitless supply.

— A COURSE IN MIRACLES

A person very close to me is struggling with depression. Since I used to believe I, too, had depression (To borrow a Prince moniker, I now refer to myself as "Joy Previously Masquerading as Sorrow"), I wrote him the following letter:

Dear _____,

I've been thinking a lot about your depression. Because I have also suffered the debilitating "dis-ease," I feel that I can understand and perhaps help in some way. Here's what I now know: The only thing "wrong" when I'm depressed is my thoughts. My thoughts start their incessant yammering, telling me I'm bad, that something is wrong with me, that life is hopeless.

But what I now believe with complete certainty is that these thoughts are false. They're the tool of what I call "the ego." The Truth (I am as the Dude created me, ACIM 162) is stronger than those erroneous thoughts.

At any time, I can throw those thoughts overboard because they are powerless. They are as insignificant as a dandelion blowing in the wind. Luckily, I'm now able to laugh in the face of those thoughts. They're simply NOT TRUE. And I refuse to buy into them. I am promised an abundant life, a life of joy, purpose, and peace. That's the only Truth.

Thoughts of worthlessness are impostors. They get away with their bald-faced lies to the extent I let myself believe them. They have no power except the power I give them. Quite frankly, I view them now as downright ridiculous. There is NO WAY I can be worthless or bad or unloved. As for the ego? It can kiss my beautiful, adored-by-the-Source ass.

15/2

PERCEPTION SELECTS AND MAKES THE WORLD YOU SEE

This world is only in the mind of its maker.

— A COURSE IN MIRACLES

Irish mystic Lorna Byrne was 15 before she discovered that her brother Christopher, whom she played with daily, had departed the planet before she was even born, when he was 10 weeks old.

When actress Laura Dern was seven, she turned to her dad and said, "I miss my sister." Laura, who was born five years after her sister Diane drowned, enjoyed an unbreakable connection to a sister she never lived with on the material plane.

Lesson 163 (There is no death. I am free) says the idea of death is so preposterous that even the insane have trouble believing it. A body (aka the ego's most effective prop) has a shelf life, but let me say it again: I am not a body. I am free.

I still commune with my daughter, Taz, who unexpectedly died of an aneurysm one week after her 25th birthday. She sends signs (222, Albert Einsteins, hedgehogs) and I talk to her every day. Recently, I got an intuitive hit to run my car radio's scan function. I use that function when I'm traveling, but I was driving the familiar streets of my hometown. I know the local stations. I chose my favorites long ago. Why would I run a scan?

The first hit was a twangy Country & Western melody. Then I got some preacher railing about abortion or something. And then I got a "station" clearly broadcasting a familiar voice. There was no mistaking Taz uttering two words that always made my heart sing, "Hi, Mom!" It so floored me that my frantic efforts to stop the scan were in vain.

So sure, I can adhere to conventional reality that Taz, because her body is no longer present, is gone. Or I can focus on enduring connection, on life being bigger than this little flesh suit, on the idea that she's still right here, as present as she ever was.

When I look through my 38 photo albums (yes, I was a proud momma), it's easy to recognize life's changing physicality. Even before she had the aneurysm, it was obvious Taz was no longer the darling five-year-old starting kindergarten with her flowered dress and her pink backpack. She was no longer the seven-year-old in the Bahamas with the parrot on her shoulder. She was no longer the 21-year-old standing among the ruins of Machu Picchu.

Now, instead of a body frozen into one reality, Taz is unfettered and free, joyfully dancing throughout the cosmos.

Call me delusional (as my friend Anita Moorjani says, whenever someone suggests she's too woo-woo, she almost falls off her unicorn), but I choose to remain grateful for all beautiful reminders that life is bigger and grander and more wildly miraculous than I will ever understand.

15/2

SHAKE YOUR ETCH A SKETCH HARD

Refuse to be sidetracked into detours, illusions . . .

— A COURSE IN MIRACLES

You've heard it a million times: George Santayana's famous line that "Those who cannot remember the past are condemned to repeat it."

I'd like to take this opportunity to point out that it is ONLY your remembrance of the past that condemns you to repeat it. If you get up every morning with a completely clean *Etch A Sketch,* with not an iota of an idea of how so-and-so is going to react or which dangerous road you think our world is heading down, you are free to write a brand-new story.

Why assume today is going to be just like yesterday? Do you know for certain your boss is an a-hole? That your partner is going to defy your needs?

I am the creator of my reality, but instead of using this oh-so-awesome gift, I create my reality based on the past. I get up each day and regurgitate the same-ole, same-ole. Even worse is my same-ole, same-ole is filtered through my fears and illusions so the "past I'm condemned to repeat" isn't even accurate.

Lesson 164 (Now am I one with my Source) asks me to put these trifling "memories" aside, to leave a wide and open space. As I look past time, vain imaginings part like a curtain, allowing me to exchange all suffering for joy.

I am the captain of my thoughts, the boss of my *Etch A Sketch,* and I can throw yesterday's soap opera overboard. I can create a brand-new reality. Starting from scratch.

15/2

DISMANTLING THE ILLUSION

There is no disease of the body apart from the mind.

— S O C R A T E S

Lesson 165 (Let not my mind deny Truth) says the only thing obscuring my perfect happiness are my thoughts and beliefs. It says my feelings and interactions with the world are reproduced in physical reality.

In 1980, Evy McDonald was diagnosed with Lou Gehrig's disease. By the time doctors finally determined her illness, she was, to use her own words, "a bowl of Jell-O in a wheelchair." The doctors told her, at best, she had six months to live.

After raging about the unfairness of it all for a day or two, she had this thought:

"Since I'm dying anyway, why not use the short time I have left to finally learn to love myself unconditionally?"

For years, she despised her body. She was overweight, for one thing. The polio she'd had as a child left her with two withered limbs and, well, she was hard-pressed to find anything she really liked about her physical body.

Three times a day, she rolled her wheelchair to the mirror and sat naked. She refused to leave until she found new positives to add to her list. Her hair was pretty, for starters. She decided that whatever it took, she would to learn to accept herself. She resolved to give all negative feelings and thoughts over to God.

At some point, she crossed some kind of miraculous threshold. She actually began to feel love and compassion for herself. She began to see her body as a miracle of creation, to see herself as a blessed being capable of great joy.

Strength began to return to her limbs. She eventually began to walk. Became able to feed and clothe herself.

Evy McDonald became the first person to recover completely from ALS, and thirty-eight years later, she's still ALS-free.

As Lesson 165 clearly states, the only healing necessary is giving up old beliefs, changing the way I think, feel, and interact with the world.

15/2

UNIVERSE DREAMS BIGGER THAN I DO FOR MYSELF

Where is the joy in my life and what have I sacrificed it for?

— ELIZABETH GILBERT

There are a grand total of two ways to do things.

Whether I'm writing a blog post or having a conversation with my BFF, whether I'm making a smoothie or plans for a European vacation, I either use the resources of Door Number 1 or Door Number 2.

Door #1, the drug of choice for many, means using the power of my own resources. Making decisions based on limited thoughts within my own head, with what I've learned from my parents, from school, from the news. To summarize, using resources of the past.

Door #2, the only other choice, uses resources beyond my limited brain. Door #2 encourages me to conduct my life in faith, accepting all gifts bestowed by my invisible Inner Source.

Lesson 166 (I am entrusted with gifts of Source) says all gifts are given without exception with nothing held back.

Whether aware or not, these gifts are reliable, constant, and far superior to anything I can conceive.

I can deny their presence, depend on the limited resources of Door #1. Or I can jump in, face-first, knowing Source intends only joy.

15/2

DEATH. IT'S NOT WHAT YOU THINK.

The last enemy that shall be destroyed is death.

— J. K. ROWLING

The Course turns everything we think we know on its head. For starters, life is not what we think. Neither is death.

Lesson 167 (There is only life) says death is an utterly ridiculous story we made up. The story provides cover so we can pretend to be limited, temporary, and separate from life. Which is ludicrous.

Life itself is eternal. It pulses, it dances, it continues long after our temp jobs (as impermanent bodies) are over. It turns acorns into oak trees, embryos into bodies. It has no opposite.

And . . . are you ready for this?

Any thought that is not supremely happy is also a form of death. Which means it's an illusion. All sorrow, loss, anxiety, suffering, and pain are illusions. Even a frown or a slight discomfort is a nod to death, which, once again, is NOT REAL.

All of these provisional buzzkills indicate our minds are asleep.

Once we awake (which we can do by either leaving our bodies or simply realigning our thoughts), our life—that pulsing, joyful dance of consciousness will continue on. As it always has. And always will.

15/2

UPDATE TO NAPOLEON HILL'S
THINK AND GROW RICH

You are already wealthy, but you have been taught not to experience your wealth.

— DAVID CAMERON GIKANDI

In 1937 when Napoleon Hill wrote his now-classic tome, quantum physics was still in diapers. Einstein, of course, had posited his famous theory of relativity, but quantum physicists didn't completely understand how it worked.

To tell you the truth, they still have trouble making sense of the crazy quantum world that is changed by simple observation. As physicist Richard Feynman famously said, "Nobody understands quantum mechanics."

However, we do know that thoughts produce energy (much like invisible radio waves) and provide the building blocks for our life experience.

The updated title to Hill's material, says Lesson 168 (Grace is given. I claim it now), should be this: *Think and BE Rich.* As in now. I do not have to wait for my good. Time is irrelevant.

The ego prefers to keep this on the down low, but Source is entirely accessible. All the time.

In the quantum world, I am connected to everything. I already have all the "riches" I could ever imagine. They exist right now as probability waves. But that's the problem. I don't imagine them.

I focus on what I don't have. This lesson assures me despair would be impossible if I had any idea how much I was loved.

So back to Napoleon Hill. He advises people to come up with a date for acquiring a certain amount of money. Sometime in the future.

But the trick in the quantum world is to "be rich now," to claim, as this lesson promises, my inherited riches and blessings today.

15/2

DO YOUR BELIEFS BLOCK THE FLOW OF THE WORLD'S LIMITLESS ABUNDANCE?

If you wish to understand the Universe, think of energy, frequency and vibration.

— NIKOLA TESLA

I'm more or less illiterate when it comes to anything electrical. I know what a plug looks like and I know how to attach it to a wall socket. Beyond that, I draw a blank.

There's a device used in electronics that provides a good metaphor for understanding Lesson 169 (By grace I live. By grace I am released).

The device is called a resistor and basically (all you electricians out there, please forgive my simplistic explanation) what it does is reduce the amount of electrical current flowing through a circuit. Resistors limit the number of electrons that can flow past a given point at any one time.

My beliefs about myself and about the way the world works serve as resistors, blocking the flow of the world's limitless abundance. My beliefs are the brakes that stop the natural, always-flowing current of good, the grace this lesson promises.

Let me give you an example. Most people believe money is limited and hard to come by. That's a resistor.

On the other hand, they don't believe health or intelligence is limited. Just because I'm healthy doesn't mean you can't be healthy, too. Steven Hawking's brilliant intellect doesn't prevent Matt Groening or Steven Spielberg from using their brain power.

But when it comes to abundance, the belief there's only so much to go around is a big, fat resistor, better at blocking the flow than tungsten, carbon, and other popular resistors.

In the world of electronics, resistors sometimes come in handy (they create heat and light), but for me, who longs for a life of ease and grace, I prefer to keep the flow as wide open as I possibly can.

15/2

WHOLE LOTTA SHAKIN' GOIN' ON

*If I'm staring at a person who needs to be fixed,
my agenda will inevitably blind me.*

— LISA GUNGOR

Lesson 170 is a big fat RSO. It basically questions our insane belief in vengeance. Which is a good thing to question, but not one that resonates with me.

Vengeance seems like a good idea only when I forget that reality fluctuates and that my five senses show me but a fragment, the one piece of the 1,000-piece puzzle that matches my inner thoughts.

Reminds me of the high school counselor who nobly passed out pencils with the anti-drug sentiment: Too cool to do drugs. Once students sharpened their pencils, the well-meaning adage became: do drugs.

Today, I repudiate all mental images and internal talk dispensed by my ego. I reject them as useless stubs employed to make me feel separate, like a vulnerable particle instead of an effervescent wave connected and flowing with all of life.

I no longer choose the insanity of rigid space and linear time, disconnected from the vibrant flow, separate from my holy bros.

Instead, I give thanks that what once looked impenetrable is pulsing, dancing, and free to realign with my true spirit of holiness.

15/2

Boom!

Review V

You are here to fly at full wingspan, for the glory of the One who sent you.

— MARIANNE WILLIAMSON

The purpose of this next review (Lessons 171 through 180) is to maximize time. It's meant to shorten my path, to "get me woke" sooner rather than later. It doesn't have a lot of words (thank ya, Jesus!). Rather it urges me to relinquish all thoughts that clutter up my mind.

Once again, I start each morning and end each evening with a mantra:

The Dude is but love, and therefore so am I.

The aim is to ingrain this mantra into my mind, as the very woof and warp of my being.

I want to know it like I know my own name.

My jukebox selection? "Can't Stop the Feeling" by Justin Timberlake.

WHY THE PARLOR GAME
SIX DEGREES OF KEVIN BACON GIVES ME HOPE

"You is kind. You is smart. You is important."

— AIBILEEN CLARK, IN *THE HELP*

The Dude is but Love, and therefore so am I.

151) All things are echoes of the Voice of Dude.

152) The power of decision is my own.

The skinny: This is a shout-out to the anonymous person who taped uplifting affirmations to the bathroom stall at the Sandbar sub shop in Lawrence, Kansas.

Your words reminding me that "I am beautiful. I am powerful. I am capable of great things" made me so happy and reminded me that the simplest of things, the tiniest of actions, can impact the world.

Your affirming words not only added joy to my day, but they elevated the energy of every person I encountered from that moment forward.

The parlor game *Six Degrees of Kevin Bacon* suggests that any two people on earth are, on average, a mere six acquaintance links apart.

I like to think of those beautiful human bonds when I get discouraged, overwhelmed by the issues in the news. It's tempting to wonder what I, one solitary person from Kansas, can do to solve the political chasm, what I, a single mom with a couple of Twitter followers, can do to stop gun violence.

And then I remember. I can invite my neighbor over for ham and eggs. I can bake a casserole for the new mom that just came home from the hospital.

We're all different, have varying political beliefs and religious affiliations. But every last one of us eventually shows up in the same bathroom stall.

One tiny sheet of paper. Five simple lines. Tiny actions sending ripples out into the universe.

15/2

THE UNIVERSE IS PROGRAMMED TO SUPPORT YOUR HAPPINESS

I am not a teacher, but an awakener.

— ROBERT FROST

The Dude is but Love, and therefore so am I.

153) In my defenselessness my safety lies.

154) I am among the ministers of Dude.

The skinny: Anytime I don't feel joyful and at peace is because I'm giving attention to something that disagrees with Source.

To use the old radio analogy, I've tuned into an "oldies station" that still believes in pain and suffering.

Today, I commit to bring a different energy to the party.

I believe that's what Jesus meant when he said, "Turn the other cheek." He wasn't suggesting I should walk around with bruised cheeks and black eyes. He was saying I should begin moving in a different direction, turn my cheek, so to speak, to a higher, brighter, more pleasing reality.

15/2

VIOLATE NORMAL EXPECTATIONS

*Know, O Beloved, that man was not created in jest or
at random, but marvelously made and for some great end.*

— AL-GHAZALI, SUFI MYSTIC

The Dude is but Love, and therefore so am I.

155) I will step back and let the Dude lead the way.

156) I walk with the Dude in perfect holiness.

The skinny: We put the majority of our attention on what we can see, touch, and measure. Nothing wrong with this . . . except for the glaring fact that it's sorely limited and driven by a disturbed lunatic that makes up lies. Hate to break up the party, but as someone once wrote on my site, "the ego is not my amigo."

Today, I consciously shift my attention to things that instill reverence, things that invoke awe, things like the northern lights, Louis Armstrong singing "It's a Wonderful World," a view of earth from space. Ask any astronaut—it changes everything.

Studies show that being in awe enables us "to recognize vastness" and "to modify our mental constructs." I can't think of two more valuable goals.

When we stand in front of, say, a full-size skeleton of a Tyrannosaurus Rex or in a grove of giant redwoods, we get goosebumps and chills. We readjust our mental structure. We preempt—at least temporarily—the maniacal little voice in our head.

15/2

NO MORE COMMENTS FROM THE PEANUT GALLERY

Reality exists in the human mind, and nowhere else.

— GEORGE ORWELL

The Dude is but Love, and therefore so am I.

157) Into the Presence would I enter now.

158) To give and receive are synonyms.

The skinny: I'll give the ego this. Even though it's a whiny know-it-all, it protects me from touching hot stoves and stepping in front of over-sized SUVs.

But mostly it squawks and carries on and encourages me to cling to such things as my heritage, my body, my position in the community. Its fears are totally irrational, its efforts are counterproductive and its short-term identities interfere with infinity and immortality.

When I know myself as love, the ego has no choice but to return to the peanut gallery where it can commence throwing worthless peanut shells.

15/2

I AM A SPECIAL EFFECTS ANIMATOR, QUANTUM STYLE

Man only likes to count his troubles, but he does not count his joys.

— FYODOR DOSTOYEVSKY

The Dude is but Love, and therefore so am I.

159) I give the miracles I have received.

160) I am at home. Fear is the stranger here.

The skinny: Before entering the hospital room of a TB patient, visitors are required to cover their entire bodies. They even don surgical gloves and face masks.

None of us balk at this overcautious behavior. TB's contagious, for goodness' sake. We go to great lengths to avoid exposure.

Yet we never protect ourselves from the bad news we see on television, the horrible tweets that pop up on our phones. The news media presents a tiny speck of a reality far removed from true Reality. It's so limited in dimension and scope of understanding that paying close attention is like having one of those "please kick me" signs pinned to our back.

The news media feeds us small bites of trivial matter, tidbits that don't really concern our lives and don't require thinking. Out of thousands of news stories and tweets I've read, not one—because I consumed it—helped me make a better decision about a serious matter affecting my life.

"News" is just one corporation's opinion. It's mostly clickbait, completely irrelevant to my well-being. Truly creative minds—whether composers, mathematicians, scientists, authors, or musicians—could care less what's trending on Twitter.

My mission now is to pay more attention to the collective rhythm and wisdom emanating from the larger whole, what I often call the Divine Buzz.

It might sound big and cosmic, but it's really the most natural thing in the world. And it's a gazillion times more resourceful and richer in content than anything I could ever hear on CNN.

15/2

THANK YOU FOR SHARING, NOW GO SIT IN THE CORNER

When the heart speaks, the mind finds it indecent to object.

— MILAN KUNDERA

The Dude is but Love, and therefore so am I.

161) Give me your blessing, my holy bro.

162) I am as the Dude created me.

The skinny: My ego wants to control the show. But it has old recipes, old solutions.

It's like a cerebral copy machine, Xeroxing the past, perpetuating problems.

Conversely, when my life is choreographed by love, I connect to the greater dimensions of my heart.

So, thank you, ego, for your two cents, but my yellow highlighter is now underlining notes from the infinitely expanding universe.

15/2

EARTH ROBOTS, REVOLT!!!

We are here to find 1008 ways to love.

— SUE MORTER

The Dude is but Love, and therefore so am I.

163) There is no death. I am free.

164) Now are we one with Source.

The skinny: I landed here on planet Earth vibrating with possibility, knowing my divinity, being excited to serve and love. I knew I was an eternal being and had no limits.

But, slowly and surely, I got "humanized."

I was told:

"Your name is Pam."

"Your gender is female."

"You are three years old today."

"That exuberant spirit? You need to tone it down."

I learned to find distinctions and differences, to recognize "the good" and "the bad."

I became an earth robot.

Today, I stage a revolution. I take an energy saber to everything I learned. I zap the labels, obliterate the differences, decimate the ridiculous defenses. And I discover that, ultimately, everything is light. Everything is love.

15/2

178

LOVE POTION NUMBER 9

We must move to the laboratory where radical change can occur—
inside our very mind, heart, and cells of our bodies.

— RICHARD ROHR

The Dude is but Love, and therefore so am I.

165) There's no denying love.

166) I am entrusted with gifts and nunchuck skills.*

The skinny: Polite society tends to relegate love to a Valentine's card. Or a chick flick. As appropriate conversation for husband and wife, maybe. But not for a government and its people. Love's okay in the bedroom. But, for heaven's sake, keep it out of the boardroom.

This lesson says love is the big cheese. It's who we are. It's why we're here.

Love is a moment-by-moment solution to every alleged "problem," both those in my own life and those that exist on a global scale.

So it's up to me. I can continue to fill my mind with the meaningless stimuli of a world preoccupied with meaningless things. Or I can cast my rod into the bottomless mystery of my own soul. Where I can tap the deep subterranean impulse that recognizes magic and repairs "defects."

Ultimately, it's the only thing that matters.

15/2

---

* Sorry, couldn't resist the nod to *Napoleon Dynamite,* one of my daughter's favorite movies.

TRUTH MERELY WANTS TO GIVE YOU HAPPINESS

Lay your interfering thoughts aside.

— A COURSE IN MIRACLES

The Dude is but Love, and therefore so am I.

167) Love is all there is.

168) I claim grace now.

The skinny: My thoughts provide an endless source of entertainment. Most of the time, they replay the past, or construct a future.

By believing today is going to resemble yesterday, I leave no room for change, no room for the endless gifts with which the universe so doggedly tries to entrust.

Instead of viewing the delicious juiciness of this one-of-a-kind moment, I kick it down the street like a discarded Coca-Cola can.

As *A Course in Miracles* so clearly states, "Without the continuity of old ideas and sick beliefs, present confidence directs the way."

Every time I head out on a new trip, I decide in advance I'm going to have a great time. I picture amazing adventures, laughter, everything working out with ease and grace.

Well, guess what? That's exactly what I get.

15/2

ONLY GOOD, ONLY GOOD

Despair is not only self-defeating, it is unrealistic.

— SUSAN GRIFFIN

The Dude is but Love, and therefore so am I.

169) By grace I live. By grace I am released.

170) Only good can come to me.

The skinny: The running thread of *A Course in Miracles* is the radical idea that I am freed from past ideas.

Once I drop all the rules, ideas, evidence, and grievances around which I've formed my life, only good can come to me.

That's an affirmation worth running in a loop. Only good can come to me. Only good. Only good. Only good.

15/2

EMANCIPATION PROCLAMATION!

There's great freedom in not compulsively interpreting other people and situations.

— ECKHART TOLLE

The next 20 lessons have a specific goal: my liberation! I do this by simply changing focus.

Lesson 181 (I trust my brothers, who are one with me) asks for a simple commitment. To move from the courtroom of my mind that imposes judgment on pretty much everyone and everything to the open field of brazen acceptance.

This is done by giving up compulsive thinking. At least for a little while each day.

I do this by asking for the aid and assistance of the Holy S. Asking to look beyond perceived errors. Admitting that if I see it "out there," it originated in "my mind."

No longer do I confuse reality with the racing thoughts in my head. I look behind the screen of misconstrued concepts that blame others as the source of my pain.

If anger comes up, I simply notice and ask for deliverance.

It is not this I wish to look upon.

Never mind that it'll undoubtedly come up again. That I'll inevitably lose my way again.

How could that matter? What matters is my commitment to look straight into the present. Not backward. Not forward.

Now!

ON THE BORDER

The world invites us to stride through the unlocked gate into realms of greater promise and possibilities.

— BILL PLOTKIN

The operative words in Lesson 182 (I will be still an instant and go home) are "still" and "instant."

I'm asked to leave behind my defenses for just a little while each day. No more is asked and no more is needed. That's why the numbers at the bottom of the page have vanished. It's not that I'm on my own. It's that I now know immediate assistance is as near as my next breath.

But because this is a daily practice and because every 24 hours has two distinct mystical periods, I like to play with the principles during what scientists call the hypnagogic state.

It's that trippy lull between wakefulness and sleep when thoughts and images swirl, flutter, and transform into endless potential and possibility. And like I said, we all get two of these precious gifts every day. It's how August Kekule, founder of organic chemistry, first envisioned the benzene ring, how Salvador Dali and Thomas Edison stimulated all those saucy new insights and inventions.

And it's the perfect gateway of consciousness to "be still and go home." This twice-daily kaleidoscopic state is an ongoing opportunity for guidance, inner peace, and wholeness. It's a special time for me and the Holy S to kick down doors, bump into new visions, and say, "hell yeah!" to the freedom I forfeit no more.

CALL ME BY YOUR NAME

Nearby is the country they call life. You will
know it by its intensity. Give me your hand.

— RILKE

Self-help tomes advise using willpower to cajole us to the gym, to deal with epic work deadlines, to prevent us from checking FB for the 34th time. Strength, inner resolve, we're told, will spur us on to glory.

But according to organizational psychologist Benjamin Hardy, "Willpower is a dangerous fad that leads to failure."

Lesson 183 (I call upon Source) seconds Hardy's assessment. When I say, "I should be more present, I should be more accepting, I should be more loving," I enlist the enculturated brain that caused the problem in the first place.

Instead, I call on the name of Source. I become oblivious to everything else. It becomes my only wish, the only sound with any meaning. Its unlimited name pulses through my body. It's as near as my every breath.

With it, I escape all bondage of the world.

It's the only prayer I need.

NO DECISION, NO FEAR

I must be a mermaid, Rango. I have no fear of depths.

— ANAIS NIN

So I have this little trick. If a lesson doesn't resonate, I return to my old standby. Lesson 184 is one that doesn't compute:

So I flip back to Chapter 30 in the text where, among other things, I'm told, "Do not fight yourself" or get "too preoccupied with every step," which lets me throw this lesson in the dumpster. Instead, I review what it calls "rules for decision."

Decisions are continuous and, most of the time, we don't even realize we're making them. For example, if I decide my daughter is gone and that I can't talk to her, that becomes my reality. It's a set structure, a "belief" that forms my life experience.

If I surrender that self-imposed structure to the Divine Buzz, then Taz and I can communicate. We can radiate love to each other, with or without physical bodies.

Then I'm able to notice the Alby Einstein (the playful photo with his tongue sticking out) Tasman sent as a sign on my morning's walk. Thanks, Taz. I especially appreciate that it was on the back of an RV. I feel your unconditional love pulsing within my heart.

So here are the steps from Chapter 30.

1. Begin each day by deciding what kind of experience I want. Amazing awesomeness works for me. Big, buoyant, generous love sounds like a plan.

2. Commit to making no decisions of my own, imposing no structure from my past, from my judgments.

The Course reassures me, "If I make no decisions by myself, this is the day that will be given me."

These two steps, practiced well, allow life's miracles to become patently obvious, obscured no longer by fear.

CHECK THE INNER DASHBOARD

Don't let the bullets take you out.

— DARREN ARONOFSKY

When making decisions (even small things), I first consult my inner dashboard. I use the following six-word indicator light: "How does it make me feel?"

If a thought is fun to think about, if it brings me peace, I milk that sucker for all it's worth. If it's less than pleasing, if it causes suffering, it's time to back away, Jack!

Lesson 185 gives me another indicator light, another handy six-word phrase. If I mean these six words (I want the peace of Dude), even for just an instant, no further sorrow is possible in any form, place, or time.

This lesson is a godsend. Because if anyone has an excuse to forfeit peace, to suffer, it's a mother who lost her only child. It's unthinkable really, to lose the precious being who grew inside my womb, nursed at my breast and became a brilliant, kind, imaginative person right before my very eyes.

Taz, who I communicate with on the daily, says choosing to feel good, wanting peace, and proving it's unnecessary to suffer is my new mission. Suffering, she points out, only isolates me from the whole of humanity. It disconnects me from the life force, like a cell phone that's too far from a transmission tower.

A mind obsessed with its own negative thoughts is like cancer, cut off from all the healthy cells. She said I owe it to my fellows (and indeed to her) to nourish a positive inner state.

She compares humans' oneness and connection to a grove of aspens. They may look like a bunch of separate trees, but a mountainside of aspens is actually a singular organism with a life force connected in an extensive root system. If I don't nurture a giving, loving inner state, I could poison the whole grove.

Grief is one thing. Suffering is another.

So thank you, Taz. And I'll say it again: I want the peace of Dude.

A TALE OF TWO PAMS

Reject your sense of injury and the injury itself disappears.

— MARCUS AURELIUS

Lately, I've been observing the two Pams who live inside my brain. I find it's helpful to narrow them down, to notice which one's in charge.

First, there's Blessed Pam. She, of course, notices how lucky she is, how amazingly awesome life is, how everything always works out.

And then there's FML Pam.

FML Pam (and if you don't know what this means, I'll just say it's a social media acronym people use to express displeasure with certain life events) tends to notice problems, just wee little ones like politics or wrinkles or a belief that something is not exactly how it should be.

FML Pam tends to be a writhing, whirling dervish that, like a pinball, careens around my head lighting up neurotransmitters of fear and worry.

When Blessed Pam is driving the car, life is good, as the popular T-shirt proclaims, reality is sweet, and celebration is the norm.

But when FML Pam calls for a Chinese fire drill and runs around the car to grab the wheel, a whole different story unfolds.

It's quite fascinating to watch which Pam is generating my thoughts.

Nowadays, when I notice FML Pam getting noisy, I simply tell her "thanks for sharing," and remind her what Lesson 186 (Salvation of the world depends on me) promises. That problems are nothing but wrong perception. And they literally wither and die when I don't feed them with my attention.

When I pump up what the Course calls my "weakened ability to be grateful," my perception changes, as does my whole world. Today, I trust that I can never be abandoned, I have everything I need, and life never stops working on my behalf.

LIFE IS NOT A ZERO SUM GAME

Love is the only rational act.

— MITCH ALBOM

A Course in Miracles turns every accepted paradigm on its head.

Lesson 187 (I bless the world because I bless myself) is a prime example. It tells me the only way to protect my assets (love, happiness, beauty, joy) is to give them away.

The material world advertises the exact opposite. There's only so much to go around, it likes to scream. It's vital to protect myself, worry, keep others at arm's distance.

If I continue to approach life from what can only be called a scarcity consciousness, I will continue to find proof of limits and lack.

This lesson encourages me to "Give gladly." It urges me to strengthen my assets by distributing them freely, passing them out to everyone.

It says I reinforce and exponentially increase my blessings when I approach life from the following mind-set:

There is more where that came from.
It is impossible to lose anything of value.
Everything I give comes back to me tenfold.

And here's the thing. I'm not asked to take any of these Course promises on faith. It's like the old Alka-Seltzer slogan: "When I try it (extending blessings), I like it (seeing blessings, grace, open-hearted people everywhere).

INVOKE FACIL!

It's all out there, ripe for the making, and it starts in your head.

— ROBERT RODRIGUEZ

Today, I add a new word to my dictionary. *Facil!* It means easy in Spanish and, because it's not a word I typically use (and therefore take for granted), it holds a rare superpower.

I can invoke it anytime I start ruminating: *Doing this Course is hard. Spiritual enlightenment is impossible.*

What if it really isn't? What if, in reality, it's facil!

According to Lesson 188 (It's here now) enlightenment requires no change, no work. It requires but my recognition. How facil is that?

"If you go in saying 'This is impossible,' you chop off your left foot before leaving the starting line," says filmmaker Robert Rodriguez. "But if in your mind it's facil, then you breeze right through it."

Instead of freaking out about how complicated and wordy and impossible the Course seems, take it from Rodriguez. Round up those wandering thoughts, encourage them to fall in line by simply asking, "What if this were facil?"

IF I HAD TO PICK JUST ONE

It's all about having a clean antenna.

— PETE HOLMES

I get this question a lot. What's your favorite country? Or city? Or destination in general?

I have a couple of pat answers. Either I answer with the country or city or destination I last visited—because, after all, that's what lovers of travel do. They fall in love with every place, everything, every person.

Or I point out that, just like you don't want pizza at every meal, you can't narrow your favs to just one. It depends on an evolving string of moods and desires. Favorites change.

The one question I've never gotten is what's your favorite *Course in Miracles* lesson. If anyone wants to know, 189 is definitely in contention. Here's why:

1. It promises a world alive with hope and blessed with perfect charity and love.

2. It promises the world, when seen anew, keeps me safe from every form of danger or pain.

3. It promises reality, the truth I block with my fears, offers endless wells of joy. My assignment is to release self-produced holograms of malice and attack. These problematic holograms are NOT REAL. I made them up and continue to invest in them by staring at them, believing in them, trying to fix them. Let me repeat. They are NOT real.

4. And this is my all-time favorite part. I don't have to do anything. The universe shows up with endless benevolence and generosity the very minute I open the valve. It promises boundless joy as soon as I ask. It shows up ASAP. In joyful and immediate response.

5. It also says, "Forget this world, forget this course." Come with wholly empty hands. It tells me to let go of every single thought the past has taught, every idea I learned before now.

So favorite destination? No idea. Favorite Course lesson? Definitely 189. Maybe I'll throw the rest away and practice it daily for the rest of my life.

IS THERE ROOM IN YOUR LIFE FOR MAGIC?

*The brain's natural instinct is to judge, but so
is the urge to boink the UPS dude.*

— MARY KARR

It's possible to live in a state of uninterrupted deep peace. It's called enlightenment.

Lesson 190 (I choose joy instead of pain) explains why most of us don't come close.

1. A false self masquerades as us. We place all our attention on this "self" that is no more real or lasting or solid than Eleanor Shellstrop from *The Good Place*. This made-up hologram blocks our connection to the sacred, limitless life force.

2. The life force got renamed, rebranded, and dishonored. The popular nickname for this realm of beauty, goodness, and infinite vastness is God. But as I've already made clear, God, as a concept, has been misused and deformed.

3. Enlightenment is regarded as the provenance of a select few. You know that false self I mentioned earlier? It likes to promote the idea that enlightenment is a superhuman accomplishment. PEOPLE!! It's our natural state. We are connected to an immeasurable, indestructible life force. Because we see ourselves as isolated fragments, we plod through life pretending to be something we're not.

4. A dumb, primitive creature mans the dials. And by that, I mean our thoughts, which compulsively judge, compare, label, and define, block us from feeling our connection.

HAKUNA MATATA

We are like Superman who must remain disguised as nerdy newspaper journalist Clark Kent, or Harry Potter who is not allowed to do magic while on holiday.

— ANTHON ST. MAARTEN

Lesson 191 basically follows the plot of *The Lion King*.

Simba, tricked by his treacherous uncle Scar, flees into exile. Out of sheer guilt, he leaves his home and his rightful place as ruler of the kingdom. He has no clue who he really is.

That's us, this lesson says. Fearful of shadows, mistakenly believing we're weak and frail and born to die.

Like Simba, we deny our own identity as we slouch around in this weird, unnatural world.

In the movie, Rafiki eventually shows up to lead Simba to a reflection pool where he sees who he really is, a full-grown king, a hero with the power to set the world free.

If I master today's lesson, I, too, can be free. Like Simba, I can escape bondage and, by changing my perspective of the world, release all others along with me.

Be glad today, this lesson says, how very easily hell is undone. I need but tell myself:

"I am the Holy Son of the Dude Himself. I cannot suffer, cannot be in pain. I cannot suffer loss, nor fail to do all that salvation asks."

In this one thought all illusions are gone.

Except one. I kinda want to hold on to Timon and Pumbaa's theme song: a problem-free philosophy, no worries for the rest of my days. Hakuna Matata.

JUST BECAUSE CREDENTIALED EXPERTS SAY IT'S TRUE DOESN'T MEAN IT IS

You have to decamp from normal reality.

— ERIC WEINSTEIN

When I was growing up, rubber beach shoes like Havaianas were called "thongs." Sometime in the 1990s, the word "thong" took on a different connotation. My daughter cringed whenever I mentioned I was donning a thong.

"Ooo, gross," she'd say.

So I decided to teach this old dog a new trick. I decided to rewire my neural pathways that have associated beach shoes and the word "thong" for five decades.

And that's what Lesson 192 (The Dude has plans for me) asks me to do with the F word.

Forgiveness is not exoneration of the world's punkasses.

Forgiveness asks for a clean and unmarked slate on which a different story can be written. It tells me that my understanding is limited, and that to believe in my faulty conclusions means I'm groveling in the dark.

When I agree to the Dude's plan (to refrain from falling for anger and judgment), I discover I've got everything I've ever wanted. No sacrifice is asked, no limitation is possible.

How can that be unwelcome? Or feared?

THAT'S A BIG BOULDER, INDY

*Just because something is rampant in your civilization
doesn't mean it has to express itself in your life.*

— ABRAHAM-HICKS

Lesson 193 is pretty simple. It promises undisturbed happiness. It says
if I see or experience anything that contradicts this assertion, I'm simply confused.

The obstacles in my life may look like massive boulders and I may
feel like Indiana Jones running for dear life, but it's all a mirage. Today,
I overcome a thousand seeming boulders with one easy seven-word
remedy: *Forgive and this will disappear.*

Why wait, this lesson says, another day, another minute,
another instant?

And with that, I'll close with this story about Rainn Wilson (Dwight
Schrutt from *The Office*). He's a practicing Baha'i, a deeply spiritual
soul, but back when he was a newly minted, struggling actor living in
New York, he temporarily threw his faith overboard. How could any
reasonable person be expected to believe there's a force that wants to
interact with us, a force that has our best interests at heart?

Except that attitude didn't feel right. Like all of us, he longed to
be connected to a bigger thing. He embarked on a quest to read all the
spiritual texts.

One night while watching a baseball game with his deeply agnostic
poet friend Phil, he shared a story about the Lakota belief in Wakan
Tanka, a sacred spirit that exists in all of us.

"Oh yeah?" Phil challenged him. "If your Wakan Tanka is so powerful, ask him to let the Yankees win this game."

At the time, the Yankees were behind by two. It was the bottom
of the ninth, two outs, not a likely proposition. Rainn, ever adventurous and open-minded, said sure and sent up an incantation to
Wakan Tanka.

"I kid you not," says Rainn. "No sooner did I send up the 'chant'
than Darryl Strawberry hit a two-run walk-off home run to win
the game."

194

BLAME IT ON THE BOOGIE

Beware the stories you read or tell. Beneath the waters
of consciousness, they are altering your world.

— BEN OKRI

Kids' computer games have undoubtedly evolved since my daughter Taz played them on the giant desktop (compared to today's laptops, that early Gateway was a veritable behemoth) in my office.

Back then, she had several games where, by pointing a cursor at an item in a scene, it would come alive. For example, if she clicked on a cupboard door, it would open, music would play, and a duet of dancing mice would pirouette across the shelf. Or she'd click on a flowerpot and it would shimmy and shake until its beautiful red petals rained to the ground.

Life is like those old computer games. When you put your attention on something, it literally comes alive. If you put your cursor on all the opportunities and love in the scenes of your life, that reality comes alive.

But if you continue to click on the monsters under the bed, they, too, are more than happy to put in an appearance. The thing is we're the ones in charge. We're the ones who decide where to point our cursors, where to send our attention.

Lesson 194 asks me to point my cursor on a happy future, to relinquish the past. No more do I permit yesterday's woes to punish me. No longer do I see the world as my enemy. I rest untroubled, recognizing that life is limitless, abundant, and strangely accommodating.

HAVE YOU CLAIMED
YOUR GIFTS TODAY?

Find a place inside where there's joy, and the
joy will burn out the pain.

— JOSEPH CAMPBELL

I know. I probably sound like an ad for a bank. Come in, open a new checking account, claim your free ice chest.

But that's not the kind of gifts to which I refer. I'm talking about the continuous gifts bestowed by the natural world. As I was driving home from pickleball this morning, I noticed a brilliant scarlet branch on a maple tree just blocks from my home. It literally made me gasp.

Every day, I'm presented with unbelievably beautiful gifts: stars that are billions of years old, fuzzy caterpillars crawling across my path, hydrangeas, dragonflies. When I bring my attention to anything in nature, I'm able to step out of the prison of conceptualized thinking. I'm able to rest and notice a state of connectedness with all things. These gifts are endless when I take time to look.

Even in inner cities, the gift of the breaking dawn signals the possibilities in a new day.

So sure, material gifts like ice chests and toasters and, for that matter, new Michael Kors purses are okay. But the gifts I claim are those that remind me I live in a galaxy that's one of a gazillion galaxies and that each of these gazillion galaxies has hundreds of billions of stars and enough gas and dust to make hundreds of billions more.

Lesson 195 (Love is the way I walk in gratitude) asks me to step up and claim my gifts. To rejoice unceasingly in my inseverable connection to all living things.

LIT WITH HOPE AND SPARKLING WITH GENTLE FRIENDLINESS

I tie no weights to my ankles.

— C. JOYBELL C.

When my friend Robbin was a little girl, she had two burning questions: 1. How were the giraffes getting to Kansas? 2. And why don't we want them peeping in our windows?

Every night, Robbin's mom insisted she close her bedroom windows to avoid . . . well, Robbin always thought she said giraffes. Needless to say, she eventually figured out it was "drafts" her mom hoped to keep out, but for quite a while, she was extremely puzzled why her mother wouldn't want those really cool, really tall animals stopping by for a visit. After all, they paid good money to see them at the zoo.

Robbin's innocent misinterpretation is a good metaphor for the perceptual mistakes we make every day when we get up expecting difficulties and unhappiness. For that matter, getting up every morning and expecting this day to be a repeat of yesterday (and we all do) is a huge misinterpretation and a giant fence that keeps the world's bounty from flowing in the windows.

Lesson 196 (I can only be hurt by my thoughts) tells me that clinging to what I know, believing it's possible to be attacked and therefore justifying my attack on others, locks out the world's largesse, along with the drafts and the giraffes.

I'm promised that if I really take this lesson in, I will proceed quickly, surely, and forever. So I repeat. It is impossible that I can be hurt by anything except my own thoughts.

THIS IS WHAT
I WANT INSTEAD

Man is what he believes.

— ANTON CHEKHOV

It's time, thank you Lesson 197, for another RSO.

Here's the sentence I refuse to rip out: The Dude's gifts are sure, eternal, changeless, limitless, forever giving out, extending love, and adding to my never-ending joy.

I often fall short of this limitless glory because my toaster's not plugged in. There's no condemnation involved. No need to damn my toaster all to hell.

If I'm smart, I simply grab the cord and plug it back in.

For the sake of clarity, let's stretch the toaster metaphor. Let's say I really, really, really want toast. I can plead and beg and pray all I want, but until I connect the toaster back to the wall, it's "Sorry, Charlie, You're SOL."

Source has no opinions on whether I employ its power or not. It doesn't judge any more than electricity judges. It's completely 100 percent non-biased.

It's always there, waiting for me to lay down my guilt, my preposterous notions that I'm not good enough, that these principles won't work for me. It patiently waits, knowing eventually I'll decide to plug myself back in.

IS YOUR BOOM BOX ON
THE RIGHT FREQUENCY?

*The universe that constantly spins out new galaxies wants to shine
through you, to speak through you, to expand through you.*

— M O I

Elizabeth Gilbert tells a funny story in her book *Big Magic*. She was
working as a cook on a ranch in Wyoming. She was drinking beer one
night with a cowboy named Hank who told her about an instructional
tape he had just purchased to learn how to imitate an elk's mating call.

Taz and I once spent an autumn near Rocky Mountain National
Park, and I can attest that Gilbert's description of a bull elk calling
for a mate is extremely accurate—an eardrum-shredding Styrofoam-
against-Styrofoam screech.

Gilbert, who thought this was the funniest thing she'd ever heard,
convinced Hank to retrieve his Larry D. Jones mating call tape. And
possibly because of the beer, they hatched the imprudent scheme of
taking the boom box out into the woods. Giddy and laughing and, as
she says, not in tune with nature in the least, they stumbled through
the woods with the artificial bull elk's mating call twanging at full blast.

Suddenly, there's a crashing of branches and a 700-pound bull elk
exploding toward them. He snorted and pawed as he prepared for war
against this rival bull elk. Luckily, Hank had the good sense to throw
the boom box as far away as possible.

I tell you this story partly because I think it's hilarious, but mostly
because it reminds me that if I can get my boom box on the right frequency, the universe is going to show up, snorting and pawing and
ready to move in my life.

Lesson 198 tells me there's no reason to oppose it, quarrel with it,
or seek for a thousand reasons it won't come. Rather, I rejoice that I
hold the boom box in my hands.

WTF!!!!!!

At any given moment, we can leave the self-enclosed world of our thought and touch down in the present moment.

— TERRY COCHRAN

Lesson 199 (I am not a body. I am free) is one of those WTF lessons. It immediately triggers a reaction.

What do you mean I'm not a body? I have mirrors. I see the wrinkles, the cellulite. That's utterly ridiculous. The ego calls it insane.

Because this lesson happens to be one that's repeated most often, let's elaborate.

My body is a limit. It's nothing but a cage. It represents my egoic mind, the illusionary part that believes I can only be one place at a time. That my thoughts are private, that everybody (or at least the everybodies not in my contact list) is out to get me.

No question my body comes in handy when taking selfies. And it's fun to dress it up, take it to dinner. But just like I'd never mistake my favorite LBD* or my high school prom dress for my identity, my body isn't who I am. It's a vehicle, as interchangeable as any item in my closet.

To limit myself to this body is to look for freedom where it can't be found. The real me is beyond all laws of time and space, unbound by all preconceptions.

It's essential to accept this idea—that's why it's repeated ad nauseam and why in about two days, we're going to review this concept for 20 whole days.

So for now, let's forget that part of this lesson and concentrate on the "I am free" part. For example:

I am free to pick a different reality today.

I am free to let go of all those made-up rules I learned when I was growing up.

I am free to create my life at will.

I am free, especially from the limitations of my body.

---

* Little black dress.

BE WEIRD. HAVE FUN.
START NOW.

I am in love with the world.

— MAURICE SENDAK

In Europe, soccer (they call it football) is huge. Really big. The best players make $50 million per year.

Ostersunds FK, a football club in remote northern Sweden, in a town just 240 miles from the Arctic Circle, knew their only hope of competing in the big leagues was Eljest. It's a Swedish term that means "be different."

Their coach, Graham Potter, a Brit who'd never really led a team before, noticed that all teams trained the same, organized the same, played the same. They were mostly owned by old white dudes.

What if he mixed it up? What if, in addition to practices, he started a Culture Academy where his players were encouraged to try something new, to step out of their comfort zones? What if he got the whole town involved?

So, in 2010, his first year as coach of this team that was lucky to get 600 fans to a game, he required his players to perform *Swan Lake*. For the community. The next year, they wrote a book. They went on to paint, to stage a rock concert, to mentor a team of refugees in Darfur.

And a funny thing happened. This little team of soccer rejects went from fourth-tier soccer when the "be weird experiment" began in 2010 to playing first-tier soccer.

In 2017, they won the Swedish Cup. They've gone on to play in the Europa League and have racked up wins against such powerhouses as Berlin and Galatasaray SK, a legendary Turkish team so impressed with their grit they gave them a standing ovation.

As their manager said, "We win every game, even if the score shows otherwise, because we learn something new every time."

So today, as we ponder Lesson 200, think of Ostersunds FK, who accomplished the impossible by changing their mind-set, being brave, opening up to a whole new weird way of being.

Boom!

Review VI

My body is nothing without me.

— TOM STOPPARD

First the—I was going to say bad news, but that's just my ego talking.

The ego feels terribly threatened when I commit to reexamine the lessons from this review every morning and night for 15 minutes. It tries to dissuade me from briefly (it takes a second) thinking about the lessons every hour on the hour. And it gets pissed that I no longer let idle thoughts go unchallenged.

If a tempting thought creeps in, I combat it like this:

This thought I do not want. I choose _____ instead.

The good news is that by doing this (despite the ego's incessant bad mouthing, it takes a teensy 4 percent of my day), I transcend my ego, I relinquish everything that clutters up my mind.

So take this, ego:

Every lesson for the next 20 days presents proof that I am more than the meat suit. Each offers evidence that the physical rules I've "mastered" about caring for my body are just not true.

Each starts with this good news:

I am not a body. I am free.
For I am still as the Dude created me.

The jukebox selection? "Three Little Birds" by Bob Marley.

NOTE TO BODY: YOU ARE NOT THE BOSS OF ME

I am large. I contain multitudes.

— WALT WHITMAN

I am not a body. I am free.
For I am still as the Dude created me.

I have nothing against my body. It's quite useful for playing pickleball, for kissing babies, for passing out hugs to fellow humanoids.

But to see my body as the boundary of my being is a myopic belief. My body is but one piece on the chessboard of who I really am.

My true self is a much wider realm made up of my joys, my ideas, my fears, my interests, and my loves. My body is a temporary clown suit happening within the larger phenomenon of me.

To give my body so much attention, as I'm encouraged to do in this culture, is to miss the whole point.

Does it really matter which purse it's carrying? Which type of mascara is trimming its eyes?

The body was made by the ego in order to strive. It's a wall I erected to make believe I'm separate from others. The linear body can be only one place at a time. Its eyes can only see so far.

Putting it on a pedestal like we all do is a mysterious case of mistaken identity.

I can pretend all I want to be my body, to dress it up like Barbie, to post its pictures on Facebook.

But making my body the "thing" is a silly game that changes nothing at all.

Who I really am is a sacred being with no beginning and no end.

NOTE TO BODY:
YOU ARE NOT THE BOSS
OF ME, PART II

If we understood ourselves better,
we would damage ourselves less.

— JAMES BALDWIN

I am not a body. I am free.
For I am still as the Dude created me.

In the department of I'm not a body, let's take Andy Mackie, a retired horse trainer. Andy's body underwent nine heart surgeries. Doctors insisted that in order to survive, it needed 15 different medications.

Andy finally tired of listening to doctors and their limitations. So he took the $600 per month he normally spent on heart meds and bought 300 harmonicas to give away to school kids. He fully expected it to be his final grand gesture.

When he didn't die, he decided to do the same thing the next month. And the month after that. Wasn't long before he forgot all about his body, the medical reports and the drugs he was supposed to take.

Rather, he got on with the business of honoring his multitudinous self. In the next 13 years, he gave out 18,000 harmonicas complete with lessons. In 2005, he even set a Guinness World record when he led 1,706 harmonica players playing "Twinkle, Twinkle, Little Star."

Andy got on with following the thing that made his heart pitter-pat. He gave up all pointless plans to protect his linear self, the packaging that, as I said, is only one small piece on the cosmic chessboard.

So today I ask, which piece of your own ginormous chessboard are you going to play? The limited slab of flesh that's prey to guilt and ends in death? Or the wider eternal self that beholds, appreciates, loves, and expands?

LET'S TAKE IT HIGHER, BABY

It's supposed to be a secret, but I'll tell you anyway. We doctors do nothing. We only help and encourage the doctor within.

— ALBERT SCHWEITZER

I am not a body. I am free.
For I am still as the Dude created me.

At the party of "anything is possible," there's always one cranky uncle who sits alone in the corner. More times than not, the belief that stubbornly refuses to budge is the one about the body being the boss. It goes like this: "My mind has no control over my health, disease, aging, weight, and any other fool thing my body decides to do."

In this review, as I claim freedom from the prison of my body, I consult a doctor.

Lissa Rankin, M.D., started out as hard-nosed and closed-minded as her colleagues, but after investigating 50 years of peer-reviewed medical literature (*New England Journal of Medicine* and *Journal of the American Medical Association,* to name a few), she found ample evidence that beliefs are the hinge on which bodies function. Minds play the starring role in determining our biochemistry. To ignore these findings, she claims, is not only grossly irresponsible, but a betrayal of the Hippocratic Oath.

She tells a story about a patient with tumors the size of oranges. After begging his doctor for an experimental drug making headlines, his enormous tumors completely disappeared. Several weeks later, a new report hit the airwaves. Turns out the "miracle drug" was not as powerful as originally thought. The patient's tumors returned. His doctor, by now savvy, gave his patient a placebo, telling him it was a stronger form of the drug and assuring him that the ineffective trials had been using too small a dose. Once again, the tumors from his stage 4 lymphoma began to shrink. Finally, the FDA pronounced the drug ineffective and pulled it off the market. The patient, who had been rapidly recovering, died within a week.

LET'S TAKE IT HIGHER, BABY, PART II

Reality is only a Rorschach ink-blot.

— ALAN WATTS

I am not a body. I am free.
For I am still as the Dude created me.

In 2012 on a show called *Fear and Faith*, Derren Brown, the popular British mentalist, cured dozens of people of everything from phobias to addictions with a powerful drug he called Rumyodin.

In reality, Rumyodin (an anagram for "your mind") was a sugar pill. It worked because his "patients" believed it worked.

Dr. Bruce Mosely, a surgeon and team physician for the Houston Rockets, performed arthroscopic knee surgery on two of ten middle-aged, former military guys. Three of the 10 had their knees rinsed (without the scraping) and the other five had no surgical procedure at all. It was an exercise in just pretend. After two years, all ten believed their surgery was a success. What Mosely discovered is that the bigger and more dramatic the patient perceives the intervention to be, the bigger the placebo effect.

Patients have grown hair, lowered blood pressure and cholesterol, watched ulcers disappear, and cured a wide range of symptoms after being treated with nothing but sugar pills. It was their belief they were getting "medicine" that cured them, not the medicine itself.

Either way, I remember every hour (and every time I need some Rumyodin) that I am not my body. I am free. I am free.

WHAT'S YOUR COVENANT WITH THE UNIVERSE?

Shake the world. Shake the truth. Shake the people. Use your salt shaker to sprinkle, melt and preserve humanity.

— ANTHONY LICCIONE

I am not a body. I am free.
For I am still as the Dude created me.

Silent Unity was started by Myrtle Fillmore, who healed herself of tuberculosis and aggravated malaria. Despite the fact she was spitting up blood, running a constant fever, and depending on a cabinet full of medications, Myrtle decided to put to the test what Lesson 205 promises: The Dude's peace will sweep away all distortions.

She'd heard the outrageous claim that the Dude would never wish disease on anyone. And that if she would simply align with that promise, the warped view of "disease" would disappear, leaving her with perfect health and wholeness.

Within two years, there was no sign of her old illnesses.

Myrtle and her husband, Charles, who also used forgiveness and alignment to overcome a disabling hip socket injury, decided to take this alignment business one step further. They decided to make a written covenant with the universe. On December 7, 1892, they committed their time, their money, and all they had and expected to have to the Spirit of Truth and to the Society of Silent Unity.

In exchange for this commitment, they made it clear they would expect the Dude to render unto them an equivalent in peace of mind, health of body, wisdom, understanding, love, life, and an abundant supply of all things necessary to meet every want. Let's just say it worked.

So I ask you today, are you willing to make a covenant with the Universe? Are you willing to give everything you've got to your highest vision and to know that, in return, you will be given everything you could ever need?

WHAT WOULD OPRAH DO?

If we don't forgive, we tie rocks to our feet.
It's too much for our wings to carry.

— C. JOYBELL C.

I am not a body. I am free.
For I am still as the Dude created me.

In this lesson, I celebrate that I am not a body. And I throw confetti, because neither is anybody else.

This container that I believe to be me is a big ruse, and today I focus on the fact that it's impossible for the real me to die or be attacked or even make mistakes.

How could today's promise—the lifting of all limitations—not be welcome? Why would I choose to live in confusion, to believe my identity is restricted to my body, to believe others can hurt or desert me?

In this lesson, I learn that my "understanding of life" is born of error and mistaken identities. And all I gotta do is let the Holy S take the wheel.

Forgiveness, my only function, is to put my stock in the formless, in the eternal. My only function is to recognize that everyone I see or think of or even imagine is not their body either. Therefore, I refuse to imprison myself by imprisoning someone else with my anger or fear or intolerance. And I recognize that anyone who tempts me to be angry is my savior and I owe them thanks.

As always, Oprah says it best: "Forgiveness isn't just letting someone off the hook. It's saying, "Thank you for that experience.""

THE ANATOMY OF AN ILLNESS: AKA THE EGO'S SECRET WEAPON

*A sick thought can devour the body's flesh
more than fever or consumption.*

— GUY DE MAUPASSANT

I am not a body. I am free.
For I am still as the Dude created me.

In 2017, the American Psychiatric Association updated its manual for diagnosing mental illness. Not surprisingly, this fifth edition of the *Diagnostic and Statistical Manual of Mental Disorders* (DSM) listed a number of new "diseases."

The first DSM, which came out in 1952, listed 26 general disorders. Today, there are more than 400.

Are we really 16 times crazier today? Or are we simply reacting to expectations, peer pressure, and the suggestion of mental illness?

Steven Pressfield, author of one of my favorite books (*The War of Art*), said that his boss at a Madison Avenue ad agency instructed him to invent a disease, because "then we can sell the hell out of its cure."

According to Lesson 207, our physical bodies are potent tools used by the ego for obscuring Truth, for hiding our bodies' inherent natural healing power.

Here's how it works:

1. You notice something's off.

2. You begin focusing on it.

3. You wonder what "it" might be (as opposed to knowing you are a child of the most high and cannot inherit illness).

4. You give it a name.

5. You Google it, tell your friends about it, join a support group.

Jill Boelte Taylor, a Harvard-trained neuroanatomist who studies the brain and became famous for her Ted Talk "My Stroke of Insight," says that an unresisted thought passes through the brain in 90 seconds.

That is, unless you decide to apply the above five steps.

FREE YOURSELF WITH THERMODYNAMICS

All my brilliant plans foiled by
thermodynamics. Damn you, entropy!

— ANDY WEIR

I am not a body. I am free.
For I am still as the Dude created me.

Yada. Yada. Yada. Unless you're a physicist, thermodynamics is probably not a daily topic of conversation.

But it comes in handy when trying to hang on to a particular identity. For example, my main identity for the past 25 years was mom to Tasman. It's how I saw myself. It's how I made every decision.

But like water that turns into vapor (when atoms gain enough energy to break through the molecular bonds of liquid), it wasn't permanent.

The love was permanent. The connection I have with Taz is permanent. But the identity was temporary.

As much as I want to cling to structure and one particular identity, it can only cause me pain.

All identities are temporary. All structures will eventually deteriorate. The universe is infinitely expanding. Trying to contain it or stop it is pointless. It will only cause distress. There's great empowerment in seeing my identity for what it is. Short-term and mortal.

The only thing that's real, the only thing that lasts is love. It's the core, the bedrock, the power. And it will forever transcend all temporal identities. Love you forever, Taz.

REALITY IS UP FOR GRABS

*A good doctor can cure your disease. Only
a great doctor proves you were never sick.*

— ZEN SAYING

I am not a body. I am free.
For I am still as the Dude created me.

When my friend Jennifer was coming off hip surgery, she focused not on the pain, not on the inconvenience, but on the fact that every single day, her body creates 500 million new cells.

With all those new cells (and, yes, my body generates that many, too), there's absolutely no reason I have to be the same today as I was yesterday.

The real question is "What do I choose to communicate to these new cells?"

The options, according to Jenn, are: "Welcome to pain and misery. Or welcome to the party of vim, vigor, and vitality."

I couldn't say for sure, but I thought she looked at least five years younger.

Speaking of the pharmacopeia in your mind, here's another miracle story from a reader named Kelly.

"My body gives me the hard proof that law of attraction principles are real and absolute.

"Not only do I bless my food—I bless my body. I have a daily ritual where I look in the mirror and say I love you! You're SO beautiful! Thank you! and then I hug myself and I talk to every single cell! Thank you, cells! I love you! Thank you! Thank you! Thank you!

"I started this when I realized that each of us is our own personal universe commanding all these cells. Essentially, what we speak, what we believe act as 'god' (or creator) to those cells.

"When I first started this practice many years ago, the excess weight I'd been carrying melted off. People asked me what I was doing, and I'd give them the utterly confusing answer 'Just loving myself.' That's not what they wanted to hear. They wanted to hear '60 minutes of cardio every day followed by juice fasts and eating only cabbage!'"

Should we tell them, Kelly, about Lesson 209, about how love sets us free?

I KNOW YOU'RE NOT
(A BODY), BUT WHAT AM I?

We speak about losing our minds as if it is a bad thing.
I say, lose your mind. Do it purposefully. Find out
who you really are beyond your thoughts and beliefs.
Lose your mind, find your soul.

— VIRONIKA TUGALEVA

I am not a body. I am free.
For I am still as the Dude created me.

The Tarahumara Indians in Copper Canyon, Mexico, run 100 miles a day. Without struggling. Without training. Without doing all the necessary drills encrusted in old beliefs.

They defy every known rule of physical limitation because no one ever told them they can't. Running, to the Tarahumara, is a joyful, sacred experience, and every Tarahumara knows the older you get, the faster you run. And like the Course says, they find confirmation for their beliefs.

In 1993, a half-dozen Tarahumara were bought to the Leadville Ultra, a grueling high-altitude marathon over the scrabbly trails and snow peaks of the Colorado Rockies. It was apparent from the starting line that the toga-wearing runners were nothing like the other runners, who were nervously monitoring their pulses, somberly preparing for what they long believed to be a "near-impossible feat."

The middle-aged Tarahumara were laughing, shooting the breeze, smoking butts, and wondering if they should abandon the sandals they made from rubber tires for the Rockport cross-trainers offered by their sponsors.

Twenty hours later, they stunned the running world when 55-year old Victoriano Churro came in first, followed by his Tarahumara buddies Cerrildo Chacarito in second and Manuel Luna in fifth.

Physiologist Dale Groom ran cardiovascular tests on the Tarahumara runners and discovered their blood pressure went down when they were running. As this review promises, they escaped the bondage of the world.

THE WORLD'S MOST ENJOYABLE "DIET"

*Let us be glad that we will see what we believe
and that we can change what we believe.*

— A COURSE IN MIRACLES

I am not a body. I am free.
For I am still as the Dude created me.

Travel writers are frequently invited on cruises. And, true to reputation, these seagoing mini-villages offer an unlimited lineup of amazing eating opportunities. Which gives me the opportunity to put my ACIM principles to the test.

The dominant paradigm (that we are nothing but bodies) suggests that a) cruises and weight gain are synonymous, and b) I will inevitably return home from a cruise with extra poundage.

Very few would argue.

Except obstinate old me, who chooses to use cruises as a laboratory.

Instead of succumbing to the extremely popular pairing of cruises and weight gain, I choose to be a guinea pig for the greater good of humanity. I employ my superpower to lose weight.

My superpower, which also happens to be your superpower, is love. Every moment we get the opportunity to love what's in front of us: every person, every event, every seeming mishap.

My cruise hypothesis is that if I love everything about each cruise, love myself more and more every moment (not always the easiest task), and love every morsel I put in my mouth, I can maintain my weight. Or heck, why not declare that I'll drop a pound or two.

The challenge, of course, is letting go of guilt, letting go of everything my culture tells me—that I should diet, that women my age have no choice but to gain weight, that going on a cruise is a recipe for looking as big as the whales on my swimsuit.

I'm happy to report that even though I enjoy some of the best food on the planet, my body continues to run the programming I installed from an early age: "I can eat whatever I want and maintain a healthy, lithe, and beautiful body."

And, yes, I often weigh less when I disembark.

FIVE STAR-REVIEWS
ALL AROUND

Life is not a roll of the dice. It is a result of what
conscious awareness we find ourselves living out from.

— MICHELE LONGO-O'DONNELL

I am not a body. I am free.
For I am still as the Dude created me.

The fifth sentence in Dr. Joe Dispenza's book *You Are the Placebo* goes like this: "On a beautiful Southern California day in April, I had the privilege of being run over by an SUV in a Palm Springs triathlon."

Say what? The privilege of being run over? That day, when he broke six vertebrae, changed his life forever. The work he's doing now as a speaker, author, and researcher would never have happened without the experiment he conducted after doctors told him his one chance of ever walking again was to have a very complicated Harrington rod surgery.

He was 23, just cocky enough to think, "I am going to heal myself. I am going to put all my conscious attention on the intelligence within me. I am going to surrender to this greater, unlimited power and allow it to heal me."

Doctors, of course, thought he was plum nuts. But nine and a half weeks after the accident, he walked back into his life—without a body cast or surgery. Within ten weeks he was again seeing patients at his chiropractic clinic and training with weights.

No matter what happens in our lives, we have the choice of how we will interpret it. For me, it only makes sense to proclaim, "This is the best thing that ever happened to me." No matter what.

YOUR BODY HAS
SELF-HEALING SUPERPOWERS

*Life is not about healing; it's about accepting
that we are already healed.*

— ANNIE ZALEZSAK

I am not a body. I am free.
For I am still as the Dude created me.

We are constantly slapped around with the insane idea that our bodies are out to get us.

One hour of television is all it takes to learn about the evil plot being waged by our bodies. Constantly-running drug ads warn us into great vigilance:

Better watch out for this symptom.

Make sure you're aware of that problem.

It's only a matter of time until your body is going to reach out and strangle you.

Here's the ad I'd like to run:

Your body is a self-healing masterpiece. It is brilliantly equipped with natural mechanisms that fight infections, repair broken proteins, kill cancer cells, and keep you in tip-top shape. The only thing capable of stopping it from doing its job is your ludicrous belief that it is not your closest ally.

MORE THAN THE DUDE LIVING THE PAM STORY

Water is water, no matter what its shape or form.
The solidity of ice imagines itself to be its edges and density.
Melting, it remembers; evaporating, it ascends.

— STEPHEN LEVINE

I am not a body. I am free.
For I am still as the Dude created me.

There's nothing empirically bad or evil about this character living the Pam story. It's just that it's completely inadequate to address the big questions of love and infinity and wholeness.

The Pam story is a diversionary tactic. It shields me from true nature, concocting a cozy image of myself as an autonomous individual, separate from the whole.

Again, nothing wrong with this mental construct except it incites a ton of fear. It knows good and well (although loath to admit), that it's self-constructed and fragile and has no real substance, no permanence, no real vitality.

In today's review, I liberate the Dude living the Pam story. I give it freedom to follow the miracle of love. To give up judgment, accept each blessing and return to the field of Divine union.

I celebrate that life never ends. It simply changes form and evolves into ever new shapes and beauty.

WHY I NEVER TALK
SMACK ABOUT MY BODY

The body is the best mind reader on the planet.

— DR. JOE DISPENZA

I am not a body. I am free.
For I am still as the Dude created me.

This sentiment doesn't usually occur to me, but some people think of spring cleaning when crocuses and daffodils make their annual debut. You know, that ritual where you throw out all clothes that haven't been in style since Chandler Bing married Monica?

I'm devoted to a different type of spring cleaning. Tossing out useless ideas I picked up during childhood, all those "You can't. It's hard. Why bother?"

Until we're five or six, our clever little brains operate in theta wave mode, which is ideal for picking up language, family nuances, and other handy tools. Unfortunately, five-year-old consciousness also picks up a lot of erroneous messages.

For example, the minute you got sick or ran a fever, your well-meaning parents trotted you off to the doctor. The message was clear: you need something outside yourself to heal.

So, yeah, I should probably lose the red turtleneck, the Ugg boots, and several other items that make better Halloween costumes, but the spring cleaning I practice is disposing of no-longer-useful ideas I've been unwittingly dragging around like a ball and chain.

FACTS ARE OPINIONS HOLDING DOWN REALITY UNTIL WE MOVE BEYOND

Our thoughts hold more medicine than many of the astonishing breakthroughs of our time.

— KRIS CARR

I am not a body. I am free.
For I am still as the Dude created me.

The body is the ego's greatest invention, its most potent tool.

A fallible, aging body provides the ultimate distraction. The irony, of course, is we become so occupied with caring for our bodies that we never stop to recognize they're simply acting out our beliefs.

The Course regards the body as a learning device, says its abilities are highly overrated.

If the body acts up, it's the mind that needs correction. But only 100 percent of the time.

Our beliefs and expectations, in fact, are so powerful that placebos (fake treatments like sugar pills, saline injections, and sham surgery) cause bald men to grow hair, high blood pressure to drop, ulcers to heal, dopamine levels to increase, and even tumors to shrink. And although pharmaceutical companies would rather keep this on the down low, placebos relieve symptoms on par with real medication.

In other words, it's our beliefs that do the healing.

Facts, despite what scientists, teachers, and CNN tell you, are opinions, holding down material reality until we can move beyond.

A THEATER OF SMOKE
AND MIRRORS

*My God smells like vanilla and is full of sass
and truth, delivered with kindness.*

— JACQUI LEWIS

I am not a body. I am free.
For I am still as the Dude created me.

Here on planet Earth, we put a lot of sway in structure, in material form, in having one particular identity. But it's all a theater of smoke and mirrors.

Material structure, by its very nature, is mortal. It's gonna change. It's eventually gonna die.

Pam Grout is a temporary identity that works for now. Like Simba singing with the warthogs, I am currently pretending to be the author of this book.

And like Simba, who eventually acknowledges his true identity in the reflecting pool, I will eventually acknowledge mine as a blessed part of life, constantly expanding and flowing, morphing into ever more beauty, more possibility, more love.

IS IT A FACT OR JUST A LONG-HELD CULTURAL BELIEF?

*I pray for the change in perception that will
let me see bigger and sweeter realities.*

— ANNE LAMOTT

I am not a body. I am free.
For I am still as the Dude created me.

WebMD and other "authorities" insist you need eight hours of sleep, that there's a disease called seasonal affective disorder (SAD) that inflicts havoc every winter, and that gaining weight is inevitable if you don't rigorously watch what you eat.

But what if these beliefs are nothing but flimsy ideas made true by believing in them, investing in them, holding them up as scientific fact?

If consciousness provides the scaffolding for the physical world (and the Course and quantum physicists tell me it does), then putting energy into any "belief" encrusts it into physical form.

Most of us can buy that we have some power over our own reality, but we don't make the correlation that groupthink, those "facts" our culture, our medical community, our media tout as true are also temporary forms of "reality."

Who's to say what is and isn't possible? Do I want to believe the widely expanding *Diagnostic and Statistical Manual of Mental Disorders* (DSM)? Do I want to believe what pharmaceutical companies insist I need? Do I want to believe that what happened yesterday is going to happen again today?

Or do I want to create a new day, a new reality, a new world?

I'M A SOOOOUUL PHONE

If at first the idea is not absurd, then there is no hope for it.

— ALBERT EINSTEIN

I am not a body. I am free.
For I am still as the Dude created me.

First, we had dial phones, tethered to the wall. Next came push buttons, phones without cords. My daughter even had a phone shaped like a hamburger.

Cell phones were next, and by 1994, smartphones that allow us to access everything from our longitudinal coordinates to Brené Brown's Ted Talk became commonplace.

So are you sitting down?

The next communication advancement (and it's being developed by none other than Steve Jobs and Nikola Tesla) is what their earthly representatives call the Soul Phone. This technology, the first stage of four that already exist, allows us to talk to people on what we call "the other side."

We can literally communicate with deceased loved ones, with important historical figures, with departed geniuses such as Jobs and Tesla who, quite frankly, still have great ideas to dispense.

Imagine dialing up J.C. and asking him what he really meant when he said, "All these things you can do and even greater"? Or Plato? What did he mean by, "Death is not the worst thing that can happen to man"?

With speaker phones, we might be able to once again hear Amy Winehouse perform "Back to Black." Or Jim Morrison's "People are Strange."

I know this sounds far-fetched, but keep in mind that until 1903, people ridiculed the Wright Brothers for believing humans could fly. For that matter, imagine telling a pioneer in a covered wagon that someday, their seven-month journey across the U.S. continent could be undertaken in less than five hours. It's coming, my friends, and it will change everything.

NO LONGER DRIVING (OR ANYTHING ELSE) UNDER THE INFLUENCE

No one can make you unhappy.
Your imagination alone does that.

— MOOJI

I am not a body. I am free.
For I am still as the Dude created me.

Within each human being is a deep well of joy and glory. The reason this is such surprising news is because we're all driving (and walking and living) under the influence of the asshole in our consciousness.

"How could you?" we reprimand ourselves anytime we eat something we shouldn't, anytime we score less than perfect 10s on job evaluations, anytime we have a "bad hair day."

We're downright mean to ourselves. We go to war with those parts of ourselves we deem as bad—the jiggly upper arms, the desire to dance in church, the pull we feel to skip work and write—and only end up crippling humanity as a whole.

The answers, we're taught, are:

Control. Discipline. Protection.

But willpower only separates us from our true nature, creates static that keeps us from recognizing that we are part of something thrilling and unfathomable that may never have happened before in the entire galaxy and may never happen again.

The Course takes it even further, claiming that unceasing (yes, 100 percent) joy is my birthright.

It reminds me that everything I see, everything I believe, is just a story I made up. It tells me that, in Truth, I am spirit. I am light. All those voices, those wars going on in my head, are nothing but chunks of the collective consciousness that I can either believe and defend against or transmute with gratitude.

The real me, the Course tells me, is kind, giving, in deep communion with all of creation. The real me is a true force for love.

WELCOME
TO NIRVANA!

Or Part II

We don't need to know. We just need to dance and sing.

— DEVA PREMAL

The lessons that remain are short, a sort of welcome mat for the realm of inner stillness that we enter into each day. Because so many of them use the G word (and because so many of us still regard G as a critical douchebag with a killer surveillance system), a large percentage of these final lessons rank as RSOs.

Don't get hung up on words or how much time is needed.

Spend as long as makes you happy. No rules, no bylaws, no judging.

Each lesson has a central message. Administer as needed. Say you forget that glory and perfect joy are your inheritance. Or you mistakenly respond to an illusion with judgment, not love.

Simply stop. Be still. Let love wash over you.

PATH TO TRANSCENDENCE

An awake heart is like a sky that pours light.

— H A F I Z

A Course in Miracles says once we take sorrow off the throne, enlightenment is our naturally occurring, organic state of being.

It says we've become so accustomed to living in the "life sucks" paradigm that it never occurs to us that another reality, a happy reality, is possible. Pain, loneliness, and fear are the context within which we live our lives. We're so conditioned to wallow in misery that the concept of life as a joyous adventure seems impossible or even unnatural. Sure, we can buy that there will be happy events. In fact, we look forward to holidays and birthdays and time off work. But to believe that happiness is possible 24/7 is a big stretch.

In Lesson 221 (Let all my thoughts be still), I recognize that happiness and everything I seek is already within me. Within every person, within every situation. There are no exceptions to this rule.

I FEEL IT IN MY FINGERS.
I FEEL IT IN MY TOES.

It is natural for you to play, to skip, to dance . . .
anything else is resistance.

— ABRAHAM-HICKS

The judging mind has a limited, yet consistent repertoire.

It goes something like this:

This is wrong.
That bozo sucks.
I better do something. And fast.

Lesson 222 (I live and move in love) reminds me that's all bullsh*t. Love is my reality. It's in the air I breathe, the food I eat, the water that renews and cleanses me.

And when I finally rest long enough to notice, I'm floored. The Divine is so conspicuous. And I can't help but wonder, "How could I have missed it, this presence that permeates all things?"

SPOILER ALERT!
THERE'S JUST ONE PROBLEM

*We either make ourselves miserable or we make
ourselves happy. The amount of work is the same.*

— CARLOS CASTANEDA

Lesson 223 (What was I thinking?) tells me the only problem I could
ever have is seeing myself differently from how the Dude sees me. The
Dude sees me as perfect, funny, loving, gorgeous, free of all problems.

P.S. It also sees everyone else that way.

A CASE OF MISTAKEN IDENTITY

I can't just sit here vibrating with my own joy—
I have to write about it, I have to share it.

— D A V I D   M A S O N

A tribe I visited in Namibia gathers for a special ritual when a mom-to-be is seven months pregnant.

They dance, they sing, and most importantly, they consciously ask the about-to-be-born baby what his or her purpose is for this human lifetime.

Each tribe member then takes a vow to honor it. They genuinely want to know and support each of their brother's highest spiritual purpose.

Imagine how different our lives would be if we'd been asked about our true identity, our spiritual purpose before we were born?

Lesson 224 (My true identity is so glorious that Heaven looks to me for light) instructs me to abandon the cookie-cutter lifestyle.

So I enlist the Holy S to "Reveal what you would have me do instead."

PUSH THE
DAMNED BUTTON

Life is not what it seems. It is so much better.

— MEREDITH YOUNG-SOWERS

So I have this car. It's a Prius. Dead-frog green, as Taz nicknamed its hue.

Among the many things I ADORE about my car is that it has a button slightly larger than a quarter. I push it and voila! the engine roars to life. I move a little lever and, like a faithful chariot, it takes me wherever I want to go.

I have absolutely NO IDEA how that happens. I've heard there are things like transmissions, axles, motors, but like Alicia Silverstone's movie, I'm completely and utterly clueless.

And that's okay with me.

It's also my position on these daily lessons. I notice my little pea brain wanting to understand how the transformation works. I want to ask, but why? But how? What exactly does it mean to live and move in Beingness?

I'm still not exactly sure. All I know is that once I started pushing the button (finding the stillness promised in Lesson 225), my life started moving forward. I quit breaking down on the side of the road. I stopped running out of gas.

I'm abundantly grateful I don't have to read every little detail of the manual or understand a drive train. Or really do anything but push the damn button. I love that it's not up to me.

A GLORIOUS NEW WORLD: A LESSON IN FOCUS

Today is your day to sing wild songs of adventure,
to soar your spirit and unfurl your joy.

— JONATHAN LOCKWOOD HUIE

My daughter and I had an unspoken policy whenever we shopped. If we got separated, she always knew she could find me in the bargain section, rifling through sales racks.

Lesson 226 (My home awaits. I hasten there) says there is no value in returning to the sales rack. Why would I want to rinse and repeat the day before? Why hit the alarm clock with the same old finger, trudge to the bathroom with the same old weary shuffle, look at myself in the mirror with the same old worn-out expectations?

Today, I forego the outdated sales racks. I give up my puny goals. I claim the imaginative, free world that's cued up, waiting patiently for me to quit throwing darts at my life.

As poet John O'Donohue once wrote, "You never know what will land on the shoreline of tomorrow."

PLASTERING OVER TRUTH

There's an improv group in my brain.
And it's way too edgy for my own good.

— APARNA NANCHERLA

Lesson 227 (I'm clad forever in holiness) proclaims my freedom. It says that edgy improv group in my brain doesn't really exist. It's an illusion that doesn't affect reality in any way.

It's a hard pill to swallow that it was me that made this mess called material reality. But as renowned physicist Brian Greene likes to say, "Once you look closely at the building blocks of the universe, you find they're dicey at best."

The exciting thing about this truth (that it's me, not some random misogynist named God) is that another way IS possible.

Today, I claim my holy release.

228

BEFORE WE CONFORMED

You must unlearn what you have learned.

— YODA

My well-intentioned parents taught me manners, sent me to school, urged me to follow certain "rules" and "constraints."

Luckily, the essence of who I am is so vast, so all-encompassing that, when I'm quiet, when I practice my daily lessons, it can't help but seep out.

Lesson 228 asks me to forego my "training" and return vastness to the center stage.

LOVERS GONNA LOVE

There are people waiting for someone just like us
to come along. Someone who will live a happier life merely
because we took the time to share what we had to give.

— LEO BUSCAGLIA

You can't make a giraffe sing an aria. You can't teach a goat to do the cha-cha. And you can't really be happy in this life without being true to who you are.

Lesson 229 (Love, which created me, is what I am) says it doesn't matter if you're a plumber, a sign painter, a candlestick maker, your true, behind-the-scenes identity is love.

We were made by love and we're here to love. Any other choice makes us miserable.

TWO THUMBS UP

All is one. The sun, stars, rain, you, me, everything. All one."

— ROGER EBERT

Famous movie pundit Roger Ebert never copped to believing in God. He spent hours and hours in churches all over the world, not to pray, but to gently nudge his thoughts toward wonder and awe.

Before he died of cancer on April 4, 2013, he wrote a note to his wife about visiting another realm. At first, she thought he was hallucinating, maybe suffering from too many meds. But he was adamant. Life, as we know it, "is all an elaborate hoax," he told her.

He described a vastness beyond imagination, a place where past, present, and future all happened at once.

Lesson 230 tells me Ebert's vision isn't "fake news," but the absolute truth beyond my meaningless imaginings.

THE MAN WITH THE SPIDER TATTOO

Really? Fated? Maybe you have some choice here.

— JERRY COLONNA

It's not every day you meet a wealthy venture capitalist with a giant spider tattoo emblazoned across his heart. Jerry Colonna, who now runs the executive coaching firm Reboot, says the tattoo reminds him of the truth we're promised in Lesson 231.

We are safe. We are loved. There is nothing to fear.

Colonna, who got the tattoo on his 45th birthday, described himself as a "freaking wreck" when he signed up for the Jungian retreat where he met Spider, the spirit guide who helps keep his fear in check.

During the retreat, while examining the beliefs that formed his worldview, he had a weird dream about mushrooms growing in the basement of his house. The retreat leader ordered him: "Go, leave the circle right now. Go into the forest and find those mushrooms. Ask them what you were too afraid to hear."

"I'm like, 'What the f*ck am I doing? I'm wandering around a forest trying to have conversation with mushrooms?'" he says. "All of a sudden I see the exact same white, long, stringy mushrooms. And I'm freaked out. I drop to my knees, and I start crying. I'm so sorry. What are you here to teach me?

"The mushrooms say to me, 'You're too afraid. Go into the forest and find your place.'"

So he spots an indentation in the forest, sits down and weeps. When he looks up, he notices a gorgeous spiderweb with dewdrops glistening like crystals.

He looks at the garden spider spinning the web and says, "Okay, I give up. What the f*ck are you here to teach me?"

And the spider says to him, "You worry too much. Your children are going to be fine. Everything is going to be fine."

In short, the message of Lesson 231.

INTERRUPTING MY MIND WITH THIS IMPORTANT WEATHER ALERT

All that I ever hope to say is that I love the world.

— E. B. WHITE

Sea otters, when they sleep, hold hands. It keeps them from drifting apart, getting lost, losing their tribe.

That's how I envision us Course students, doing these lessons together. We're all here holding hands until we wake back up and realize we could never drift apart or get lost or lose anything.

The only reason we think we've drifted or that we're lost is because of our grievances.

Lesson 232 (Be in my mind, Yo Dude!, throughout the day) is yet another attempt to "go toward the light."

Our brilliance, our unending luminosity is temporarily obscured by our complaints, our loudmouth thoughts that like to pretend something is wrong.

Today, I'm encouraged to release my mind's regular programming and rejoice in a higher truth.

And every time the old programming tries to run its commercial message ("something's missing," "you're not okay," "gotta strive harder"), I'm just going to lay back, relax, and grab my fellow otters' hands.

SPIRITUAL LESSONS FROM NETFLIX

The only thing you really want from life is to feel
enthusiasm, joy and love. If you can feel that all the time,
then who cares what happens outside?

— MICHAEL SINGER

If you have Netflix, you'll notice a category called "Because you watched . . ." that lists all the movies or TV shows or documentaries that fall into the same genre. Netflix assumes you'd appreciate these offerings because well, they're quite similar to options you chose earlier.

Likewise, Amazon recommends books and products that are related to items you've bought and even viewed in the past.

This is exactly how the universe works. It continuously sends people, ideas, and events that mirror the frequency you emit, the channel you've chosen to speak for your life.

It doesn't charge for these gifts that match what you've previously selected. But it also doesn't discriminate. It doesn't judge or doubt that what you've chosen in the past is what you still want. It doesn't think, "Well, her parents and her culture obviously had it wrong, so I'm going to send her different kinds of stuff."

No. It sends an exact match.

Lesson 233 asks me to subscribe to the Dude's watch list. To let Its wisdom pick the features in my life. Its lineup provides a day of countless gifts and mercies.

THE CLIFFSNOTES
IN MY BRAIN

Thinking the physical world is all that matters is like shutting oneself up in a small closet and imagining there is nothing beyond it.

— EBEN ALEXANDER

One of the great joys in my life is knowing the universe is bigger than anything I can conceive, knowing miracles (or what we call miracles) reside right on the other side of the veil.

My brain, a veritable network of millions of neural pathways, imposes a tremendous barrier to Truth. It takes all available input and boils it down to what I call "CliffsNotes for Dummies."

Sadly, my CliffsNotes are restricted to what I've picked up from my culture, my family upbringing, and the six o'clock news.

As Lesson 234 reminds me, I would be astounded at the limits my brain has placed on Reality. From now on, I officially appoint my brain as secretary of my neurology and digestive system and leave the rest to Source, to Truth, to the Reality of Pure Bliss.

I'D LIKE TO THANK MY MOTHER, MY SECOND-GRADE TEACHER, MY . . .

*The world you see is a stage you have constructed
with your thoughts, and everyone you meet is an
actor you have hired to play out your script.*

— ALAN COHEN

Black Panther cost its creators a staggering $200 million, not bad when you consider the futuristic African nation, its spaceships and skyscrapers had to be generated out of thin air.

Since I'm not getting paid to create drama out of thin air, I'm going to give myself an Academy Award for the incredible "drama" I've created thus far in my life.

In a world that brims with beauty and plenitude, I deserve an Academy Award for the convincing "story" of lack and struggle I sometimes create.

The special effects I've employed to overlook the world's unending largesse are truly mind-bending.

Today, I take a bow and ask myself, "If I've been this successful at creating separation and pain, what else can I create if I begin focusing on love and infinite possibilities?

WHO RULES THE KINGDOM OF YOUR MIND?

Rule your mind or it will rule you.

— HORACE

Deranged people circle the kingdom walls shouting, "The sky is falling." Town criers preach despair. An airplane flies overhead with a banner: "Danger, danger. Take cover."

But there's also a dot, dot, AND. There's also a bigger story going on.

Lesson 236 (I rule my mind, which I alone must rule) says I'm the one in charge.

Letting my mind's kingdom fall prey to anguish is a scary rabbit hole. For me, it's an indefensible way to live.

Which is why in the kingdom of my mind, I frequently pose this question: "AND what else is true?"

When the drums of distress start reverberating throughout the kingdom, it's time—for me at least—to get up, look around, and see what else is happening.

Listening for the beat of love beneath the dominant melody enables me to rule the precious kingdom of my mind.

EL DIO AMOR

I cannot quite embrace the gods of antiquity. Gods so petty as to feel threatened by human hubris, destroy Babel, chain Prometheus to a rock, etc. Nah. Look around: there are French cheese and wine, Mozart and Bossa Nova, love and sunsets . . . all ours for the taking. Surely, He/She/It loves us some.

— VIVIAN ALLVIN

My daughter Taz was fluent in Spanish, a skill she acquired through classes and lots of practice.

When she walked into her first Spanish class, she was given a new name (Luisa, I think it was) and a new temporary identity.

Every good language teacher knows the power in leaving behind the old name, the old identity, the old learned habits. The "new person" has access to more possibilities, making it easier to learn the new language.

Today, instead of clinging to my old identity, I take Lesson 237 to heart. I arise in glory and allow the light in me to shine upon the world throughout the day.

AN ARIA TO POSSIBILITY

Spiritual practice is just training our minds towards reverence,
like moving a potted plant to a sunny spot by the window.

— LANA MAREE

If an opera diva can break a glass with her voice, it's pretty obvious that the words we speak about our lives carry a vibration that shapes our future. Who needs a tarot card reader?

Back in the day, I used to call my friends and moan: "Woe is me! I am depressed."

Now I prefer a) not to call my friends to blather on about something undesirable, and b) if I need to mention it, I say something like "My thought-maker is temporarily malfunctioning."

As neuroscientist Alex Korb says, "If you break your arm, you don't tell people, 'I am broken.'" Why would I need to say, "I am depressed" when my thought-maker (i.e., my squirrely brain) is just doing what squirrely brains do: running thoughts?

It certainly doesn't mean that's who I am.

I can use my "I am" to argue my limitations or I can use it to speak Truth: I am free, I am blessed, I am joyful.

THE BRATTY VOICE INSIDE MY HEAD

People who judge you are just not your people.

— CONSTANCE WU

My brain is a magnificent instrument. It keeps track of where I left my keys, remembers that 3 times 9 is 27, and files away lessons on how to drive.

But it often acts as my number-one nemesis.

It chatters incessantly. It categorizes, compares, labels, judges, and defines. It gets its jollies perpetuating the idea that life is a problem to be solved.

When the heart over-functions, we get dizzy, light-headed, and develop heart disease. When cells over-function, we get cancer.

When our brains over-function, we become slaves to a ridiculous little asshat in our heads that lies through its teeth.

That's why, whenever I can, I separate myself from the voice. I observe it, notice it's back on the treadmill, spinning its fearful little stories.

And I smile.

RECALCULATING

Fear is a darkroom where negatives develop.

— USMAN B. ASIF

Lesson 240 (Fear is not justified in any form) needs no paraphrasing.

Fear is deception. Its only job is to prove I am something I could never be. It attests to a world that doesn't exist.

This lesson doesn't equivocate. Not one thing in this world is true. No matter what the form. It was created to attest to an illusion.

Let me not be deceived today! There is no fear in me, for I am part of Love Itself.

NONSTOP CELEBRATION

Life is short, wear your party pants.

— LORETTA LAROCHE

In 2012, on a pre-baby trip to the Serengeti, Kristen Bell and Dax Shepard decided to make a YouTube video of their African adventure. The music? What else but Toto's immortal tune "Africa."

After driving five hours to see the annual wildebeest migration, they jumped out of their rental car and commenced dancing. They got so carried away that they failed to notice the African game rangers who didn't see the humor in clowning around with a million wildebeest. The game rangers wasted no time slapping the American actors with a $50 fine.

The video is loads of fun—Dax in a tux, Kristen flitting along the Serengeti plains. And personally, I can think of few better uses for $50.

The ego (AKA the dominant paradigm) encourages us to view the success of others with envy. It tells us Dax and Kristen got to dance with wildebeests and we didn't. It tells us Richard Branson gets to own an island and we don't. It tells us James Cameron is a talented film-maker and we're not.

But it's a classic case of separation.

In Spirit, any good that happens anywhere is also mine to enjoy.

So I can promulgate the malicious rumor of separation (green-eyed monsters are a sure sign the ego has me by the neck) or I can take it from Lesson 241. Today is a special day of celebration. My good fortune and everyone else's.

PRIORITIES

I will never again cast a curse on myself.

— ROB BREZSNY

Time to get out and celebrate. Time to remember how lucky you are, time to give praise to the highest of holies. As Rob Brezney likes to say, "Let's break open the forbidden happiness."

Sure, I have a to-do list. In fact, I have two of them.

On mine:
Dream up better questions.
Have the best day of my life.

The other to-do list is for Source, God, the Field of Potentiality.

Here's what it says:
Handle everything else.

HOUSTON, THERE IS NO PROBLEM

A blazing fire makes flame and brightness
out of everything that is thrown into it.

— MARCUS AURELIUS

Amor fati! This two-word Latin phrase helps me cope with last year's massive rip in my understanding of the universe.

Losing your only child is brutal terrain. I'm often tormented with overwhelming emotions. Some days I stay in bed long after the sun rises. I occasionally question whether life is still worth living. Tough to admit as the writer who regularly blogged about being the luckiest person on the planet.

So if I'm going to love my fate no matter what, as amor fati means, I have no choice but to rely on the Course promises that a) This body, this material world is a mental construct, b) The only problem I could ever have is one of perception, and c) I have the power to control my thoughts.

I draw strength from Victor Frankl, who found meaning even though the rest of his family perished during the Holocaust. I remind myself that I got to spend 25 years with this incredible being of light and love. I was a 37-year-old singleton with no real prospects in sight when she chose to hang out with me. Literally, she was a life-changing gift— the most amazing, the most compassionate, the wisest person I ever met.

And I turn it over to the Holy S, who reminds me:

1. If it's not wholly joyous, it's not God's will.

2. If it's not wholly joyous, it involves some decision I erroneously made.

3. Because it was me who made the less than joyous decision (see #1) and because this decision was never forced on me (see #1), I can change it at any time.

4. I just have to go back to the point where I made the erroneous decision and ask the Holy S to decide instead. I repeat. I don't have to fix anything.

5. Over and over, It assures me that Taz now belongs to the infinite. And that someday soon I will, too.

"You'll spend eternity with Taz," it says. "In fact, you're in eternity with her now once you change your perception."

CLAIMING JOY AND EASE

*As characters in the universe game, we are
no more our bodies than we are red and black checkers
on a game board. Bodies are merely a means of interacting
with a probability database—the quantum field.*

— ALEXANDER MARCHAND

For three decades, I've enjoyed a pretty sweet gig as a travel writer. I get paid to jet off to really cool places, to do things I'd probably never get to do on my own.

Lesson 244 (I am in danger nowhere in the world) often comes in handy.

Two days before I was scheduled to leave for an assignment in Turkey, the State Department issued a travel advisory. I pay no attention to such things, but several worried friends emailed me the alert. One of the other journalists backed out.

So I had a choice. I could believe the ego's messaging (danger ahead!) or I could focus on today's lesson.

I am forever grateful that I chose to claim safety and ease. Not only did I visit ancient archaeological sites, tea plantations, and remote mountain villages, but I stayed in the same sultan's palace where Madonna and her 25-year-old boy toy stayed during her infamous flash-the-crowd concert.

Turkey also displayed another potent metaphysical truth: "To give and receive are one in Truth." Everywhere we went, Turkish families invited us into their homes, fed us the most stupendous meals (Turkish cuisine is beyond spectacular), and honored us as treasured guests. I have never felt more loved, more secure, or more sure that people everywhere are infinitely beautiful, kind, and filled with love. There is no better way to learn about abundance than to give it away.

DON'T CONFUSE A TEMPORARY PROBLEM WITH ETERNAL TRUTH

Worrying is like praying for something you don't want to happen.
— ROBERT DOWNEY, JR.

A month ago, I banged my shin into a coffee table. It hurt. It bled. It made an embarrassingly huge scab. I couldn't wear skirts, shorts, or dresses without people asking, "What happened?" So I wore pants. It was easier than explaining how I accidentally injured myself in my own living room.

I'm happy to report that today, there's absolutely no sign of this unsightly wound. My shin, with no effort on my part, healed itself on its own. My body was able to completely restore this temporary boo-boo without my participation.

The three key words in that sentence are "without my participation." All problems are temporary. They will heal themselves on their own . . .

Unless I decide to participate, to throw myself into action. Here's how that works. I recite the problem to my loved ones, usually embellishing it to sound even more ferocious than it actually is.

I start worrying, using my powerful consciousness to add energy to something I don't even want. I Google, check out books at the library, even join a support group.

Most people applaud my efforts, hold up big 10s for my hard work, my commitment to eliminate my problem.

But what those judges don't realize is my active participation clogs up the healing force of the universe. It literally builds a wall, adds material heft to the thing I am working to dislodge.

Today, I remember my shin, how it fixed itself. And I will repeat Lesson 245: Peace is with me. I am Safe.

WHY THE F-WORD
AND I ROLL DEEP

No man could look upon another as his enemy,
unless he first became his own enemy.

— MAHATMA GANDHI

Most of us think forgiveness is an act we're forced to perform when horrific jerks do us wrong.

Forgiveness is realizing that no one HAS the power to do me wrong. To believe someone or something outside myself can hurt me is what started all the problems in the first place. It negates the Truth of who I am.

Being pissed off unplugs me from the FP, this wild and crazy force that's constantly trying to bless me. It erects a big wall between me and my highest good.

Believing outside forces can hurt me stunts my growth. Blinds me to all the miracles. Creates an illusory world that makes me want to hide, feel guilty, close down.

Each of us is here to strengthen the life force—in ourselves and in each other. If we point fingers and believe something outside ourselves can hurt us, we put the squeeze on this unbelievably cool and ever-present life force.

Lesson 246 reminds me of the real reason I want to forgive. Because I want to be happy.

Forgiving, it says, removes strain and fatigue. It takes away fear, guilt, and pain. It makes me invulnerable. But I'm down with forgiveness because it brings me joy.

ONE THOUGHT AT A TIME

I encourage everybody to open their ears and their eyes and especially their minds, wide.

— CHRISTOPH WALTZ

Christoph Waltz won the Oscar, the Golden Globe, and the BAFTA for his portrayal of King Schultz, a dentist turned bounty hunter in *Django Unchained.*

During pre-production, however, he was bucked off a horse and sent to the hospital with a dislocated pelvis.

Some people might have thrown in the towel. But not Waltz, who claimed total responsibility.

"I hadn't ridden a horse for 40 years. It's a skill like playing an instrument. You have to do it every day," he said.

And that's the perfect description of how we ACIM students "change our minds and therefore change our world."

Here's my daily practice:

Instead of focusing on "what I see," I focus on "what I want." Over and over and over again. Yes, I get bucked off the horse. Yes, I hit the ground of apparent problems, dislocate the pelvis of limitations.

So I just keep getting back up in the saddle, directing my mind to focus on what I know to be Truth.

NO LONGER SUBJECT TO
THE RUMORS OF MY MIND

Emancipate yourself from mental slavery.

— BOB MARLEY

Whew! So relieved Lesson 248 didn't come up ten months ago. To suggest tragedy, chaos, and unhappiness are nothing but a ridiculous rumor doesn't typically sit well.

Polite company tends to be heavily invested in the inevitability of sorrows and trials.

Even making a joke about suffering not being a standard part of the human condition can get a gal burned at the stake.

So I'm hoping that now—after 10 months of thumbing our noses at illusions—we can finally just come out and say it. Life doesn't have to suck.

The only reason we think it does is because that's the reality cemented into our consciousness by years and decades and centuries of conditioning.

Even death is a false idea to strike from the record books.

To believe there's no way to escape suffering and pain and lack is to disown the truth.

This lesson asks us to disown falsity, to disown all the inevitable sorrows to which we've been so faithful.

NELSON MANDELA: POSTER CHILD FOR *A COURSE IN MIRACLES*

Man's goodness is a flame that can be hidden but never extinguished.

— NELSON, MY HERO, MANDELA

A few years ago, when visiting Robben Island, I bought a replica of Nelson Mandela's prison bracelet. Engraved with 46664, the number he was assigned during his 27 years of prison, this bracelet that I wear nearly every day reminds me that no matter how it looks on the outside, there is always a greater story going on.

I think of South Africa often when I get discouraged that things never change. Or wonder what I, one person from Kansas, can do to affect that change.

It wasn't that long ago that ending apartheid in South Africa seemed impossible, much like it seems impossible to fix all the rifts on our planet today.

But during my lifetime, it went from impossible to possible. Almost overnight.

Nelson Mandela probably didn't own the big blue doorstop (reading material at Robben Island was verboten), but he understood Lesson 249: Forgiveness ends all suffering and loss.

He intuitively knew that if he spent his time in prison letting his anger fester, he would turn bitter and cold. That's why he befriended his white prison guards, showed kindness to those who mistreated him.

He recognized the white guards were just as enslaved by the system as he was. And when he was finally released after 27 years of hard labor, he launched a forgiveness tribunal. He invited the very guards who abused him to his inauguration.

Mandela's shining example reminds us that forgiveness changes everything. It also reminds us to never give up, never lose your sense of humor, and never forget to dance.

A PLACE OF JOY, ABUNDANCE, CHARITY, AND ENDLESS GIVING

It is with your thoughts, then, that we must work,
if your perception of the world is to be changed.

—A COURSE IN MIRACLES

Depending on who you talk to, Tinder is:

a) The world's most popular dating app

b) An uber-easy scheme for hooking up

c) A surefire recipe for rejection

Tinder is an app for viewing pictures of available humanoids. If you like the way they look, you swipe right. If not, you swipe left. I've worked harder putting on eyeliner.

Either way, the direction you swipe is 100 percent up to you.

Like Tinder, *A Course in Miracles* tells me I get to choose which feelings and thoughts to hook up with. I decide whether to embrace or reject the circumstances of my life. Why would any idiot swipe left?

Lesson 250 encourages me to swipe right, to pick pictures that make me happy, pictures I'd actually like to "date."

THE ONE WHO
WILL CATCH ME

Let me fall if I must fall. The one I am becoming will catch me.

— BAAL SHEM TOV

In 1977, comedian Garry Shandling was in a car accident that left him in critical condition. He was hospitalized for two weeks with a ruptured spleen. In what's often called an NDE (near-death experience), he recalls a voice giving him a very clear choice: "Do you want to stay and continue being Garry Shandling?"

Lately, I've been asking myself a similar question. Thankfully, mine doesn't involve wrecks or death or crushed spleens, but I've been wondering what I want to do with this collection of molecules named Pam Grout.

The current arrangement seems rather static, wooden, even a bit boring. My thoughts are restless, ready for a change.

At the same time, as I observe my thoughts and notice there is disappointment, sadness, lack of clarity, I also know there is a bigger part of me woven into the despair. This other part is much wiser, much more loving. It's working behind the scenes with this message: "Relax. I got this. Just fall into my arms."

That's what Lesson 251 (I am in need of nothing but the truth) offers. I have everything I need. I have everything I want. All that I denied myself is restored.

All I have to do is rest in the loving arms of "the one I am becoming" who is already here, probably with a big net, ready to catch me.

SEVENTY-SIX TROMBONES IN THE THOUGHT PARADE

The mind places footnotes and second thoughts and qualifications where once there was simply radiance.

— PICO IYER

Words, language, and thoughts are my stock in trade. To admit they're mostly irrelevant might just put me out of a job.

Lesson 252 calls them burning impulses which move the world. It reminds me that words and thoughts are pawns of the ego, deliberately used to muck up the radiance.

Today, I want the radiance, the limitless love.

I remind myself every hour that my thoughts are electrical impulses. No need to underline them with yellow highlighter. No need to endlessly wallow, examine, or take them seriously.

Today, I watch my parade of thoughts from the sidelines, recognizing they're only electrical impulses, and I wave fondly as they march on by.

TWEAK AND YE SHALL FIND

When you act out of love, good things happen.

— MICAH TRUE, EL CABALLO BLANCO

When I ask "can" and "will" questions ("Can I make more money?" or "Will I find my soulmate?") my mind relies on old lessons from the past. It leafs through my catalog of beliefs and concludes, "Probably not. Doesn't look promising."

Anytime I access reality with the question, "Can I do something?" I consult with an old reality. I access old beliefs that my ego has long told me are facts: "Human beings are only capable of A, B, and C."

Lesson 253 says banish the old ABCs with the new H-O-W? Simply add these three letters to your question.

"How can I make more money this year?" and "How will I find my soulmate?" are vastly different questions that produce vastly different results. When we add H-O-W, we enlist the aid of the Holy S, who is more than happy to show us.

Its specialty is bypassing absolutes, snubbing its nose at that damned asshat who pretends to know everything.

H-O-W allows me to be still and open to a spanking-new possibility.

BACK AWAY FROM
THE DIALS, MA'AM

The only true wisdom is in knowing you know nothing.

— SOCRATES

Lesson 254 basically gives me four words that, when practiced diligently, propel me into a whole different reality.

"I need do nothing."

Yes, it says nothing. Zero. Nil. Jack squat. Zilch.

When I start hatching schemes and composing plans, all of which are laughably limited and focused on self-preservation, survival, and looking good, I get in my own way.

The Dude always has a much broader, more loving perspective.

I'm not saying I never make intentions. I just know my limited brain has a very tiny vantage point. And that until I see through the Dude's eyes, it's probably best to keep my opinion to myself.

255

I'M GONNA MAKE HIM AN OFFER HE CAN'T REFUSE

Disbelief in magic can force a poor soul into believing in government and business.

— TOM ROBBINS

The above line, uttered by Don Vito Corleone in *The Godfather,* is what's known as a Hobson's choice. It might look like a choice, but there's really only one option.

The phrase originated in the 16th century with Thomas Hobson, a stable owner in Cambridge, England. While the enterprising livery owner had 40 horses, his customers were given one choice—the horse nearest the stable door.

Today, I'm offered just such a Hobson's choice: perfect peace, as Lesson 255 offers, is the horse by the stable door. It's the only choice being offered. I can gaze at all the other horses (the kids overslept, the sink is clogged, there's an accident on the freeway), but the only item on the universal menu is perfect peace.

So sure, I can opt for the illusory severed horse head. I can pretend the other horses are more important. Or I can decide now to surrender to ultimate reality: I have no cares and I remain forever in the peace of heaven.

As Henry Ford liked to say about his Model T, "You can have any color you like. As long as it's black."

SCOOP UP THE NEW DAY

*Participate relentlessly in the manifestation
of your own blessings.*

— ELIZABETH GILBERT

"Hozho" is said to be the most important word in the Navajo language. When you live "in hozho," you're in alignment—with your Creator, with your brothers, with the betterment of the whole world. That, says Lesson 256, is my only goal today.

In hozho, I'm not trying to triumph over my enemies (I recognize there ARE no enemies), and I'm not actively seeking anything (I know I already have everything).

Franciscan priest Richard Rohr spent a summer taking a census of four communities in New Mexico's Acoma Pueblo. Because it was hot and sticky, he'd jump in his orange pickup and, at sunrise, watch as mothers stood outside the doors of their homes with their children. They'd reach up with both hands to scoop up the new day, pouring its blessings over their heads and bodies.

So today, as we seek to live in hozho, read this Navajo prayer aloud:

> In beauty I walk
> With beauty before me I walk
> With beauty behind me I walk
> With beauty above me I walk
> With beauty around me I walk
> It has become beauty again
> It has become beauty again

TODAY I COUNTERACT THE OPERATIVE IN MY MIND WITH FORGIVENESS

Why should James Bond have all the action,
fun, money, and resort hotel living.

— PAUL KYRIAZ

My ego (that whiny voice that likes to inform me that so-and-so "done me wrong," that this circumstance is a huge problem) is a double agent. It pretends to know everything. *But he really did call you a skunk. You really DO have a good excuse.*

It pretends to be my friend. It pretends to work on my behalf. Unfortunately, it lies through its teeth. It has no allegiance to the higher cause. It's employed by the patriarchy, loyal to the cultural consensus that people are not to be trusted, that lack and limitation is the state of the world, and that fear is the only emotion worth cultivating.

This pernicious double agent ego infiltrated my mind sometime before I was five. It transmitted disinformation, told me I was different from other people, that I was both better (sometimes it whispers that fictitious story) and/or worse (another popular tactic) than everybody else.

It gained my trust by scaring me, showing me its deceptive surveillance of the wretched and the ugly. This double-crossing mole told me that life is hard, that abundance was for other people.

Today, I have but one goal. To stand with and for Truth. Lesson 257 promises me peace. And any operative that presents conflicting counterintelligence, I will immediately report to the authorities (the Holy Spirit) to handle as it sees fit.

TODAY WOULD BE A REALLY GOOD DAY TO FORGIVE SOMEONE

In the end, only lovers seem to know what is going on inside of God. To all others, God remains an impossible and distant secret, just like the galaxies.

— RICHARD ROHR

The F word. You can't really practice the Course without bumping into it. It's like brushing your teeth, taking a shower, ingesting a multiple vitamin. It's an ongoing daily prescription.

Although the F word is widely misunderstood, there's just one thing to keep in mind. It's like Reykjavik in the game *Trivial Pursuit*. Only instead of being the answer to every seventh question, something I noticed about Reykjavik back in 1979 when the popular board game first came out, the F word covers literally everything.

Here's a partial list of the many uses for forgiveness, the Swiss Army knife of spiritual practices:

Need physical healing? Try forgiveness.
Desire a better relationship? Employ forgiveness.
Wanna manifest your dreams? You got it. Use forgiveness.

WHO'S STILL SITTING ON YOUR LAP?

Getting over a painful experience is much like crossing the monkey bars. You have to let go at some point to move forward.

— C. S. LEWIS

Marvel Comics' Kitty Pryde walks through walls. I walk through X-ray machines, every time I board a plane. TSA, I'm told, is looking for such contraband as scissors, cigarette lighters, pool cues, and, of course, guns and bombs.

By scanning our carry-on bags, airport security intends to avert all potential threats to our safety and well-being.

I'd like to invent a compulsory X-ray machine that detects all the grudges, resentments, and other stories we humans carry, not only on to airplanes, but into all areas of our life. For most of us, there's a whole crowd of people still sitting on our laps, riding shotgun on our backs, and clinging to our legs like dead weight.

That old boyfriend who cheated on you in high school? That boss who failed to notice all your hard work? Although neither has made a physical appearance in more than 20 years, they're still an oppressing presence in your energetic frequency.

Quite frankly, those invisible energetic connections are more dangerous than any shoe bomb.

You can cut off all ties. Refuse to ever see that dirty rotten person again. But as long as you hold fast to any belief, any story that this "villain" performed some sinister deed, they own you.

They thwart your superpower. They intercept all the blessings and miracles that the universe wants to bestow.

Lesson 259 asks me to remember none of it is true.

Instead of being "insane" today, I remember love is my superpower. Love that rearranges molecules. Love that alters reality. Love for all people. Love for all rocks, minerals, and vegetables. Love for every blessed thing.

Today, I surrender every story, every belief, every "bad guy" that hinders my superpower. In doing so, I recognize all those bogeymen never really existed at all.

ARE YOU PICKING UP WHAT SOURCE IS LAYING DOWN?

Don't be a garbage can for anything that does not feed your intellect, stimulate your imagination, or make you a more compassionate peaceful person. Refuse to open your mind to other people's trash.

— LES BROWN

Before he married Gladys Knight or became an Ohio congressman or started teaching people to follow their dream, Les Brown was a student of Johnnie Colemon, an amazing New Thought minister from Chicago. After graduating from her Johnnie Colemon Institute, he agreed to recruit participants for her Universal Foundation for Better Living. He came into her office one day with his head down.

"I just don't understand," he said. "I've been working my butt off. And I've only been able to sign up seven people."

Johnnie took one look at him and said, "Les, that's because you've only got seven-people consciousness."

Source consciousness is infinite. There is literally no limit to its generosity.

It shows up in my life depending on how much I pick up what it's laying down. I can pick up "seven-people consciousness." Or I can be like high-energy motivational speaker Les Brown, who, like Lesson 260 promises, threw that ridiculous limit aside and took up instead with his true Divine identity.

THE CELEBRATION COURSING THROUGH YOUR BODY

You are defined by how great your thoughts are.

— HENRY WINKLER

When Henry Winkler was 72, he finally won an Emmy.

That was 65 years after he began imagining himself as an actor.

When the imagining began, he was only seven, not exactly succeeding in school. He'd been pegged "the class dunce, not that bright." His parents practically disowned him because they thought he was lazy.

It's ironic he went into acting, a field where reading is part of the drill. Monday's script read-throughs on *Happy Days* when he played the leather-jacketed, bequiffed Arthur Herbert Fonzarelli filled him with dread.

But along the way, he learned something important, something Lesson 261 tells us. We live and move in a ginormous field of love and information.

He was unable to learn using his eyes. Or his brain. He had to learn by getting still, by listening, by accessing the ginormous field of love and info coursing through his body.

"I just wait," he says.

And without fail, whatever he needs to know literally drops into his awareness.

The trick, he says, is getting beyond the neurosis in his brain. Once he washes his cares out of his body, everything he needs to know is right there.

As he said, "Your inner voice, your instinct, knows everything."

THE LIFE-CHANGING MAGIC OF KONMARI-ING MY THOUGHTS

If it sparks joy, keep it. It not, dispose of it.

— MARIE KONDO

The reason Marie Kondo's 2014 bestseller *The Life-Changing Magic of Tidying Up* sold eight million plus copies is that, by discarding crap that doesn't spark joy, life gets profoundly easier, lighter.

Today, I'm going to use Marie Kondo's method, as Lesson 262 requests, to spend my day in perfect peace.

Principle #1: Let go of thoughts (things) to make room for thoughts (things) that matter. I look at my thoughts, determine if they "spark joy" and, if not, ba-boom! Out of here.

Principle #2: Override all instincts to keep certain thoughts that HGTV or a fashion magazine told me would brighten my life. That's the ego talking. And remember, "the ego lies."

Principle #3: Identify things (thoughts) that make me happy. Joy is my goal. I honestly examine my thoughts for *tokimeku* (Japanese word meaning flutter, throb, palpitate). What kind of energy does it produce in my body? If it doesn't make me happy, I give it a heartfelt and generous good-bye.

Principle #4: Resist the urge to repurpose old thoughts for "loungewear." Or to keep a thought out of guilt. Or because I paid a lot for it back in the day. Just like that old T-shirt that I might someday use if I ever paint my cabinets, those thoughts that served me in the past are no longer useful. Sayonara, sucker!

LOOK BEYOND THE MADMAN'S DREAM

Sometimes I use X-ray vision to look into the dancer and see who this dancer is right now, at this exact moment in time.

— TWYLA THARP

Like Superman, I was raised in Kansas and have a thing for wearing tights. Unlike my fellow Kansan, I rarely leap tall buildings or fly. I also don't have X-ray vision.

But I do have what ACIM 263 calls holy vision. It allows me to see beyond appearances. It allows me to see beyond lack and limitation. It allows me to see the reality that is covered up with my distorted thinking. My brother J.C. was so good at using holy vision that people who hadn't walked in years literally got up and busted a jaunty Nae Nae.

I, too, possess this superpower. It's like a magic wand. When I commit to use it, reality changes right before my eyes. The ugly morphs into the beautiful, the darkness into light, the sadness into joy.

Today, I use my superpower to see all things as perfect, pure, and pristine. I use it to bless everyone I see, to bless everything that crosses my path. And as I look beyond seeming appearances to the incomparable truth beneath the veil, I call forth life and restore all things to their original state of perfection.

SETTLE FOR MORE

While you're caught up in why he didn't return your call,
galaxies all across the cosmic horizon are tumbling
into the unknown faster than the speed of light.

— DEEPAK CHOPRA

We humans are an awful lot like Dobby, the house elf in the Harry Potter books. Thankfully, we don't have the green tennis ball eyes or the long bat-like ears, but we do treat ourselves in much the same way.

Like Dobby, we continually settle for less. We refuse to fully accept our good. The universe is trying like bloody hell to pour out blessings, and we're so busy composing snarky tweets that we don't even notice.

When Professor Dumbledore hired the heroic elf to work in the kitchen, he offered ten Galleons a week and weekends off. But Dobby wanted no part of it. He insisted on a single Galleon and only one day off per month.

When Dobby, who always referred to himself in third person, explained his pay negotiations to Hermione, he said, "Dobby beat him down, miss. Dobby likes freedom, but he isn't wanting too much, miss."

That's us. Never wanting too much. Never seeing our own beauty. Never recognizing that we have the power to create worlds.

And like Dobby, who often inflicted injury upon himself, we punish ourselves for simply being who we are. We may not hit ourselves in the head or iron our own hands, as Dobby did, but we certainly iron our hair, hit ourselves psychically every time we look in the mirror, and constantly try to "improve" our perfect selves.

I prefer what British artist Ruby Etc. posted on Instagram. "The only problem with my body? My brain for assimilating the concept of problem areas."

So today, I say to myself, to Dobby, and to every humanoid on the planet, "You are a perfect angel goddess rock star, and I am so very, very proud of you. C'mon down and scoop up your gifts."

TODAY WOULD BE A REALLY GOOD DAY TO FORGIVE SOMEONE, PART II

The conquest of the physical world is not man's only duty.
He is also enjoined to conquer the great wilderness of himself.

— JAMES BALDWIN

For about a year, I've nursed a grudge against someone who holds a lot of cards in my life. Despite my big talk about working the Course, I viewed this "horrible ogre" as the one exception to the Course's request to forgive.

In this person's case, I felt oh so justified in hanging on to my story. He really is an unreasonable prig. He really is boring. And mean. And OMG, it's just so unfair that I have to endure him every time I want to see this other very special person in my life. My sister and I have spent hours dissecting all the reasons this asshat prevents us from really being there for someone we love.

After hours of avoiding the inevitable, the Voice of the Holy S finally tugged on my pants leg.

"Pam," it said. *"I've had about enough of this sh*t. You are nothing but a poser. How dare you write a book about a practice you're not faithfully practicing."*

So I decided to take Lesson 265 (Creation's gentleness is all I see) at its word. To concede that maybe (probably not, but maybe) I misunderstood this person, maybe I deceived myself, maybe these judgments are only in my mind.

My ego stood resolute, but I was able to give a teensy kernel of willingness.

Funny thing. Not 30 minutes after throwing up my hands in defeat, this person who hasn't contacted me in a year (even when my special person was hospitalized) sent me a text.

TODAY WOULD BE A REALLY GOOD DAY TO FORGIVE SOMEONE, PART III

All that is asked of you is to make room for truth.

— A COURSE IN MIRACLES

I hate when this happens. When lessons like 266 insist all nimrods in my life are saviors in disguise. That they're sent by the Dude itself so I can find *my* Holy Self.

Fat chance, my ego says, but, if you insist, I'll try the four questions Byron Katie suggests asking about all stories that cause me pain.

1. Is it true the ogre I referred to yesterday is really a dickwad?

Me: Well, you better believe it's true. He's the most small-minded person I've ever met. He lies. He makes up stories. How else could a person be expected to react to hi—

"Pam," I hear the Holy S say. "It's a yes or no question."

Me: Okay, yes, it's true.

2. Are you absolutely 100 percent sure it's true?

Me: Well, no. There's a tiny possibility that it's not true.

3. So, how does holding on to this thought make you feel?

Me: Angry. Ready to attack. Quick to defend. Wanting to build walls. I waste long hours plotting my revenge.

"So, in other words," the Holy S points out, "not a good look."

4. So who would I be without that thought?

Me: Um, gosh. I can hardly imagine. I've worn that thought like my own hair. I've held on to it for so long it seems like gospel truth. But maybe, just maybe, it's possible I'd feel a tad bit better if I deleted that story from my hard drive. It might lower the energetic wall that has come between me and this person.

Byron Katie's "The Work" then asks for a turnaround.

Me: I'm the one who's boring and small-minded and holding on to my story.

How could that also be true?

Me: Well, I've bored anyone who will listen with why this person has "done me wrong." And I've been sure (aka small-minded?) that I'm right. And I've held on to this story ever since he sent me the nasty texts. In fact, I haven't had any communication with him for twelve long months.

So, okay, okay, I get it. And once again, I offer just a tad bit of willingness.

PINCHING MYSELF OVER MY EXTREME GOOD FORTUNE

Let me be clear. I do feel like a contest winner.

— W. KAMAU BELL

In a profound and heartbreaking scene on *Parts Unknown*, the late Anthony Bourdain told W. Kamau Bell, as they gaze over the Kenyan landscape, that he has to f***ing pinch himself because he can't believe he gets to do and see all this.

I know the feeling. I'm frequently dumbfounded that a preacher's kid from small-town Kansas has been blessed to experience Kenya, Turkey, Japan, Peru, and many of the same countries as the celebrity chef. But even more sublime is that I also get to experience, to feel, and to know the life force that Lesson 267 so eloquently promises, that Anthony Bourdain temporarily forgot in 2018.

I get the joy of knowing I am surrounded by love, that peace fills my heart and floods my body. I get the peace of knowing that every single thing I need is given to me, that my every breath infuses me with strength.

As for Anthony Bourdain, whose shocking suicide stunned us all, we have to ask:

Didn't he know how much we loved him?

Doesn't he realize how beautiful he is, how much joy he gave us?

Having these thoughts reminds me of what our Source thinks about us as we go about our lives, not appreciating the truth of who we really are.

When I forget who I really am, Source steps in to remind me of the one answer to all the big questions. (1. Who am I? 2. Why am I here? 3. What is my purpose?)

The answer to all three is love. I am love. I'm here to love. My only purpose is to be love.

FINDING NEEDLES
IN HAYSTACKS

It's kind of fun to do the impossible.

— WALT DISNEY

The Course minces no words: There is no order of difficulties in miracles. Translated, that means, "Nothing is impossible. Nothing is out of reach."

Anything we can dream (moving mountains, changing water to wine), we can accomplish.

So far, I haven't skipped across any bodies of water, but once, in Greece, I did experience a miracle that involves water and is, by all standards, statistically impossible.

My friend Nixie and I rented motor scooters to drive around Mykonos. I was wearing jean shorts and because who doesn't want to take a break at a gorgeous white sand beach, we stopped, laid down our towels, and gamboled into the crystal clear ocean. We oohed and aahed at the handsome dudes, downed a shot of ouzo each, and chatted with a topless jewelry maker.

When it was time to jump back on our scooters, I reached into my pocket, where I had deposited the key, and discovered that alas, it had floated out into the ocean. A big giant ocean.

Most reasonable people would have panicked. But Lesson 268 is very clear: if I "let things be exactly as they are," I am free from all loss. Free from pain. Wholly safe.

So I walked right out to where the key was, plucked it out of the water, shook it off, jumped on my motorcycle, and commenced to circumnavigate the island.

I used to tell that story to demonstrate how clear Greek oceans are. But what it really demonstrates is this principle—there is no order of difficulties in miracles. And my Source, at all times, has my back!

SEEING THE CHRIST IN GENGHIS KAHN

Whenever you deny a blessing to a brother, you feel deprived.

— A COURSE IN MIRACLES

Get out your cape. Today you're going to employ your secret superpower. You are going to call forth greatness in your fellow humanoids. And you're going to do it with nothing but the strength of your thoughts, the jurisdiction of your consciousness.

Lesson 269 states: My sight goes forth to look upon Christ's face.

Christ's face, in this instance, is a pattern of high-energy photons that your thoughts are going to retrieve and transform into love.

Quantum physicists call it the observer effect. While the fact we impact what we observe wreaks havoc on everything we thought we knew, it's actually welcome information. Because it means we're not stuck with the 3-D reality we think is reality. We can actually surpass perception, transcend illusion, and see only love.

I started by thinking of famous people, movie stars. I saw Christ in Gary Gulman, the comedian who created HBO's *The Great Depresh.* Then I thought of Judd Apatow, who happens to be his producer. It's easy to see greatness in the Ron Howards and Brian Grazers of the world.

Then I moved it up a notch. I saw Christ's face in my partner, Jim. That, I must admit, is sometimes a bit more challenging. And then I thought of my friends, my family.

The final test was seeing it in people I judge, people I cast as ogres in my personal melodrama.

As the Course tells me, all confusion comes from believing that anyone (politicians, angry predators, needy relatives) can deprive me of anything. If I see this in anyone, I accept it as a part of me.

Instead, I wish happiness and joy on every single person that crosses my mind. I send out love photons to everyone I see on the streets, everyone I talk to.

It's so much fun. And guess what happens? It proves a long-standing Course tenet. The more I give, the more I receive.

CAVEAT EMPTOR, OR HOW BIG IS YOUR TELESCOPE?

I've learned that fear limits you and your vision. It serves as blinders to what may be just a few steps down the road

— SOLEDAD O'BRIEN

Light has been dancing and rebounding off the sun for more than 13 billion years. Eight minutes after a photon leaps off the sun, it bounces off the Earth.

This ongoing disco is available to anyone with a telescope. Needless to say, there's a wide chasm between a mass-produced telescope sold at a toy store and, say, the Hubble.

The main job of a telescope is to gather light, to collect radiance. The kiddie scopes made in China have a very different goal—to separate consumers from their money. Rarely do they deliver on their 486X magnification promises.

Lesson 270 urges us to use the better telescope. Depending solely on our body's eyes precludes us from all the signs and opportunities and, yes, blatant love that is disco dancing for our good.

The very fact that these limited eyeballs show heartache, limitation, and death is proof that they, like the kiddie telescopes, are here to separate us from reality. They focus in on a narrow band of experience, completely denying the brilliant dimensions beyond the physical senses.

All of us have access to the high-end Hubble. The Course calls it Christ's vision. And you don't have to go to McDonald Observatory to tune in. High-end "Hubble" vision is as simple as refusing to use the body's eyes, focusing in instead on receiving the gift. Today, I let my Hubble vision translate all I see into a glorious and gracious world.

GET YOUR GRATITUDE ON

Beauty is a construct made by the capitalist system to make us see flaws that don't exist to sell us things we don't need.

— MEME FROM CHRISTINE SMITH'S EPISTLE

Gratitude is my wingman.

I use it like duct tape. Of all the tools in my kit (and believe me, when you have a thinking cap like mine, you need a lot of tools), it's the one I most often pull out. It's a multipurpose utensil whether I hope to heal a relationship, fix a physical boo-boo, or just feel happier. Lesson 271 calls it "using Christ's vision."

Gratitude is particularly useful when I notice myself marching across the desert toward some mirage that looks an awful lot like a problem. After I lasso my racing mind that's squawking "poor, pitiful me!" "oh no!" "death is surely imminent," I give it the following one-two punch.

Step One: (Again I can only do this after I recognize I'm making it worse by fretting and awfulizing) I say thank you "Mr. Problem." I know you're a gift in disguise, another rat coming up from the cellar, one I probably need to look at and call out. Thank you for so clearly showing me I still have resistance. But you better watch out! Because I'm calling Orkin.

Step Two: I recognize that this temporary scare tactic is one of hundreds of thousands of superpositions in the field of infinite potentiality. This impostor (be it seeming illness, poverty, a disgruntled boss) is tiny, barely worth noticing.

As always, I can either turn my "problem" into a big hairy deal, or I can say "Hallelujah! Thank ya, Jesus" and with the power of my command, send it back into the native nothingness from which it came.

NO MORE JERKY KNEES

We hit delete on a lot of inconvenient miracles.

— PETE HOLMES

Most of us know our shoe size, our height, and our credit card numbers. But how many of us cop to our premature cognitive commitments?

We all have them, those beliefs about reality that cause our brains to edit out everything that doesn't fit our perceptions. PCCs are basically knee-jerk reactions that create a false sense of safety and security. What they really are is a prison trapping us in yesterday. Lesson 272 makes no bones about it: Illusions will never fully satisfy, will never deliver happiness.

Today, we pass illusions by. We let love happily replace all fear.

MAYBE TODAY'S THE DAY

Everyone says, "Get in the moment." You ARE the moment.

— KYLE CEASE

Forgiveness is like a thick, absorbent paper towel that sops up spilled coffee, wine, and melted chocolate.

Forgiveness, more than being a concession you make for grouches and assorted bad guys, is a means for wiping away old patterns and no-longer-useful ways of thinking. It's how you find the stillness promised in Lesson 273.

If you do it right, those patterns—and their resulting consequences—are potentially gone forever. Maybe today's the day.

Just like you don't go digging through the trash for that discarded sheet of Bounty, forgiveness refuses to dig up negative thoughts from yesterday's rejection. It doesn't sort through sticky yogurt containers and bacon drippings for that memory of Mom's disapproval.

Forgiveness changes everything. The patterns that have been moving you around like a pawn on a chessboard disappear. You're free to create a new life. Dreams start unfolding easily and effortlessly.

Everything you've ever wanted is right there on the eighth-floor apartment. It's right there waiting. But you gotta throw out the old paper towels.

A MINI-LESSON IN MIRACLE-MINDEDNESS

*Miracles are like pimples. Once you start looking
for them you find more than you ever dreamed.*

— LEMONY SNICKET

In the Cook Islands, a bare-chested 60-something medicine man with waist-length dreads plucked a small black rock out of the river, handed it to me, and said, "Put this in the north corner of your living room and you'll become a millionaire." Turns out curing cancer with his encyclopedic knowledge of jungle botany isn't all that medicine man knew. Or was it coincidence that by the summer of that year, *E-Squared* ruled the *New York Times* bestseller list?

One summer, I was unloading my dishwasher when my editor at *People* magazine called and asked, "Would you want to go to a party and interview Blake Shelton?"

Last November, an agent from Creative Artists Agency, the Hollywood agency that represents Viola Davis, Jennifer Aniston, James Cameron, and Nicole Kidman, emailed me in Kansas to ask if she could represent me as a speaker.

I hadn't made an intention to manifest any of those things. What I had done—and what I still do every day—is make the intention to erase all beliefs, thoughts, and emotions that block the power of Source.

Lesson 274 (Today belongs to love. Let me not fear) basically says that any thought that's not of love is fear. And that fear erects a solid energetic wall that keeps cool things like abundance and partying with rock stars (okay, so Blake sings country) at bay.

Did you get that? The universe WANTS all of us to have abundant lives and party, not only with rock stars, but with EVERYONE!!

YOU BE YOU

The moment you doubt whether you can fly,
you cease forever to be able to do it.

— J. M. BARRIE

We use photo albums and scrapbooks to preserve memories. They're a snapshot of a specific time period. Nobody mistakes them for current news.

My nonstop judgments and labels are basically scrapbooks, displaying yesterday's collective beliefs.

True reality is expanding energy, life in constant motion.

Once I "snap" a photo in my mind, I separate and freeze it into a reality no more current than a dusty photo album. When I begin to label "this is good," "this is a giraffe," "this is my aunt Susan," I abandon infinite possibility. I swallow the collective belief. I fall from grace.

Lesson 275 says it's unnecessary to label and judge. It says I'm forever protected and there's no reason to be anxious. Ever. About anything.

The Dude, it promises, "will tell me what to do and where to go; to whom to speak and what to say, what thoughts to think, what words to give the world."

I'LL HAVE WHAT SHE'S HAVING

*I used to walk down the street like I was a f*cking star.
Every day, I fought hard for that delusion until
eventually it became the truth.*

— LADY GAGA

In college, when time seemed endless, my friends and I discussed everything from "Do humans really have free will?" to "Who is hotter? Butch Cassidy or Sundance Kid?"

A frequent query from these endless jam sessions was this: "If you could be famous, which field would you choose?"

Rock star? Statesman? Pro athlete? Movie star?

ACIM Lesson 276, in a roundabout way, asks this very question.

In whose voice do I choose to speak?

The voice of the ego that likes to separate and hold certain individuals outside the powwow?

Or the voice for love, the biggest rock star/statesman/movie star on the planet?

Today, I walk down the street like Lady Gaga, knowing I'm a f*cking star. And I speak for the voice that blesses and loves every one of the other six billion rock stars/statesmen/movie stars.

PIN THE TAIL
ON THE REALITY

*Learning is slowed less by lack of intelligence than by a reluctance
to let go of bankrupt ideas and exhausted ways of seeing.*

— D. PATRICK MILLER

When I was a kid, birthday parties featured three things: cake, presents, and pin-the-tail-on-the-donkey.

Maybe you've played it? A picture of a donkey is tacked to a wall and one by one, participants are blindfolded, handed a paper tail, and spun around in circles.

The object is less "zero in on the donkey's backside" and more "laugh at your disoriented friends stumbling around the room."

Worldview 1.0, the reality we've labeled as fact, is much like this childhood game. We're bound (or blindfolded) by make-believe laws. We actually believe the world is limited, that we're separate from other humans, that our identity is a weird, needy flesh suit.

At least children know when it's time to take off the blindfolds.

The number of "laws" we've made up, that we've literally concocted out of thin air, would be laughable if we didn't take them so darn seriously. We've even made up science to prove this long list of limitations.

The Course tells us there's only one thing that binds us, only one thing that limits our eternal, endless selves. And that's our belief in limits, our belief in arbitrary "laws."

To get an idea of the number of "made-up laws" we've imposed upon ourselves, check out any Facebook quiz or women's magazine or library of how-to books.

It's a fact, we're told that our bodies need X amount of daily protein, vitamin C, hugs, education, and on and on and on. The list of "laws" to ensure our body's safety is long indeed. But again, these "laws" only apply as long as we believe them.

Today, I commit to forsaking all made-up laws. I claim instead my freedom and know the only law to which I'm bound is the law of love.

My New Mantra

The bad news: You're falling through air with no parachute. The good news: There's no ground.

— CHOGYAM TRUNGP

My mind likes to replay old news. It gets on a repeating loop, endlessly cycling for temporary adrenaline boosts. Watch out! Better duck!

Today, whenever that happens (notice I use the word when, not if), Lesson 278 reminds me to use these four letters: NRRN

Not relevant right now.

Anytime I think about the past, say an editor rejected one of my brilliant ideas, I pull out my trusty letters.

Not relevant right now.

Or when I start thinking about digital images I need to replace the two my editor didn't like:

Again, not relevant right now.

What IS relevant right now is that there is a gentle breeze swaying the catalpa leaves in the backyard. There is a cardinal sitting in the bush beside my window. There is the soothing sound of my partner turning the pages on his latest mystery novel.

There is so much to notice in this moment that the rest is (shall we say it together?): not relevant right now.

EXPAND YOUR REALITY

Are you willing to consider the possibility that
God might know a few things you haven't thought of yet?

— EDWENE GAINES

When my Sunday School teachers informed me that God had a plan for my life, I panicked. What if he wants me to leave my family, be a missionary in some country with leeches or tarantulas?

I wasn't ready to commit to God's will because, well, look what he did to Lot's wife. Or to Job. My gosh, who needs all those seeping body sores?

So it was with great relief I found *A Course in Miracles*. God's will, for those still scarred by pillars of salt and lion's dens, is unceasing joy. Or as Lesson 279 promises, freedom, complete and unbridled.

IT'S RIGHT ON YOUR TAIL

Are you looking for me? I am in the next seat.
My shoulder is against yours.

— KABIR

After surviving a brutal car accident that ruins his hands, brilliant neurosurgeon Dr. Strange, played by Benedict Cumberbatch in the 2016 movie, goes looking for truth, for answers, for wisdom.

In his search, he's followed by a strange figure in a dark hoodie. It's all we, the audience, can do to keep from yelling, "It's right behind you, dumbass. It's been following you the whole time."

And that's exactly what Lesson 280 is trying to tell me.

What I am seeking has been there the whole time.

I don't have to jump through hoops. Knock myself out.

I just have to stop.

Limitless freedom, peace, and joy is literally tailing me. Its shoulder is against mine. It's sitting in the next seat.

Today I stop. Use this moment. This very moment to experience the Divine.

DIGGING IN DAILY TO MAKE SPIRITUAL TRACTION

To be enlightened means to be light in all senses of the word.

— CARLOS SANTANA

Carlos Santana, the Grammy-winning guitarist, delights his concert audience with hits like "Oye Coma Va" and "Black Magic Woman." But after four or five songs, he starts rapping about the light within, about finding the Divine Spark.

He talks about the importance of gratitude and about the nobility of life, how all of us are united by what he calls "the universal tone." Like a preacher, he encourages his audience to take responsibility for their thoughts.

Inevitably, some clod shouts out, "When are you going to play 'Maria, Maria'? I just wanna rock."

And he'll say, "Hey, man, I'm grateful you paid for a ticket, but here's something you might need to hear even more."

Like me, Santana is a *Course in Miracles* fanatic. If forced to pick three items for a deserted island, he says he'd take his guitar (well, duh!), Miles Davis's *Sketches of Spain,* and his beat-up copy of *A Course in Miracles.*

He reads from his Course every day and, even on the road, lights incense, a candle, and asks for release from his ego that, like all of our egos, tries to guilt-trip him.

He reminds himself of Lesson 281 that "he can be hurt by nothing but his thoughts."

"I like the idea of spreading a spiritual virus that instead of making people sick makes them totally alive."

BE YOUR UNAPOLOGETICALLY WEIRD SELF

I'm in love with everyone.

— MICHAEL BECKWITH

I have plenty of "bad thinking habits," but envy isn't one of them. I've always been able to celebrate others' success, partly because I know I'm connected to everyone and also because I totally get it, that if they can do it, I can do it, too.

In keeping with my motto, "Celebrate what you want to see more of," I'd like to celebrate that every last one of us is weird and different and that's a beautiful thing. Diversity is not something to be threatened by. Or to avoid. It's to be celebrated.

As Lesson 282 reminds me, I will not be afraid of love today.

Instead of reaching for the spring-loaded trigger, I will burst out laughing. Old defensive habits probably worked in cavemen days, when saber-toothed tigers were trying to rip elk meat from our baby's mouth. But it's the 21st century.

And it's time to create new habits, new beliefs. It's time to quit gnawing on old miseries and enjoy the now.

Even if I'm asked to apologize. Even if I did nothing wrong.

So if I'd asked to forgive today, why not? As one of my gurus says, "If someone asks for my cloak, I might as well give them my 'Vote for Pedro' T-shirt as well."

Remember it isn't agreement with others I need. It's agreement with myself.

I YAM THAT I YAM

We have enslaved the world with our dismal
thoughts and meaningless laments.

— A COURSE IN MIRACLES

Lesson 283 says, "Nah-nah-nah-boo-boo." Pretend all you want to be powerless, limited, lacking in creativity or love or peace.

But the Dude's not buying it.

My name, like Its name, is I AM.

And whatever I attach to I AM___ (I am miserable, for example, or I am overweight, or I am tired) invokes the entirety of the power of the universe. These proclamations are sent out into the world thousands of times a day.

Today, I claim my true identity by attaching the following proclamations to my name:

I AM joyful.

I AM peace.

I AM the light of the world.

What's your I AM _____ for this glorious day?

NO WORRY BEFORE
ITS TIME

Events don't cause stress. Your views
of those events cause stress.

— EPICTETUS

After fire destroyed the home of Harvard professor Ellen Langer, her insurance agent came to view the damage and file his report.

"This is remarkable," he said. "Eighty percent of your possessions have gone up in smoke. Your call is the first where the damage is worse than you reported."

Most people, after a devastating loss, double down on negativity. They throw every ounce of their emotional energy into their loss.

Langer, who spent 40 years researching how perceptions and beliefs effect our lives, refused to go there.

"I'd already had the loss," Langer explained. "Why should I also give it my soul? Why would I want to pay for it twice?"

Langer understands Lesson 284: I can elect to change all thoughts that hurt.

Once I set a belief in stone, my psyche goes out to seek confirmation.

Langer turned what most would call a devastating fire into a game. She got to stay in a hotel, she made new friends with the staff, she got to march her dogs through the lobby every morning. Consequently, she can't remember a single thing she lost in the fire.

"It's remarkable what you find when you strip away the mindless insecurity and negativity," she said.

ALWAYS GET YOUR HOPES UP

Our ability to shape energy is like breathing.
We do it all the time without even realizing it.

— DAMIEN ECHOLS

When I began focusing on what could go right (instead of the more popular viewpoint touted on CNN), I found that my so-called problems had a way of fixing themselves. I discovered the less I did, the better my life worked.

The more I identified with the invisible realm of goodness, joy, and beauty, the happier I became. The less I planned, the more magic became available.

Planning, by its very nature, is based on what we know. We can't plan for *firturjelsk,* for example. Or ask for *wemerk.*

Why?

Because our limited pea brains have never heard of them.

The invisible realm has a much bigger vantage point, so when we start focusing on all that's good, the flow opens up, and experiences way better than we can imagine mysteriously line up for our enjoyment.

That's the message of Lesson 285. Today I wake with joy, expecting but happy things to come. I ask for them and realize my invitation will be answered. What would be the use of pain to me, what purpose would my suffering fulfill? Today, I ask for only joyous things as I allow my holiness to shine bright and clear.

REACH FOR THE SKY

*The world you see does nothing. It has no effects at all.
It merely represents your thoughts.*

— A COURSE IN MIRACLES

CNN used to hire me every summer to write about new roller coasters.

The really insane ones—the ones with the 85-degree vertical drops, the seven inversions—often have a camera right where the coaster plummets 185 feet.

If you look at the photos these theme parks somehow manage to process and have waiting for purchase when you step, wobbly-kneed, off the ride, you notice teenagers have big smiles on their faces, their hands in the air. The adults? They look terrified, even though they know, theoretically, they're perfectly safe.

Life is like those roller coasters. It sometimes looks like I'm in danger, but, as lesson 286 reminds us:

The time has come to laugh at such insane ideas. Nothing external to your mind can hurt or injure you in any way. No one but yourself affects you.

So today I join the teenagers, put my hands in the air, and shout with glee, even when the coaster appears to be heading downhill.

THE EXISTENTIAL SHOCK
OF BEING TRUE TO MYSELF

*The downside of spiritual law is once you understand
a lesson, you can no longer play dumb.*

— SARAH BAN BREATHNACH

Might as well make it easy today. Lesson 287 gives me one goal. One simple goal.

To be love. To radiate love. To be my true self.

And if I'm tempted to erect impediments to receiving, allowing, and participating in love, I will clear them away with three simple questions:

1. What could possibly be better than being true to my deepest being, being connected to my inner Source?

2. What could possibly substitute for happiness?

3. What gift could I possibly prefer over peace?

Today, I pooh-pooh all futile substitutions for love and celebrate that nothing is better than Truth.

SPARKLY WITH ENERGY

*The more you praise and celebrate your life, the
more there is to praise and celebrate.*

— OPRAH

I'd like to interrupt this book with an important noncommercial announcement.

You are already a master at creating reality.

You can't not be.

By virtue of being alive, this power is yours. Like all things vital to your well-being—air and sunshine, to name a couple you already take for granted—the energy to create worlds is your birthright. You do it every day, at every second.

The trick is to let go of the default "reality" you focus on now.

Once you do, the minute you let go of the "reality" you were mistakenly taught, it's impossible to avoid joy, peace, and daily blessings. They will stalk you like Freddy Krueger.

You have been taught that "life is a struggle," that "nothing comes easy." You have erroneously mastered the idea that people are not to be trusted, that it's important to "be careful."

And look how good you've been at creating THAT reality. In fact, it would be highly appropriate to get up right now and take a bow.

And while you're standing, go ahead and do the "Harlem Shuffle" because once you let go of the "old reality" you created so successfully, the one with the deck of cards that proclaims "sickness is inevitable," "abundance is limited," "good things sometimes happen, but not all the time," you can customize your reality to your liking.

Congratulations! You are now free to roam the planet.

CAN YOU HANDLE THE TRUTH?

*If your mind isn't cluttered by unnecessary things,
this could be the best day of your life.*

— FROM A MESSAGE LEFT ON MY VOICE MAIL
BY THE ZING, AKA ETHAN HUGHES

Discovery Channel's *Mythbusters* investigates urban legends, internet rumors, and other mistruths.

While it's not terribly hazardous to believe a penny dropped off a skyscraper can kill a pedestrian, it really cuts into your potential when you believe the gazillion myths we perpetuate about the world, about forgiveness, about God.

Lesson 289 (The past is over. It can touch me not) says that until my mind gives up my past, until it surrenders the countless cultural myths, the real world—the infinite Divine Broadcast that airs possibility, joy, and freedom—will be hidden from my sight.

It's like the explosive scene in *A Few Good Men* when Lieutenant Kaffee (played by Tom Cruise) has Colonel Jessup (played by Jack Nicholson) on the witness stand. Kaffee is badgering Jessup, wanting to know whether or not he ordered a Code Red.

Jessup, getting redder and madder, finally erupts: "You can't handle the truth."

Once I give up my past, once I'm able to look at every person and event in my life and see its beauty, its radiance, its shimmering love, I will finally be privy to and able to handle the truth.

THE MOST IMPORTANT QUESTION

*Let your mind be cleared of all the foolish
cobwebs which the world would weave.*

— A COURSE IN MIRACLES

Let me guess. You probably binged some series last night—maybe *Stranger Things* or *Game of Thrones*.

Whatever it was, you didn't for a moment believe it was factual information. You knew the story to which you sat glued was the creation of some evil genius scriptwriter. You might have cringed at Daenery's dragon meeting its shocking death or forgotten to breathe as Winona Ryder sat waiting on the couch with an ax, but you knew the moment you turned off the TV, it was basically irrelevant to your life.

That's how I view most of what the world calls "reality." It's made up. It's a mental construct that was created not by a scriptwriter, but by a world gone mad. This cultural Kool-Aid that we call "reality" has gone unquestioned for far too long. The "news" that we so worry about is no more real than *Game of Thrones*.

I only THINK I'm bound and gagged by the world's reality.

Lesson 290 (My present happiness is all I see) gives me one goal. To recognize "It's not real, people!" At any time, I can suspend my investment in these fictional stories of separation and problems and dysfunction. Why be deceived an instant longer?

Today, "I see my present happiness and look on nothing else except the thing I seek."

291

SHHH!!!

Within you, there is stillness and a sanctuary
to which you can retreat at any time.

— HERMANN HESSE

The message of Lesson 291 (This is a day of stillness and peace) is basically, chillax!

When I don't, I clog up the connection. When I give the floor to my inner anxieties, my fears, my time-sucking melodramas, I'm like Cinderella's stepsisters—cramming life's unending beneficence into my tiny shoes of old judgments and antiquated programming.

Not taking time to align my mind with my eternal, fearless, abundant self is like wearing one shoe. Or applying lipstick to only my top lip.

Today, I surrender to that place of complete trust, knowing I am connected to everyone and anything is possible.

DAMPENED BY LOW EXPECTATIONS

Mama exhorted her children to "jump at de sun. We might not land on the sun, but at least we will get off the ground."

— ZORA NEALE HURSTON

Before throwing his hat into the political ring, New Jersey senator Cory Booker was advised to go see Momma somebody or another from the projects.

Evidently "Momma" wielded a lot of political pull. So being a sharp guy, a Rhodes scholar and a Yale lawyer, he, of course, chose to pay due diligence. He knocked on Momma's door, sat down for a chat, and soon enough, let her take his hand and tour him around the projects.

"Young man," she asked. "Tell me what you see here."

Not sure exactly how to answer, he began a list: "Well, there's a lot of trash. Broken down cars, kids with no direction—"

"Young man." She stopped him right there. "As long as that's all you can see, that's all you'll ever see."

And he got it. He realized that it's our vision, our ability to imagine a better future that brings a better future about.

"The world outside is a reflection of what you have inside," Booker says now. "If all you see are problems, that's all there will ever be."

Lesson 292 says: A happy outcome to all things is sure. So we can waste our time looking at the trash, the broken-down cars, or we can move straight to the Dude's guarantee: Joy is the final outcome for all.

WHAT "THEY SAY" IS COMPLETELY IRRELEVANT

With a sense of real joy, from the depths of your being,
you open up to a place where grace can come in.

— BOBBY MCFERRIN

They say you should follow the rules.

They say you need eight hours of sleep.

They say you should avoid sugar, stay away from gluten.

They say love hurts.

They say lots of things that are only true if I decide to subscribe to them.

The real question is what do I say, what do I believe, what do I want to be true?

My money's on Lesson 293: All fear is past and only love is here.

A THOUGHT EXPERIMENT

A story only has the power you give it.

— JAMES CORDEN

So you're driving down the highway with Prince riding shotgun. You're innocently gazing at cornfields and windmills and a giant billboard advertising the world's largest prairie dog. You're having a fabulous time. How could you not be? You're hanging with one of the greatest artists of all time. One that everybody else thinks is dead.

Suddenly, a red Corvette pulls in front of the car. You barely notice. You're singing "Purple Rain" at the top of your lungs.

Prince, however, stops singing. He stiffens up. That car reminds him of the one-night stand that broke his heart. The one that inspired his famous 1983 hit, "Little Red Corvette."

That bi***!

The red Corvette itself means nothing. It's wholly neutral, as Lesson 294 explains. Prince, if so inclined, can lay his story on it. He can see the Corvette through the lens of his date's promiscuity. You, on the other hand, see a red car. Period.

Our bodies, like that red Corvette, are wholly neutral. Without our stories, without thoughts of fear (*I need to schedule a mammogram. I forgot to take my Lipitor, yada-yada.*), our bodies serve as useful vehicles as long as they're needed. The American Medical Association would prefer the Course keep this on the down low, but after they've served their purpose (to serve and give love), our bodies can easily be cast off without sickness, aging, or pain.

DONNING MY HOLY SHADES

Let go all the trivial things that churn and
bubble on the surface of your mind.

— A COURSE IN MIRACLES

The Shermans, our neighbors when I was growing up, had three rambunctious boys. Their constant poking and prodding bore a striking resemblance to the antics of the Three Stooges. Whenever the Shermans dared appear in public—say in church or at the movie theater—the parents strategically seated one son on the outside, a parent in between, the next son, the other parent and the last son on the other side.

This seating chart saved a lot of problems. I've discovered two words that, like the Sherman boys, are better behaved when separated.

The words are "I" and "know."

When uttered together, the door of further investigation slams shut.

These two words are sneaky, because—*isn't that why we're sent to school? Aren't we supposed to know stuff?*

This lesson reminds us: there are more sides to every story.

When "I" and "know" sit next to each other, an unbelievably powerful force is locked into a tiny box.

When I'm convinced and therefore attached to such stories as "The world is skidding to disaster" or "So-and-so is such an a-hole" or "I'm just not good at _____ (insert your own personal nightmare)," I basically thwart the field of infinite potentiality in its hell-raising-anything-goes tracks.

Lesson 295 (The Holy Spirit looks through me today) asks me to use different eyes today, to refrain from putting the Dude in handcuffs. It tells me that whatever "I know" pales in comparison to what's possible when I see through its eyes of love.

TELL IT LIKE YOU
WANT IT TO BE

*We have perfected the attitude of worry. If we don't
have something to worry about, that worries us.*

— MICHELE LONGO O'DONNELL

"Manifesting" is a popular concept in self-help circles. But it's actually a misnomer. Thanks to a quantum physics principle called entanglement, you are already connected to everything you could ever want to manifest.

What you draw from this field of endless possibilities is what you focus your attention upon. Whatever you invest your energy in is what coalesces around you.

Because the dominant paradigm teaches us to focus on problems, that's what we manifest, that's what we believe is reality.

Lesson 296 asks me to focus instead on gratitude, on what is going right (so many more things than you can even imagine). When I let that truth speak through me, problems dissolve into the nothingness from which they arose.

Things I casually mention drop into my lap. A few years ago, I noted in my journal I'd love to go to Turkey. I didn't obsess about it. I simply "set it and forget it," a concept I sometimes call the crockpot principle. During Ramadan, I was invited to breakfast with two Turkish families who live in my hometown. Hmm, I thought. That could be the indication I was getting close, like the birds that show up when you're nearing your destination after a long ocean cruise. Soon enough, I got the official invitation from the Turkish Ministry of Tourism.

MACHETE AND ME: A FORMULA FOR FORGIVENESS

The treasure you seek is in the back of the cave.

— JOSEPH CAMPBELL

My ego thinks it's a tough guy. It constantly bullies me, urges me to judge, to leap to conclusions.

Lesson 297 tells the ego (nicely, of course) to shut the f*ck up. Look deeper, it says, look beyond appearances. There, you will find tender hearts and shared humanity.

Hollywood actor Danny Trejo is my go-to example. Known for his intimidating mug (long hair, sprawling moustache, heavily lined face, acne scars and ginormous chest tattoo), he's often cast as a thug or a lowlife. Let's just say his blade-wielding Machete, a character he has reprised in many films, emits a threatening persona.

Until you look deeper in the cave.

Underneath, Danny Trejo is the exact opposite of Machete. He's kind, giving, and, yes, even gentle. He recently rescued a toddler trapped in an overturned, partially crushed car. He stayed long after emergency personnel arrived, comforting the frightened young boy and sweetly introducing him to a game of superheroes.

Here's my simple forgiveness formula: Any time my "enemy" looks creepy and menacing, I think of Machete and walk right by him toward the treasure in the back of the cave.

FALLING OFF MY UNICORN

A new world is what people fear most.

— FYODOR DOSTOEVSKY

Our strict adherence to conventional reality precludes us from recognizing miracles, miracles that are happening all around us.

Lesson 298 promises a return to reality, an end to all that intrudes on my holy sight.

Who in their right mind walks into a restaurant, takes a look at the menu, and orders the dish they least desire?

Likewise, who would go shopping at Nordstrom and opt to carry the rack's ugliest outfit up to the sales counter?

Yet that's what most of us do in our thinking, in our conversations. We focus on things we don't want to happen. We focus on the fear, on the negative, on the lack.

And those decisions have a much bigger impact on your life than one ugly dress or a dish you can't stand. You literally get exactly what you order from the universe. It's an unalterable law.

So sure, I can habitually return to the worn-out groove of death and its many minions (sadness, fear, anxiety, doubt, anger, etc.) or I can march my happy little ass right up to the universal counter and order what is truly mine: being unfettered and wildly alive.

BEST PARENTING ADVICE. EVER.

Children are remarkable for their intelligence, for their curiosity, their intolerance of shams, the clarity and ruthlessness of their vision.

— ALDOUS HUXLEY

Along with potty training and socialization, most parents give their children some kind of spiritual training, some kind of guidance into the higher dimensions.

Sadly, the most popular spiritual training involves reining in natural impulses, comes with a list of rules, no-no's, and a set of 10 commandments.

Lesson 299 (Eternal holiness abides in me) suggests instead:

Make it clear to your children that the No. 1 method for connecting with their spiritual nature is to follow their joy. Impulses of curiosity, bliss, and joy is the language of Source. It begs for an intimate relationship with no doubt about what to do next or which path to follow.

Because we're taught the opposite (you need to do this, you need to get good grades, you need to forget about running around and whooping like a wild banshee), most of us spend our lives wondering "What does Source want from me?" "What am I supposed to do with my life?" It's all there in living color.

If we only follow our joy.

YOU ARE INCREDIBLY PRECIOUS

O God, help me to believe the truth about
myself no matter how beautiful it is.

— MACRINA WIEDERKEHR

Today, I find serenity, unclouded, obvious, and sure. Lesson 300 encourages me to: Let no false perception keep me in its hold.

Or as Macrina Wiederkehr, a Benedictine nun from Arkansas, reminds me:

"You are incredibly precious! In the sacred moments offered to you each day, robe yourself with that truth. Linger with it in each new moment given to you and consider how you might bless those you encounter simply because of the truth of who you are. Hold on to your ephemeral staff and memorize these words: I am incredibly precious."

I'm invited today to see myself as I really am. The truth always astounds.

BRAND SPANKIN' NEW

I am the sky. My beliefs are the clouds.

— KYLE CEASE

My friend Jay was flying to California. The night before, he tried to check in online. He entered his confirmation number several times and was puzzled by the error message.

"Oh well," he said.

He was busy, had lots of things to wrap up, and finally decided he'd just check in tomorrow at the airport.

Next day at the kiosk, he got the same message. Finally, with less than an hour until his flight, he stormed up to the Delta desk and demanded, "What's the deal?"

The gate agent took one look at his ticket and said, "Oh, that's a United number."

United, for those who don't know the Kansas City airport, is in a completely different terminal. He had to catch a bus to get there. Jay's perception about his airline tickets, like so many of our perceptions about the world, were false.

We literally make up a story ("I'm on Delta") and proceed to go to the wrong terminal. As the Course says, the mechanisms of illusion are born from those illusions. And as long as we keep the illusion that nothing is quite good enough (our bodies, our finances, our relationship, our careers), that's the terminal we live in.

Lesson 301 is like the attendant who kindly pointed out that Jay was basing his thoughts (and therefore assumptions and actions) on a false perception.

At any time, I can abandon the terminal of separation, the one where nothing's quite good enough, and catch a free bus to the terminal where errors vanish, false perceptions disappear, and everything is perfect in every way.

TODAY'S FORTUNE: ANYTHING YOU DAMN WELL PLEASE

To miss the joy is to miss all.

— WILLIAM JAMES

Taz's friends used to play a game with fortune cookies. They'd break open their designated cookie, read the fortune, and add the phrase "in bed."

For example:

"You will inherit an unexpected sum of money" . . . in bed.

Or "This Friday will be an exciting time for you" . . . in bed.

You can imagine the giggles and excited red faces this provoked in a gaggle of junior-high girls.

Tosha Silver, author of *Outrageous Openness*, suggests replacing "in bed" with a different phrase.

To any complaint ("I'll never have enough money," or "I just can't find the right guy," for example), she adds ". . . without Source."

As Lesson 302 tells me, without Source, my complaints might have validity. But once I offer up my fears, my demons, my challenges to Source, light shines them away. I realize they are but vain imaginings.

WITH Source, my complaints have no power. WITH Source, I can do anything I damned well please.

TIME FOR AN INTERVENTION FROM THE RELENTLESS 24/7 MEDIA

Violence is interesting, which makes it a great obstacle to world peace and more thoughtful television programming.

— P. J. O'ROURKE

Crisis, conflict, and violence are the prevailing themes of our 24/7 media. If a stranger talked to us the way newscasters do, we'd tell them to go jump in a lake. Likewise, if our partners and other S.O.'s made us feel the way headlines often do, our friends would line up for an intervention. "Toss the jerk out on his head," they'd say.

Living in fear sells products, creates economies, elects politicians, and keeps the flying monkeys on the job. But it's not the truth about the world.

Lesson 303 assures me collaboration, goodness, and love are the norm. It tells me that when I "let earthly sounds be quiet," the sights to which I've become accustomed disappear.

To escape the straitjacket of the relentless news media, I simply change the question. Instead of asking "What's wrong?" I ask the ongoing question that re-ups everything: "What's right? What am I thankful for?"

GLIDING THROUGH LIFE

*Glide through life as if all of creation is
yearning to honor and entertain you.*

— ROB BREZSNY

If you've ever taken a walk with a three-year-old (and if you haven't, put it on your bucket list now), you know they notice and appreciate everything.

Look, a ladybug! Look, a pebble! Look, I can kick it down the street.

That's how I feel when I "let not my world obscure the sight of Love," as Lesson 304 teaches.

I learn that perception is a mirror, not a fact. I learn the world I observe is my state of mind, reflected outward.

When I bless the world and look with the light of love, I'm just like a three-year-old, still pointing, still saying, "Look!!"

GIVE ME FIVE

*Virtually all the ills that people experience are a
result of mindlessness, one way or the other.*

— ELLEN LANGER

Lesson 305 promises peace—deep and quiet.

While it doesn't give specific instructions, I'm partial to the follow-ing technique:

Notice the now.

Instead of trying to count breaths or repeat a mantra or sit on a cushion with a stiff back, I like to give five. I actively behold five new details about wherever I happen to be.

You probably think you know the room, the coffee shop, the wherever-you-happen-to-be like the back of your hand. But do you really?

For that matter, try looking at the back of your hand and notice five new details. Next time you see your partner or a friend, take it upon yourself to notice five new details.

When you begin to "notice the now," everything you took for granted suddenly springs to life. People, places, and things literally jump out of the box into which your ego tried to stuff them. Through the simple act of noticing, you begin to recognize how frequently you restrain your experience.

Today, as I give up control, as I enter the now, I find peace, undis-turbed and wholly changeless.

BELIEVE THE FAIRY
TALE IS TRUE

The more you look for synchronicity, the more magical your life becomes. You are the magician that makes the grass green.

— ROBERT ANTON WILSON

The ego is like the annoying tall person who sits in front of you at the theater or the baseball game.

Until it showed up, you had a perfectly clear view. It was a cinch to see the light, the brilliance, the vision that Lesson 306 promises.

But once that damned ego showed up, wearing a wide-brimmed hat, carrying a monstrous bucket of popcorn and completely blocking the view, your vision morphed into a Wes Craven horror flick.

Today, I happily skip out of the theater, where transcendence is the only thing I could ever see.

ONLY ONE CHANNEL

Be quiet, still and solitary. The world will freely
offer itself to you to be unmasked, it has no choice,
it will roll in ecstasy at your feet.

— FRANZ KAFKA

When I was growing up, television programming ended at midnight. The national anthem was dutifully played and a black-and-white test pattern popped up until programming resumed the next morning.

Today, there's nary a minute when airwaves aren't broadcasting. Never stops. Never ends.

The same can be said about Source. There's never a lapse. The Divine Buzz never ceases transmitting guidance, blessings, signs, and miracles.

I, on the other hand, frequently tune in to a different channel. Let's just call it the grievance channel, the channel where something is not quite right.

That's why in Lesson 307 (and over and over throughout this Course), I'm reminded there's really only one channel. And if I'm seeing something besides beauty, light, and never-ending joy, I'm running a self-created test pattern of grievances.

The grievances obscuring the Divine Buzz are subtle, so subtle I don't always recognize I'm running them.

That's why every morning, I solicit help. I turn my day over to the Holy S and my intention for extraordinarily epic.

NEW AND DIFFERENT TIME ZONE. WHY I REFUSE TO BE BULLIED BY TIME.

Forget the to-do list. Create a to-be list.

— KELLY SULLIVAN RUTA

Here in the United States, we practice a ridiculous ritual called Daylight Savings Time. If nothing else, tinkering with our clocks is a potent reminder time is a construct we made up, a construct we can change.

As Alby E. used to say, "Time is but an illusion, albeit a persistent one."

So here's my proposal:

Let's rewrite the construct of time as a prison ("I never have enough." "There's too much to do.").

Instead of a number on a clock face, let's approach time as an unlimited gift of pure presence. As a deep moment just to be.

Congress created Daylight Savings Time.

I get to create my personal approach to time.

Do I want surface time? Ferrari, go, go, go time?

Or do I choose deep time: where all is possible, all is unlimited, all is here?

Lesson 308 (This instant is the only time there is) reminds me the only interval of time is now. No past. No future.

ROADSIDE FLARES

We're surrounded by things we cannot see.

— LOUIE SCHWARTZBERG

An old boyfriend of mine, a rational, left-brained advertising man, was sitting at his office desk one Tuesday when he suddenly got up, jumped in his car, and drove home. This never happened. He had trouble leaving work at day's end.

He pulled into his driveway at the unheard of hour of two in the afternoon . . . just in time to thwart a thief making off with his new TV.

This was a guy who wouldn't dream of uttering words like God or grace or guidance. As I recall, his favorite description of me was "way-too woo-woo." Yet, even though he'd never before left his office in the middle of the afternoon, he somehow picked up a signal to stop work immediately, to drive home now.

Lesson 309 says the universe is "there forever and forever." It constantly leaves bread crumbs, persistently sends up roadside flares—even when we're not paying attention.

IN GOOD WE TRUST

You must never allow something that happened to you
to become a morbidly treasured heirloom that you carry,
show people, put back in its black velvet pouch and then tuck
back into your jacket where you can keep it close to your heart.

— AUGUSTEN BURROUGHS

You know that story you tell about yourself? The one that describes you as dysfunctional or poor or desperately in need of something you don't have now?

That story is only true as long as you: a) continue to tell the story, b) continue to believe the story, and c) continue to live from that story.

Lesson 310 suggests writing a whole different stage play. One of thankfulness, joy, and unbridled fearlessness.

LIES MY EGO TELLS ME, PART II

When we live in our egoic minds, when we limit awareness to our physicality, we remain as paupers.

— ANNA ENEA

My ego is a loudmouth with lots of rules and limitations.

It orders me to sit in a corner by myself, to separate myself from all that I am. It uses judgment as a weapon against truth.

Its finest trick, according to Lesson 311, is to show me a partial picture. Urging me to believe that a single puzzle piece plucked from a 1,000-piece puzzle gives me an accurate picture of reality.

I can't really destroy the ego, but I can quit identifying with it. I can quit letting it call the shots. Today, I throw my singular puzzle piece back in the box, where the Holy S can use it to re-establish peace of mind.

A LIBERATED WORLD

By believing passionately in that which
does not yet exist, we create it.

— NIKOS KAZANTZAKIS

Who in their right mind buys a pizza, eats one slice, and then throws the rest into the trash can?

Yet, that's what I often do with my time. I throw away precious hours of my day in mindlessness, in judgment. Instead of being fully present, fully enjoying my oneness with daisies and squirrels and the driver beside me picking his nose, I analyze and scrutinize. I'm often, it seems, one judgment away from reality.

Lesson 312 says: I have no purpose today except to look upon a liberated world, set free from all judgments I have made.

As I liberate myself from my ridiculous blah-blah-blah judgments, I discover an all-absorbing, lustrous, and inexhaustible reality.

TO SEE ANEW

What are we believing that costs us our freedom, our happiness
and the awareness of our own true nature?

— BYRON KATIE

The ego is a master of disguise. It pretends to support spiritual enlightenment. It loudly applauds spirituality as a worthy, glorious goal.

"Too bad," it says, that it takes so damned long. Lesson 313 tells my ego to shut the h*ll up. It says instead:

1. THERE IS NO NEED TO WAIT. Love, peace, and joy are as close as my next breath. These attributes are literally who I am.

2. THERE IS NO NEED TO WORK HARD. The notion of working at being love or peace or joy is laughable. It's like working to breathe. Or working to make the sun come up.

3. MY OWN PERSONAL SUPERHERO IS ALWAYS ON CALL. ACIM says it like this: We are never left comfortless. At any time, the Holy S, our very own superhero, stands by waiting for our call. It never takes a break. It never demands overtime. Or maternity leave. It's ready and eager to respond to my every need.

I VOTE FOR LOVE

Use the present to be free.

— A COURSE IN MIRACLES

Lesson 314 (I seek a future different from the past) gives me an opportunity to see reality from a different angle.

The past tells me, "Uh-oh! We're in trouble."

But what if that's not true. What if it's only the judgments I've imposed that create a potentially scary future?

If it's true we live in an intelligent, benevolent, and connected universe (and I have ample proof that we do), I might as well relax, trust there's something a whole lot bigger going on.

When I come from a place of possibility, when there's peace in the planet of my own mind, change happens without my input.

A TALE OF TWO PERCEPTIONS

The ego wants all of us to have big buts.

— JAMES TWYMAN

A Course in Miracles has lots and lots and lots of pages, but it sorta boils down to this:

At every moment, I either perceive the world from love or from my ego.

The ego is the pernicious voice in my head that I often refer to as the asshat. It typically pipes up with some version of "Eeks! Fix this! Run!"

It usually goes something like this: "This is a mistake. Don't even try. It's too hard, too risky, too much work."

Love, on the other hand, says things like: You are more than enough. (And so is everybody else.) You have an important role to fulfill. (And so does everybody else.) Your mere presence is enough to change the world.

Lesson 315 is about making the choice. Which voice has the floor?

PAM AND THE TERRIBLE, HORRIBLE, NO GOOD, VERY BAD DAY

*Refuse to accept apparent delay and detour
as anything other than the perfect path.*

— U. S. ANDERSEN

Despite rumors to the contrary, I still occasionally feel like unflavored gelatin. I recently had one of those days. I was in Grand Haven, Michigan, recording the audio version of my book *Living Big* at a fancy-schmancy studio owned by Amazon.

My flight was delayed so I got in late, I had a headache, had to show up bright and early, and the producer was quick to point out my glaring inability to pronounce such words as *Dostoyevsky* and *joie de vivre*.

Now, I know good and well the only thing wrong in this situation was my attitude and my grumpy thoughts, but like a squid, I kept squirting out woe-is-me ink that put up a smoke screen between me and my highest intention, unceasing joy.

Finally, after leaving the studio and being unable to even muster the energy to walk very far along the gorgeous Lake Michigan beaches (I didn't even leave my normal beach affirmation), I returned to my hotel room and went to bed.

I woke up the next day feeling bright and sunny and was even grateful for the horrible, terrible, no good, very bad day. Here's why:

1. It made me achingly aware of how far I've come. Being disgruntled used to be a way of life. Going back for a little peek confirmed that it's not much fun.

2. I was able to be kind to myself in spite of it all. Okay, so I had a less-than-stellar day. So what? I used my magic words ("It's okay!") and shrugged it off as the perfect unfoldment and realization (see point 1) that I'm on the right path.

3. Lastly, I finally learned how to pronounce my favorite word: *Joie de vivre,* a French word that pretty much describes my life now that I've officially broken up with discontent and grumpiness.

JOY IS MY GPS

Sidewalks are littered with postcards from God.

— WALT WHITMAN

On a cruise to Bermuda, the captain made lots of jokes about finding the little speck of an island in the middle of the huge Atlantic.

Did I worry? Heck no! The ship's navigation equipment took us right to King's Wharf, right on schedule.

Even though Captain Dimitrios didn't constantly man the wheel (I know, because I sat next to him at dinner one night), we made it safely to our destination.

Lesson 317 says all of us have navigation equipment. Rather than be a slave to time and human destiny, we can set the destination of joy into our GPS. As we set sail (in any direction), the GPS will quickly tell us which way to go.

The ego tries to override our navigation equipment. It wants to man the wheel, supervise every step.

Today, I let the universe do the navigating, knowing the way is certain, the end secure.

WHY POSSIBILITY TRUMPS FACTS EVERY TIME

The man who views himself the same at 50 as
he did at 20 has wasted 30 years of his life.

— MUHAMMAD ALI

I'm a journalist, bound by the ethics of my profession to report the truth, to provide reliable, unbiased information.

But here's the rub. I no longer believe there is one truth to report, one single perception. "Reality" is up for grabs.

While reporting for, say, *People* magazine or CNN, both outlets for which I write, I will continue to gather "facts."

But here's the criteria I use for the rest of my life:

Is the story of service? Does it enlarge the conversation, strengthen the life force?

When I view "reality" through the lens of possibility rather than a solidified, this-is-just-how-it-is viewpoint, the new and magical is set into motion.

ANATOMY OF A GUILT TRIP

*The problem is not the problem. The problem
is your attitude towards the problem.*

— CAPTAIN JACK SPARROW

My dysfunction of choice has always been guilt. Maybe you've been on the same hamster wheel? The one where you obsessively worry about all the things you could have, should have, why didn't I? do better.

I wrongly believed that if I beat myself up, I would become a better person. If I listed my faults and came up with a plan to improve them, I would finally get the guy, the financial situation, the (fill in the blank) I so desired.

What I finally came to realize is guilt (and all its mean girl cousins) is a deterrent to miracles. Each "why didn't I?" only made the wall between me and my highest good more impenetrable.

As I began to dismantle each shaming thought, to take my focus off the "facts" of my pitiful existence, a higher Truth began trickling in. I am okay just the way I am.

Every wrinkle on my 60-something face, every age spot, every time I felt wronged or angry and acted less than the perfect human I aspired to be is okay.

Self-love isn't about getting a massage every other week or treating myself to a bubble bath—although they're nice gifts and never discouraged. Self-love is about accepting myself exactly as I am. Warts and all.

Guilt is as foolhardy as any military Strategic Defense Initiative. The only thing it deters is the always-flowing stream of universal good.

YOUR DEED TO THE WORLD'S MOST VALUABLE REAL ESTATE

*Eventually you will see that the real cause of
problems is not life itself. It's the commotion the mind
makes that really causes the problems.*

— MICHAEL SINGER

Terry Crews is a former pro football player, one of the stars of *Brooklyn 911*, and a former *Time* magazine "Person of the Year."

Even though he grew up with an abusive father in Flint, Michigan, where, as he says, he DID drink the water, he made the decision to employ Lesson 320: I am limitless.

Despite the boundaries of his culture, the brainwashing of his hood, he decided he was going to take charge, interpret life on his own terms.

In other words, he took control of the real estate of his consciousness. Instead of believing in limits, he created opportunities and possibilities. Instead of being tied to his back story, he decided who he was going to be.

By giving up limits, he went from poverty-stricken Flint hoodlum to incomparably successful movie star.

So today, as I repeat the phrase "I am unlimited" I take over the deed to the most exclusive and important piece of real estate—my consciousness.

STRIVING SUCKS
Or what self-help books fail to mention

If ever I am sad or hurt or ill, I have forgotten what God thinks and put my little meaningless ideas where His Thoughts belong.

— A COURSE IN MIRACLES

I know. I know. Many of my books are listed in the self-help section. But here's why I'd like to invent a new category:

Striving is unnecessary. Nothing is missing. Nothing is wrong. No matter how it appears to the naked eye, you, me, all of us are perfect just as we are. When I seek to "fix" something, I add weight to the illusion that something could be wrong. I begin seeking, I begin striving, which only trains me how to stay broken. Wanting to change sets off warning bells, sends up a red flare.

There's no need to follow the seven (or eight) steps. Most of us believe there's a linear progression. We go from A to B to C, etc. When I live in miracle mind (aka my natural state), answers arise spontaneously, people I'm meant to meet show up in the same aisle at the grocery store. Everything works without effort.

There's custom-designed guidance. One size (or diet plan or strategy for meeting your soulmate) does not fit all. Everything I need to know is already inside me. Any worthy pilgrimage always brings me straight back to myself.

So, I'd like to propose a name change. Instead of self-help, how about Self-Connecting to the Bigger Thing. Look for it at your local bookstore.

HIT THE ROAD, SMACK, NO MORE, NO MORE

Words are like eggs dropped from great heights; you can no more call them back than ignore the mess they leave when they fall.

— JODI PICOULT

When I talk smack about my life, even little things like, "Oh, I wish I'd gotten up earlier," "I wish that idiot in the passenger lane hadn't cut me off," I create a resonant field of issues and problems.

Instead of playing beautiful symphonies with my words, instead of utilizing them to create dreams, I often waste them moaning about problems.

Lesson 322 says, "fuhgeddaboutit." Those problems are just the ego talking. And the ego's not real.

Grievances hide all the gifts that "await me in shining welcome." Beyond the illusions is the Dude's overriding message: "Sacrifice remains forever inconceivable." The only thing I could ever lose is my fear.

LIGHTEN UP, FRANCIS!

Stress doesn't really go with my outfit.

— MEME THAT POPPED UP IN MY FB FEED

Today's lesson is provided by Bill Murray's sergeant in the movie *Stripes*. On the first night of boot camp, when members of Murray's platoon introduce themselves, a surly, uber-intense recruit stands up and announces: "The name's Francis Sawyer. But everybody calls me Psycho. Any of you guys call me Francis, I'll kill you. Also, I don't like anybody touching me. Keep your meat hooks off. Anyone here ever tries to touch me, I'll kill ya."

At that point, Army Sergeant Hulka, played by Warren Oates, jumps in with this now-famous line: "Lighten up, Francis!"

And that's what Lesson 323 asks me to do. To close all those open tabs in my brain. To gladly "sacrifice" all stress, anxiety, all sense of loss and sadness. To take my meat hooks off self-deception and false images. In other words, lighten up!

GET USED TO IT

*Once you buy into what @PamGrout is talking
about, #Weird Sh*t starts to happen.*

— COPIED FROM TWITTER

The asshat abhors Lesson 324.

"Like hell I will," it responds to all suggestions that it step aside and let the One Who Knows lead the way. It pitches a fit at the slightest hint that the Dude is chomping at the bit to get involved in my life, to connect with me, to provide me with guidance.

The ego is very protective of that job. It lives to plan, to work things out.

The ego comes up with a finite plan, a restricted process for getting from Point A to Point B.

It doesn't have a clue.

Here's an example. The ego wants to win the lottery.

There's nothing wrong with winning the lottery, but that's a finite way to achieve abundance. The Universe is frickin' infinite. It knows three bazillion ways to achieve abundance. So planning to win the lottery gives the Universe a grand total of one option.

Today, as I merely follow and not lead, I allow the universe to haggle with the details.

HI, *NEWMAN!*

When you're looking so hard to get on your path, you're putting up resistance that keeps you from finding it.

— ESTHER HICKS

Remember Newman? The ongoing *Seinfeld* character who annoyed Jerry to no end. There was the episode with the flea infestation, the time he narced on Jerry for making out during *Schindler's List*.

We all have Newmans in our lives, those nemeses at whom we shake our fists.

Lesson 325 reminds me that, just like *Seinfeld* writers created Newman to play Jerry's foil ("It was just fun to hate Newman," Jerry once said), my mind creates problems to duplicate my thoughts.

Everything I see starts in my mind. The Course describes it like this: "My mind creates an image of something it values, projects it outward, esteems it as real, and then guards it with care."

It's tempting to dismiss the Newmans in my life, to scapegoat them, to shove them out the door. But when I recognize it was me who wrote them into my script, I can forgive them, forgive myself, and send them lovingly back to Apartment E.

DRIVING A FRED FLINTSTONE CAR?

When you believe something, you have made it true for you.

— A COURSE IN MIRACLES

Lesson 326 is another reminder that thoughts have power, that the world I see is a representation of my state of mind.

When I devote my mind to the physical world, I'm locked in the ego's chamber of habitual patterns.

It's like driving a Fred Flintstone car. It doesn't take an engineer to figure out that when Fred treats the family to a drive-in brontosaurus burger, he's basically running, dragging Wilma, Pebbles, and the lumbering vehicle's massive granite wheels along for the ride.

Can we all agree Fred's car is not the most effective way to travel?

I have the capacity to use my mind for spiritual vision. The material world (my body, the stuff I see in the news) is but one piece of the chessboard.

I can use my mind to access the eternal part of myself or I can rely on feeble human effort. By thinking I have to perform or meet some standard or jump through hoops.

But here's the thing I forget. It's already mine. I don't have to earn it. Lesson 326 tells me it's a gift, and nothing can ever change that. Nothing can ever take it away. No matter what I do.

STOP THE SHOULD STORM

As long as your experience of self and life is defined by the mechanical, conditioned, and compulsive movement of thought, you are bound to a very, very limited perception of what is real.

— ADYASHANTI

It starts the moment we're born. We're measured and weighed, compared to other babies in the nursery. Gotta make sure we're the proper height, the proper weight.

Then we're taught language. Given rules. Told to forsake our imaginary friends.

It's not that the Dude deserted us. It's just hard to make contact through all the words, through the ongoing "should storm" of guilt and shame.

Even the self-help literature (and, yes, I'm one of its dispensers) makes us feel guilty. Oh no! I'm having a negative thought. I'm not vibrating enough joy.

You know what? It doesn't matter. If you simply let go of all "shoulds," you will be guided, blessed, and constantly taken care of. As Lesson 327 promises, I need but call. I will be answered.

WHAT'S POSSIBLE
IS FAR MORE IMPORTANT
THAN WHAT IS

Without leaps of imagination or dreaming, we lose the excitement
of possibilities. Dreaming, after all, is a form of planning.

— GLORIA STEINEM

We have a choice. We can place our attention on "what is" or we can dream of what can be. By placing our attention on new possibilities, we animate a completely different future.

Here are the headlines I like to envision:

New Ebola cases in Africa fall to zero
U.S. Democrats and Republicans hug it out on the
Senate floor
The Middle East celebrates 10 years of peaceful coexistence
Snow returns to Kilimanjaro
Pam Grout appears on SuperSoul Sunday

SO THE MOTHERSHIP CAN FIND ME

What good are all the courses, initiations, and headstands if, in the end, the ego does the leading.

— TOSHA SILVER

I wouldn't go on a date without brushing my teeth.

Or write a resume without adding my phone number.

So why start my day without tuning in to his Dudeship?

Lesson 329 says when I'm in "whiny baby mood," as Anne Lamott calls grumpiness, the mothership can't find me. It can't rescue me.

My only mission—and I choose to accept it—is to remain open to the transmission of the always-circling mothership.

WHO WANTS TO KNOW?

*The mind is the strutting actor on the stage who knows
how to complicate the simple and unweave the rainbow.*

— PICO IYER

There's love. And there's fear.

There's the Divine. And there's the ego.

One always makes you feel good. The other doesn't.

I get to decide to which I'm going to listen.

Lesson 330 says it's a no-brainer. Why hurt myself? Why give myself images of pain?

When I can just as easily accept my freedom, indulge my joy.

It pays to stop and question, "Who's asking?"

HOLDING A LUMINOUS VISION

Stay free inside the game. Find the glory inside
yourself so you can dance with a little more abandon,
with a little more shaking of those hips.

— BILLY FINGERS

Anyone who has ever donned a pair of Spanx understands the state of today's world. We squeeze our big, beautiful selves—our radiant, multidimensional spirits—into a tight, uncomfortable garment known as a body.

Our divine magnificence gets cuts off by the tight restriction of the cultural Kool-Aid.

We fall lockstep into the beliefs and traditions of our culture, however false and limiting they may be. Little by little, we learn the "correct" energetic-frequency rules, allowing only a small percentage of who we really are to radiate.

Lesson 331 says the Spanx are completely unnecessary. It says fear is a dream. Death is an illusion. Life is eternal. Today, I'm asked to give up suffering, abandon all sense of loss and sadness, forfeit all anxiety and doubt.

The Dude can then propel me into a dazzling new story. One with a guaranteed happy ending.

RED ALERT

Refusing to forgive is like being in a dump truck with tin cans
dragging off the backside. Clatter. Clatter. Clap. Clap.

— GLENDA GREEN

Important Safety Notice. Holding on to unforgiving thoughts will cause you to lose life's normal orientation of happiness. Believing in fear will keep your mind in chains. Avoid making any quick movements that could cause you to judge and injure yourself. If you continue believing your mind's futile thoughts, you are guaranteed to feel unwell.

Please don't drive, drink alcohol, operate heavy machinery, or pass judgment on anyone within your vicinity while consuming fear and believing its ugly thoughts.

If this happens, please discontinue its use immediately, which will allow light, hope, and peace to shine through.

WHAT "THEY" SAY
IS IRRELEVANT

*You move totally away from reality when you
believe there is a legitimate reason to suffer.*

— BYRON KATIE

Lesson 333 (Forgiveness ends the dream of conflict here) asks me to shine away conflict and doubt. It asks me to take responsibility for designing my own life.

Most of us believe our job in life is to set boundaries, to figure out what's not working and then to eradicate it.

People who do us wrong?

Gone.

Parents who didn't act like Ward and June Cleaver?

Out the window.

This attitude totally negates who we are. It's like signing the paper to a new house, walking in the front door, and storming out because there isn't any furniture. There's only one person who can furnish the house. It's up to you to create the kind of life you want. It's up to you to shine the light.

So often we get indignant: "I deserve much better than this." And you're right. You do. But it is your responsibility alone to create "much better than this."

Yes, you may be in a relationship that isn't loving. You may have a job that doesn't trip your trigger. But there is only one person with the power to change these things.

Calling out a search party for the next guy, the next job, the next self-help book is like calling the fire department to blow out the candles on your birthday cake.

Take what you have now. Take the relationships you have now. Take the job you have now. Take the home you have now. And let the Holy S turn them into something beautiful.

REWRITING MURPHY'S LAW

Reading the morning news is like
opening the bedroom door in Poltergeist
and seeing sh*t flying all around the room.

— ELIZABETH HACKETT

Murphy's law, a famous adage that most of us live by, states: "Anything that can go wrong will go wrong."

Lesson 334 begs to differ.

It is only our belief in problems that perpetuates the problems. Our constant struggle to awaken is the very obstacle to its accomplishment.

Whenever I am being my mind's bitch, I am not living in my natural state of joy. I am not living my Truth, which is that I am already free and infinite.

Instead of looking for the next teacher, the next book, the next process, I would like to suggest we spend time following the Dude's law that states: "Anything that can go right will."

Once we start noticing all that's going right, that is all we will see.

ROLLING IN ECSTASY

Every leaf speaks bliss to me, fluttering from the autumn tree.

— EMILY BRONTE

One afternoon, when Taz was four, she was playing "mom" in the backyard with her friend, Ashley. Ashley had taken her turn being "mom" and had dutifully washed the pretend dishes, hung up the pretend laundry, and ordered her pretend daughter, Taz, to pick up her toys.

When Taz's turn came, she said, "Okay, now I'm the mom. I'm going to go meditate."

It was one of my proudest moments. My daughter believed that's what moms do first.

I don't remember her friend's response, but I do know this. The most important thing I could ever do is get in tune with the Divine Buzz, to know, as Lesson 335 promises, this moment is all there is.

I can read all the books, follow all the steps, write affirmations to the moon and back, but until I begin to feel the invisible, yet palpable buzz of right now, I will spend my life searching.

It's all right here. In this moment.

SWITCH ON THE INVISIBLE

The world is sneakier than I thought, more mysterious
and filled with wonder than I boiled things down to.

— LISA GUNGOR

Lesson 336 tells me the highway no longer leads to interesting places. Its sights and sounds, at best, show me distortions of yesterday. Today, I happily enter uncharted territory by tuning into what's invisible.

I appoint Sakima, an aid worker from Afghanistan, to be my role model. She works with Afghani families caught between the forces of sectarian violence. Many have sons who, out of desperation, have joined ISIS or the Taliban.

But Sakima refuses to see them that way. Even when they point guns at her head.

"I know who you are even if you don't," she says to them. "You can't fool me."

She sees beyond their "story." She sees them as God sees them, as a spark of herself. Instead of vengeance and bloodshed, she holds peace. She's able to call forth the invisible.

Her vision of love and truth is so strong that she's able to enter dangerous situations, even war zones, without fear.

Today, I recognize the power in seeing things differently. The current story of differences and danger is an unreliable guide. I practice instead seeing God in everything.

I NEED DO NOTHING, EPISODE II

Hard work is damn near as overrated as monogamy.

— HUEY LONG

We, in the West, tend to be action-oriented. The Course urges us to save time by "not doing." In fact, we're told to practice little else. "Doing nothing," Lesson 337 purports, is a grand "statement of allegiance."

Consider:

A caterpillar does jack sh*t before emerging from the chrysalis, ready to fly.

Eckhart Tolle sat on a park bench for two-and-a-half years before becoming what Watkins Review called "the most spiritually influential person in the world."

Nelson Mandela was imprisoned on tiny Robbin Island for 27 years before becoming president and one of the most revolutionary leaders of our time.

DON'T BUY YOUR DIAGNOSIS

Reality is so vast that there is no way from our small place in the universe to see it all. We create cultural constructs of our knowledge and try and make the whole vast infinite universe fit in our tiny little boxes.

— LYSSA DANEHY DEHART

Whatever affliction you believe about yourself is a hoax. It's a tiny box that you continue to animate by your belief in it.

I know it seems like stone-cold fact that you are depressed or financially challenged or still suffering the aftermath of something your parent did or didn't do.

But it's just not true.

Get Lesson 338 (I am affected only by my thoughts), apply it without exception, and you will be released from all fear. Nothing will be able to frighten you. Nothing will be able to endanger you. You will have no enemies and will be safe from all external things.

So how do you want to describe yourself today: As a hot mess? Or as hot sh*t?

THE MYSTERIOUS CASE OF
TOP-SECRET COLLUSION

The world is neither good nor bad nor defective, nor is it in need of help or modification. Its appearance is only a projection of one's own mind. No such world exists.

— DAVID R. HAWKINS

Lesson 339 (I will receive whatever I request) suggests we're the ones who asked for our pain, who asked to be frightened. Needless to say, it provokes the following reaction:

There is no way I asked for this sh*t. You can kiss my lily-loving ass.

Rather than argue, this lesson gives us a break. It says we're simply confused.

It says we've spent the last 2000 years colluding with the ego, getting our intel from a little voice inside our head that tells us we're powerless and that it's better to play it safe.

The ego is a crafty mother that has been yanking our chains for too long. It's loud and it lies and it dishes up the fake news that we are nothing but crumbling bodies destined to die horrible deaths.

It tells us that other people are scary. That we must protect ourselves. But it's all smoke and mirrors.

It's time, guys. Let's quit colluding with the ego. Quit colluding with our wounds, with our problems.

Let us resolve today to ask for what we really want: to join forces with the light, the love, the beauty. Let's be fearless!

#MeToo Escaping the Abusive Relationship of My Ego and Its Henchmen

Your story doesn't hold a candle to who you really are.

— John O'Donohue

I've heard all the stories: Weinstein, CK, yada, yada! And here's what I know.

There's not a misogynist alive that's half as bad as the abuser in my brain. Perhaps you know him? The voice that tells me and everybody else that's living and breathing that something is wrong, that something needs to be fixed.

A Course in Miracles calls this voice the ego. It's the opposite of love and it shows up as fear. It's a big fat liar and, pardon my French, but it's full of caca. It runs on three main themes: "Do Something. You're screwed. Run."

It shoves us away from what we've been put on this earth to do—to love, to connect, to create ridiculously beautiful things.

Lesson 340 (I can be free of suffering today) tells me there's a much more compelling voice. One that knows how to be free. So let's celebrate today. Be glad!

And know, "There is no room for anything but joy and thanks today."

ANYTHING YOU CAN DO . . .

To change your life, start immediately.
Do it flamboyantly. No exceptions.

— WILLIAM JAMES

The soundtrack of my childhood (thanks to my mom, who was a pianist and church organist) was hymns and Broadway tunes.

I was particularly fond of "Annie Get Your Gun" where Annie Oakley and Frank Butler, playing one-upmanship, sang "Anything you can do I can do better. I can do anything better than you."

I think of that song whenever I think about J.C. You know the cute guy with the beard and sandals that, according to the Bible, told us point blank that, "Any miracle he can do, we can do better. We can do any miracle better than him."

So far, I've yet to walk on the Sea of Galilee or turn water into my favorite glass of Cabernet, but neither activity resides on the top ten of my bucket list.

I'm more motivated by miracles of love, where people who used to hate each other realize they don't. Or where some limiting belief that kept me stuck in an old pattern gets turned into a whole new possibility.

Lesson 341 says it's time to start performing miracles. To start one-upping J.C. He'd have it no other way.

DRINK IT UP, MY FRIENDS

Love God and do what you want.

— ST. AUGUSTINE

I used to believe if I surrendered to the Dude, I'd be required to work with starving babies in countries with Ebola and typhoid and other unmentionable diseases. I attribute this to the stream of foreign missionaries that came through my home when I was a kid.

Lesson 342 tells me the only thing the Dude asks of me is to expand His goodness and to love as much as I possibly can.

By simply showing up and using the gifts I was given, I receive even more gifts. To name just a few:

1. I was invited to Verona, Italy, where I danced to a 12-piece orchestra at a 16th-century estate that once hosted Winston Churchill and Lady Di, and I stood on Juliet's famous balcony. For good measure, I even shouted, "Wherefore art thou, Romeo."

2. I was slathered by volcanic ash and sand at the Puning Hot Springs and Spa near Mount Pinatubo, Philippines.

3. I was hosted in a Renaissance castle (complete with moat) just outside the medieval town of Kutna Hora, a UNESCO World Heritage site in the Czech Republic.

4. I walked 40 miles of the Cotswold Trail in England. It's where the PBS show *Father Brown* is filmed.

5. And I got to help break the Guinness World record for most zombies (I used beet juice for blood) dancing to Michael Jackson's "Thriller."

I love that about the Dude. He only wants my good, only wants to bless me, only wants me to use my gifts to expand His glory.

343

THERE'S MORE WHERE THAT CAME FROM

Believing in scarcity alters how we look at things. Our single-mindedness to scarcity leads us to neglect things we actually value.

— SENDHIL MULLAINATHAN

Lesson 343 (I am not asked to make a sacrifice to find the Dude's mercy and peace) defies the scarcity principle that runs our planet.

When we operate from a scarcity mind-set, we hoard, refuse to share, and lead with an overly protectionist stance. This misguided stance squeezes the life, the light, and the love right out of us.

Things of true value (in fact, that's how you can tell how valuable something really is) are not scarce. They've never been scarce. Ideas, appreciation, gratitude, and love are infinite, and multiply like mold on an old slice of bread when offered freely.

When we assume scarcity, as we're taught in this society, we limit our potential, we limit possibilities. It impacts how we think about ourselves and about others.

Today, I'm encouraged to believe in my own vast untapped potential. And to recognize that others have the same infinite resources within.

Nothing real, nothing of value is finite. Everything real is self-generating, multidimensional, and only expands when given freely.

IT'S ALL PRESENT NOW

Children see magic because they look for it.

— CHRISTOPHER MOORE

Preschoolers don't sit in front of a pail of Legos thinking, "Nah! Not feeling it today." They don't worry about ISIS.

Never crosses their mind to question their ability, worry what someone will think.

They plunge in, unhindered, free, happy.

My friend Carla tells a wonderful story about her daughter who was dancing with great abandon. A well-meaning adult, watching nearby, said, "Wow! I'm impressed. Are you going to be a dancer someday?"

Carla's daughter stopped, looked her square in the eye and retorted, "What do you mean? I already am!"

Lesson 344 seconds Carla's daughter. We already are everything we want to be.

Shall we begin?

WINNER, WINNER, CHICKEN DINNER

We can never perceive what is real.
We can only perceive what is real for us.

— BARBARA DEWEY

Your beliefs recreate and reproduce themselves in physical reality. Which is why thoughts become things. Why what we focus upon expands. The external world is the display screen of your innermost beliefs. Blaming life for your misfortunes is like accusing your smartphone of running lousy apps. You're the one who downloaded them.

Few of us truly understand the potency of our thoughts and beliefs. A thought is a seed, a unit of mental energy that plays out in the world as powerfully as gravity or the principle of aerodynamics.

A thought that carries sufficient intent, emotional impact, and conviction of belief (whether true or not) takes root and stimulates materialization.

You might want to read that last bit again. Beliefs (whether true or not) stimulate materialization.

So if you believe life is an unending struggle, that bodies have no choice but to deteriorate, or that most guys are jerks, that's the script that will play out in your life.

Lesson 345 reminds us that putting faith in erroneous beliefs absconds with our miracles. So today we say, "Scat!" to all falsehoods and claim only miracles.

HOLY AMNESIA

Love allows you to transcend the great fear, the great suffering that comes from a temporary, mistaken-identity problem.

— THE WAY OF MASTERY

Lesson 346 (I forget all things except Love) promises I will wake today with miracles correcting my perception of all things.

I will know that "My safety, peace, and joy are totally beyond question. And that any perceived problem is not a problem of fact, but a problem of understanding."

No more do I short-circuit the Divine Spark with petty whining, judgments, and unresolved emotional issues.

Today, I throw all that aside.

And I rest in that which transcends all laws of time.

PUTTING ON MY
BIG-GIRL PANTIES

Argue for your limitations, and sure enough they're yours.

— RICHARD BACH

When I was a kid, I loved playing hide-and-go-seek. One of us would be "it" and the rest of us would hide in Mom's closet, underneath the coffee table, or, if we were playing outside, behind the neighbor's shed.

The whole point was to find someone who wasn't *really* missing. One exuberant "olly-olly-oxen-free" was all it took to reunite us.

Lesson 347 points out that I'm still playing a childish game of hide-and-go-seek. Not only do I spend most days covering my eyes and counting to ten, but I waste my time searching for things that aren't missing.

My culture trains me to find problems, limitations, and mistakes. It trains me to then devise plans to fix them.

The Course says my time would be better spent recognizing that, in reality, nothing is missing, recognizing that it only appears missing because I spend time looking for it.

When I say, "I want this," I make the assumption I don't already have it.

When I say, "I need to be healthier or more spiritual," I embark on a journey to find the very things that are already my birthright.

It is only my decision to seek something that creates the perception it's concealed.

A Course in Miracles reminds me that I already have all the love, all the abundance, all the joy I need. And at any time, I can quit playing make believe and just say "thank you!"

I can pretend to be lacking. Profess the need to be skinnier. Or wealthier. Or shacking up with Mr. Right.

Or I can acknowledge that I'm the one who made the obstacle course. And can call olly-olly-oxen-free.

LARRY DAVID OR
MR. ROGERS?

My most profound lessons about life, love, goodness
and courage were revealed through gratitude when
Heaven and I were barely on speaking terms.

— SARAH BAN BREATHNACH

Back in Paleolithic times, survival depended on keeping a mental file of which berries were poisonous, which rocks made the best tools for fending off mastodons and giant sloths.

Lesson 348 says those days are long gone. It says there's absolutely no reason to hang on to pointless information regarding our survival. We're literally surrounded by the Dude's love. There's absolutely nothing to fear, no cause for anger.

Today, instead of working to ensure my survival, I celebrate all that I have. I see my life as a grand unfolding of grace.

Mr. Rogers, here I come!

ET TU, GROVER?

We are all just standing on piles of collective fiction.

— ASHTON KUTCHER

I take my inspiration wherever I can get it. Grover—yes, the Muppet Grover—taught me everything I need to know about fear.

In *The Monster at the End of This Book,* an '80s children's book, the lovable Muppet warns his readers that, whatever they do, they should not TURN THE NEXT PAGE because (gulp!) there's a monster at the end of the book.

As the reader bravely continues to flip through the pages, Grover gets more and more freaked out. "STOP!!" he warns. "You turned the page. You must STOP turning pages."

In his desperation, Grover, who claims to be "so scared of monsters," attempts to nail the pages shut. He tries to tie the pages down. He even builds a big brick wall.

But despite Grover's attempts to avoid this long-feared serial killer, the reader keeps turning pages, getting ever closer to the monster and the chilling conclusion at the end of the book.

Finally, when the reader reaches the last page, he discovers that the evil monster is none other than the furry blue Grover himself, harmless and nothing like he feared.

As Grover learns to embrace the monster within, he realizes that Franklin D. Roosevelt was right. Fear is self-generated, overblown, and never worth our energy.

MANIFESTERS WHO DO TOO MUCH

She would think things so hard that they showed on her face.

— AMANDA PALMER

I got an email the other day from a reader of one of my books. "Help," she said, "I can't figure out what I'm doing wrong. I meditate every day. I've made at least three vision boards. Every morning, I make lists of positive aspects. I've got a focus wheel. (These last two are practices recommended by Abraham-Hicks.) And nothing is happening."

I was exhausted just reading her email. And here's what I told her after I took a few deep breaths: All those practices are fabulous. I'm a fan of Abraham-Hicks myself.

And I know how tempting it is to work hard, to try, try, try.

But when I "try so hard," I negate Truth. I put up roadblocks to all the good that wants to manifest before my eyes. This is important to say again.

Everything I'm trying to manifest is already mine. It's right there in my field of potentiality, twiddling its thumbs. Except when I'm on a different wavelength (the wavelength of *I don't have it*, the wavelength of *Better put on my running shoes and move faster, try harder)*, it's invisible.

Just like a filmmaker decides upon which of many objects his lens focuses, I get to decide if I want to zero in on the stuff in the foreground (what I have now) or if I prefer pointing my lens on something else.

Reality is never static or complete. It's an unending process of movement and unfoldment. I'm the cameraman. I choose what to unfold, what to put in my lens, where to point my viewfinder.

PERCEIVE ALL THINGS AS KINDLY AND GOOD

*My gratitude quest has taken me across time zones,
and up and down the social ladder. It's made
me rethink everything from globalism to beavers,
from hugs to fonts, from lightbulbs to ancient Rome.*

— A. J. JACOBS

Lesson 351 reminds me that I will behold whatever I choose to behold. And it points out that if my choice of beholdment (is that even a word?) differs from the Dude's then, well, it might not make me dance with joy. If I choose to behold, you know, something like my brother's greed or my sister's fear, I'm at odds with my highest being.

And that's where it begins. That's when my mind starts riffing that there's a problem.

I've found I can cut it off at the pass by fiercely practicing gratitude. Not only do I get all the psychological bennies—lifts depression, helps me sleep, incites generosity—but when I count my blessings like a mofo, my radio dial stays tuned to the same channel as the Dude.

THESE GHOSTS AREN'T CONJURED UP WITH OUIJA BOARDS

We live our lives in a state of nearly perpetual reaction and self-protection.

— RICHARD MOSS, M.D.

If you caught the 10-episode Netflix series *The Haunting of Hill House,* you're already a pro at ACIM Lesson 352. You know that all the sorrows of the world (or the ghosts, in the case of Hill House) are self-created and no more than our own psyches of guilt and fear jumping out from the dark to rattle us.

Like the five siblings who grew up in the old Gothic fixer-upper, we project paranormal images from our past, created by ongoing judgments, ongoing beliefs that the rapidly escalating tension is real.

Hate to be the sop that spoils the cliffhanger, my friends, but that TV is nothing but a screen, projecting harmless waves of energy. And just like the Dudleys, the Hill House caretakers who choose to go home every night, we can return to peace and safety whenever we choose.

Today's lesson reminds us we always have a choice. We can ratchet down the suspense and be restored to peace by—guess what?—simply turning off the TV, simply forgiving the horror story we've long chosen to scare ourselves with. At any time, we can go home to our Source.

LIFE-CHANGING REMINDER TO TATTOO UPON MY BODY

I don't have issues. I have subscriptions.

— GREG TAMBLYN

I've noticed an odd tendency among readers of my books. They make the disturbing assumption that I have my sh*t 100 percent together.

While that's certainly a beautiful notion and, in Truth, we are all perfect, beautiful, secret agents for the Dude, I sometimes forget.

So here's the tattoo-worthy reminder:

Successful people also feel fear and doubt and have bad ideas.

It's vital to remember this. Because when we feel fear or doubt or have a bad idea, we too often decide there's something wrong with us and that we'll never write that book or find that relationship or do the thing that our heart is bugling out for us to do.

I gain the strength to follow my heart's bidding by hanging out regularly with what I call my possibility posses. As songwriter Greg Tamblyn reminded me yesterday, everybody needs to find a group of abnormal people to commune with.

We're abnormal in that we tell stories that defy what society tells us is normal. We tell stories about miracles and possibilities. We witness to the fact that when we get on the right frequency, the bigger thing has ample room to work with us, to guide us, to bless us. And when one of us is having an "issue" or even a "subscription," the rest of us can gently point out that: "Yep, that's one story. But there are a gazillion others."

All of us are all full of stories. Why not be abnormal and choose the ones that instill peace and joy and light?

IT'S IMPOSSIBLE TO FALL SHORT OF THE GLORY OF GOD

We are players, actors on many stages. We yearn to wonder, we long to be amazed, to be enthusiastic, to be expressive. In short, to be alive."

— MATTHEW FOX

Although the term "fake news" is nearly as popular as "Despacito," it recently hit me that the first purveyor of vicious falsehoods was probably the fundamentalist church. It created its entire doctrine around the idea that "all men have sinned and fallen short of the glory of God." Think about it. The first thing a young child learns sitting in the pew is that he (or she) was born into original sin.

My message, same one that J.C. and the Holy S came to spread, is that every one of us, without exception, is born into original blessing. Every one of us is entitled to an infinite outpouring of the Divine.

This flow never stops. It can't. It's impossible for it not to love, to bless, to comfort, to pass out miracles. Sin, in fact, is nothing but a mistaken identity, an oft-repeated item of fake news.

THE ONGOING ANTICS OF MY MIND

*We all have a lot of enculturation
that has muddied up who we are.*

— NATALIE SUDMAN

The asshat churns up thoughts. By some estimates, the average human brain regurgitates 60,000 to 90,000 thoughts per day.

The war begins when I pluck a particular thought out of the normal litany and declare it to be "a problem."

When I make myself wrong (say, for being afraid to speak in public) is when it owns me.

Fear is a standard song in the jukebox of the human mind. It's the most normal thing in the world. I know fear's Apple ID, its first pet, the name of its kindergarten teacher.

The trick is to put a period at the end of those thoughts. I'm afraid. Period. I think I can't speak. Period.

It's only when I start adding humiliating extra clauses (I'm afraid and that means there's something wrong with me, I'm panicking and that means I'm inferior, I'm terrified and that means I should just run away) that it grows into an insurmountable thornbush.

What if I simply recognized that there's nothing bad or unnatural going on here?

Under the thornbush, waiting patiently for our awareness, is this truth from Lesson 355: There is no end to all the peace and joy and miracles that I can give.

BEAM ME DOWN, SCOTTY

*Why do we accept the programming from
our youth as the source of all truths?*

— NAVAL RAVIKANT

Other than the bit about drinking eight glasses of water, most of what I learned as a kid is limiting and self-defeating.

Today, I pledge to reinstall the attitudes I had before I learned it was "wrong" to jump on the bed. I discard these six childhood lessons:

1. "Wipe that silly grin off your face."
   Replacement: Loosen up. Claim your silly.

2. "Be careful."
   Replacement: Throw caution to the wind. Take risks. Fall flat on your face.

3. "Don't speak to strangers."
   Replacement: Speak to everyone. Speak until there ARE no strangers.

4. "Don't leave the house without clean underwear."
   Replacement: It doesn't matter what kind of underwear (or shoes or purse) you're wearing. What matters are the dreams written on your heart.

5. "Stay in line."
   Replacement. Anything is possible and you are free to adapt any guidelines you choose. But there is no line.

6. "Always look out for number one."
   Replacement: Give everything you've got to everyone you see. No exceptions.

A MULTIPLE CHOICE OF PERCEPTIONS. CHOOSE WONDERMENT.

What power is this. I can't say. I just know that it's there.

— ALEXANDER GRAHAM BELL

A few years ago, at a workshop in British Columbia, I was spouting my normal controversial belief that joy is possible in every situation. Some of the workshop participants weren't buying it. *Oh yeah! What about this? What about that?*

One participant, whose father worked for an international corporation, told the group about her family's housekeeper in the Philippines. She loved life with a deep and abiding joy, found astonishment in everything. Her unabashed contentment and happiness provided a continual source of inspiration to the wealthy family who employed her.

One day, a tsunami or earthquake or typhoon (I don't remember the exact natural disaster) struck. The wealthy family fretted after hearing that their housekeeper's family home had been swept away, completely obliterated in the storm. When she showed up for work the next week, they tiptoed around, wondering how they could help. They fully expected her to be morose, to have lost her unbridled enthusiasm for the beauty of each moment.

"Oh, we are having so much fun," she said. "My whole family, including all the aunts and uncles and cousins are living together in the basement of a church. It has been so fantastic all of us being together."

Say what?

How was this even possible? How could she find joy in what most of us would rate as one of the top worst things that could ever happen.

Stubborn gladness, my friends, is an internal decision. Life is sometimes gonna throw curveballs. But it's up to us to cultivate joy and find the wonderment that, like air, always surrounds us.

THE EASY WAY
TO GET FOUND

Many people never disband their armies,
never go beyond what they know.

— REBECCA SOLNIT

So far (knock on wood), I've never required the aid of a search-and-rescue team. These selfless, often volunteer do-gooders devote their time to finding and providing aid to campers, climbers, hikers, and other humans who, for whatever reason, aren't attending to weather, geological landmarks, the direction of the sun or, for that matter, their intended route.

They end up lost, distressed, and sometimes, sadly, in imminent danger.

Although the necessary skills vary (depends on if it's a mountain rescue, a ground search, a rope rescue, a swift water rescue, etc.), every search-and-rescue pro knows this one fact.

Children are far easier to find than adults, because well, they're willing to admit they're lost. They don't stray far, they curl up in a shelter somewhere, they know they need help.

When it comes to ACIM Lesson 358, it pays to, as J.C. suggests, "Become as a little child."

Sure, I can keep stubbornly seeking for the path, continue backtracking and crisscrossing and struggling for the answer, or I can curl up and rest, knowing I am safe, invulnerable, and never really lost.

WHEE!

He's so optimistic that if his house is on fire,
he roasts marshmallows.

— AISHA TAYLOR

The plane was about 20 minutes from landing in Vegas. The pilot came over the loudspeaker.

"Okay, folks!" he said. "It looks like high desert winds are going to prevent us from landing. We've been asked by traffic control to circle above the airport until the weather shifts. It's going to be bumpy, so please fasten your seatbelts."

Sure enough, the plane started dipping and bumping and rocking like a mad bull. It got so bad that . . . you know those air sickness bags in the pocket with the airline magazines? The passenger in 16A used hers. Which started a fad.

People were exchanging worried looks and grabbing each other's hands and proving the old "There are no atheists in foxholes" aphorism.

Suddenly, from the back of the plane, there's a giggly, high-spirited, "Whee!"

The two-year-old in 28D had his hands in the air. He was having the time of his life. Every time the plane bucked, he'd celebrate with a full-throated whee!

He wasn't yet encumbered with fear, he hadn't yet learned to worry for his safety. He was fully present to the moment.

Lesson 359 tells us to be more like the two-year-old in 28D. "Rejoice," it says, "that misery is replaced with joy. And that sin is merely a mistake."

Whee!

360

BEEN-THERE-DONE-
THAT-NO-THANKS

*Nanny Ogg looked under her bed in case there was
a man there. Well, you never knew your luck.*

— TERRY PRATCHETT

The world I see is old news, like ABC (already been chewed) gum. Been-there-done-that-no-thanks.

The old reality is reductionist, judgmental, a know-it-all. My brain, specifically the prefrontal cortex, engineers reality. It crunches and tags data, filters and constructs information according to the default programming I've set up. This programming decides what to let in, what to suppress, and what to believe is possible.

The higher, more subtle energy realms end up getting deleted, while the regularly scheduled programs—sensations in our bodies, nearby material things—get enhanced and directed to center stage.

Today, I attend to the bigger, non-visible world. I put my faith in the new story, the inclusive, everyone-belongs story.

WHY I NO LONGER MARCH IN THE STREETS

Turn your light on for those with no vision.

— PHARRELL WILLIAMS

I used to ADORE a good protest! I marched against war, against guns, against racism.

Nothing's more exhilarating than carrying a sign and chanting in resistance with fellow comrades.

But it finally dawned on me that being AGAINST something only adds energy to a reality I no longer want. It gives things I don't like more credit than they deserve. And it negates my power to create something better.

Now, I prefer to be FOR things. I prefer to create better things. Things that make the old things obsolete.

Remember dial telephones? Black-and-white TVs? Card catalogs in libraries? Nobody carried placards to protest those things. Rather, someone came up with a better vision.

Fighting against something only makes it more real. Forgiving (aka: no longer resisting) makes room for new things to burst forth. It makes room for a new vision.

There's still no shortage of things I'd like to change. It's just that now I go about it by using my true power to imagine new things.

I use two very significant words. What if?

TALKING AND
THINKING TRASH NO MORE

The bliss, the wisdom, the creativity, the laughter,
the friendships, the joy, the serenity and peace
that have been, for the most part, seen as an impossible
dream will become your most ordinary state of being.

— THE WAY OF MASTERY

Talking trash was forbidden in my family. Even repeating the word "butt" was grounds for "the look" or, worse, a spanking.

What WAS allowed, perhaps even encouraged, was THINKING trash, as in, "I probably shouldn't, I probably couldn't, I better not."

This trash thinking creates a cloud of debris (like Pig-Pen from the Peanuts cartoon) that blocks universal flow.

Lesson 362 assures me that, whether I'm aware of it or not, there's a part of my mind where stillness and peace reign.

I often fail to recognize the stillness and peace, because my trash thinking clogs up the transmission. Unlike the cloud around Charlie Brown's friend, my energetic cloud is largely invisible. But it's just as effective at keeping the world's goodness locked out.

It's why I attempt to keep my personal climate as pure and positive as possible. It's why I get up every morning and declare, "Something extraordinarily epic is going to happen to me today." It's why I meditate and actively look for blessings.

Above all else, I choose to listen. And I affirm that Source really, really, really wants me to hear its "Psst! Hey you!"

THE DUDE'S MOCCASINS

Silence is God's first language.
Everything else is a poor translation.

— THOMAS KEATING

You've probably heard the proverb, "Do not judge a man until you walk two moons (or a mile) in his moccasins."

So today, I'd like to give you a little taste of what it's like to walk in the Dude's moccasins.

You: "I really want to travel."

The Dude: "Awesome sauce! I'd love to set that up for you. Where do you want to go?"

You: "Ummm, well, maybe Paris. Or wait. No, I really want to go to the Caribbean. Except, no, I always wanted to learn to tango in Buenos Aires. But wait, can I really afford it?"

These are the kind of messages the Dude gets all day, every day.

On one hand, we want a new car, but on the other, won't that mean higher payments? We hope for a positive outcome, but isn't optimism a bunch of baloney? We want to be committed to so-and-so, but what if she leaves?

The reason we don't turn water into wine and heal illness with one touch is because our thoughts are scattered all over the place. Instead of being one constant, well-aimed tuning fork, our thoughts are like a junior high band of trumpet players.

The force is literally bouncing off walls. Go this way. No, wait, go that way. It's knocking around like a lightning bug in a Mason jar. This amazing all-powerful force that works with the certainty of mathematics is being dissipated because we have no clear bead on what we really want.

It's not that the Dude isn't materializing your thoughts. It's just you're thinking way too many, completely opposite things.

GRATITUDE, PLEASE

Absolutely everything is available to us—sorrow and joy, grievance and forgiveness, horror and transcendence—it's all on the menu. It's up to us where we put our attention.

— JOSH RADNOR

Tuning in to gratitude each morning is a piece of cake when life is humming—I'm healthy, I'm in love, there's scads of moolah in the bank. But the real mystical power of gratitude comes when I'm falling apart, stumbling in the dark, crying myself to sleep.

ACIM suggests "giving thanks in all circumstances," but it doesn't say I have to high-five my "enemy" when giving it. Sometimes it's all I can do to force—through gritted teeth—a sarcastic "thanks a lot."

But it's that daily litany of gratitude that enables me to drop back into alignment with my inner source of power, wisdom, strength, and love that, damn it, is far greater than my own.

Counting my blessings, more than penciling a written list, is to practice alchemy. Looking for the good in life physically changes things. Financially changes things. It literally reconfigures atoms and rearranges molecules.

Epilogue

Memory of joy and liberation can become
a navigational tool, an identity, a gift.

— REBECCA SOLNIT

Hip, hip, hooray! You made it across the finish line. You completed the 365 lessons. (Either that or you've skipped ahead and that's okay, too.)

Now that you're regularly hooking up with the Voice, you don't need me or this damned book (or any other) to find answers.

Now that you know the mind-blowing secret (that you are connected to everyone and everything in the universe), you can deploy this connection on a moment-by-moment basis.

If you ask nicely (even sometimes when you don't), the Holy S will take the wheel from here. It will guide you and tell you exactly what to do. In every situation.

As for you and me, let me just offer thanks for joining me on this trek. I trust we will all meet up again someday at some weird planetary soul convention. We will look back, slap our knees, and guffaw at all the preposterous things we used to believe.

That we were helpless and all alone. That we were manning the dials on this little orb hurtling through space.

But for now, it's time to go out and do this thing! Fully, with great aplomb, with great love and joy.

And I will end with this page from the calendar that was lovingly created for me (and now for you, too) by my infinitely talented, amazingly awesome daughter, Tasman McKay Grout.

Something

AMAZINGLY AWESOME
BODACIOUSLY BRILLIANT
CAPTIVATINGLY COSMIC
DELICIOUSLY DELIGHTFUL
EXTRAORDINARILY EPIC
FEROCIOUSLY FANTASTIC
GLEEFULLY GLORIOUS
HILARIOUSLY HISTORIC
INTRINSICLY ILLUSTRIOUS
JUBILANTLY JOYFUL
KEENLY KENETIC
LUMINOUSLY LUSCIOUS
MARVELOUSLY MAGNIFICENT
NOTORIOUSLY NOTEWORTHY
OUTRAGEOUSLY OVER-THE-TOP
PROFOUNDLY PERFECT
QUIXOTICALLY QUANTUM
RIDICULOUSLY RIP-ROARING
STUPENDOUSLY STUNNING
TOTALLY TANTALIZING
UNDENIABLY UNIQUE
VIBRANTLY VICTORIOUS
WILDLY WONDROUS
(e)XPEDITIOUSLY eXTRAORDINARY
YABADABAINDUBIOUSLY YUMNIFICENT
ZEALOUSLY ZEN

is going to

happen

this year

FROM THE BOTTOM
OF MY HEART

Do not the most moving moments of our
lives find us all without words?

— MARCEL MARCEAU

Where do I begin? I owe an extraordinary debt to so many people who have picked me up, put bandages on my broken heart, and supported me during the writing of this book. I exaggerate not when I say it has been the most challenging year of my life.

If it wasn't for my readers, I'm not sure I'd even be here. You have kept me going with your kind words, your encouragement, your sightings of 222. I love that Taz has become special to so many of you. She truly was (and still is) a remarkable person.

Jim Dick already knows how much I appreciate him. It would be impossible to repay him for his steady, calm presence in my life. He's an unwavering rock. He also makes killer pancakes and veggie rice.

I'm also in the debt of countless writers who have inspired me over the years, Hay House for saying "yes!" and providing me with a steady stream of lessons in patience (Amor Fati!), and Anne Barthel, my permanently busy editor who fielded my never-ending questions, made time to read the extra books I created as giveaways on the landing page, and put up with my continuously rotating copy. Thanks for playing what had to be a challenging role as a go-between.

A special thanks to Molly and Ivy Kahn for driving 1,840 miles to be by my side at the hospital and to Mary Condron who dropped everything last Thanksgiving to join me in India.

Shout-outs as always to my possibility posses, the whole Sheridan clan, my sister, Becki Sasser, Joyce Barrett, Kelley Hunt, Melanie Loyd, Robbin Loomas, Cindy Novelo, Cindy Whitmer, Anita Moorjani, Mike Dooley, Taz's amazing friends, and every person who senses in their heart that something a whole lot greater is afoot. 222 Forever!

ABOUT
THE AUTHOR

Pam Grout is a freelance writer who has published with *Scientific American Explorations, Outside, Men's Journal, People* magazine, *Travel + Leisure, a*nd many other publications. She is the author of 20 books, the creator of the TV series *Going Rogue,* and the wacky proliferator behind two popular blogs. Her current focus is the 222 Foundation she started to honor her magical daughter, Tasman, who has been guiding her from the nonphysical since October 15, 2018. Pam can be reached at www.pamgrout.com and @PamGrout on all the socials.

Hay House Titles of Related Interest

We hope you enjoyed this Hay House book. If you'd like to receive our online catalog featuring additional information on Hay House books and products, or if you'd like to find out more about the Hay Foundation, please contact:

Hay House, Inc., P.O. Box 5100, Carlsbad, CA 92018-5100
(760) 431-7695 or (800) 654-5126
(760) 431-6948 (fax) or (800) 650-5115 (fax)
www.hayhouse.com® • www.hayfoundation.org

———

Published in Australia by: Hay House Australia Pty. Ltd.,
18/36 Ralph St., Alexandria NSW 2015
Phone: 612-9669-4299 • *Fax:* 612-9669-4144
www.hayhouse.com.au

Published in the United Kingdom by: Hay House UK, Ltd.,
The Sixth Floor, Watson House, 54 Baker Street, London W1U 7BU
Phone: +44 (0)20 3927 7290 • *Fax:* +44 (0)20 3927 7291
www.hayhouse.co.uk

Published in India by: Hay House Publishers India,
Muskaan Complex, Plot No. 3, B-2, Vasant Kunj, New Delhi 110 070
Phone: 91-11-4176-1620 • *Fax:* 91-11-4176-1630
www.hayhouse.co.in

———

Access New Knowledge.
Anytime. Anywhere.

Learn and evolve at your own pace
with the world's leading experts.

www.hayhouseU.com